"*A Couple Cooks* is a beautiful book celebrating the joys of cooking together in the kitchen. If any book could inspire your partner, this is the one. From the delicious and approachable recipes to the breakdown of who does what, this book is a must for every couple!"

—TIFFANI THIESSEN
ACTRESS AND AUTHOR OF COOKBOOKS *PULL UP A CHAIR* AND *HERE WE GO AGAIN*

"This cookbook brings a sense of possibility, mindfulness, and joy to the dreaded daily question, 'What's for dinner?' Not only is this cookbook full of practical recipes for couples and families; it brims with inspiration for how to create a meal plan, cook as a team, and enjoy the process of preparing meals!"

—YUMNA JAWAD
CREATOR OF *FEEL GOOD FOODIE* AND AUTHOR OF THE *FEEL GOOD FOODIE COOKBOOK*

"Alex and Sonja's latest cookbook is the guide to cooking as a team of two! You won't just find delicious recipes here—they also share pro tips for dividing up tasks in the kitchen, setting the mood for at-home date nights, and throwing fun, flawless dinner parties. This book is a must for any dynamic kitchen duo."

—JEANINE DONOFRIO
AUTHOR OF *LOVE AND LEMONS SIMPLE FEEL GOOD FOOD*

"*A Couple Cooks* is a must-have addition to the culinary collection for couples everywhere. It's a trove of delish recipes, perfect for everything from a cozy date night to a full-blown holiday bash. Sonja and Alex show us not only that they are a real-life match made in heaven but also that they are the perfect match in the kitchen."

—JOCELYN DELK ADAMS
BESTSELLING AND AWARD-WINNING AUTHOR OF *EVERYDAY GRAND*

"Alex and Sonja bring warmth, flavor, and connection to the table. *A Couple Cooks* celebrates the same joyful spirit and shows how they make cooking together fun with recipes like Risotto with Asparagus, Peas & Pine Nuts, French Toast Waffles, and Cozy Vegetable Pot Pie: feel-good recipes that bolster the sense that it's worth doing it (life! cooking!) together."

—SARAH COPELAND
AUTHOR OF *THE NEWLYWED COOKBOOK, EVERY DAY IS SATURDAY,* AND *INSTANT FAMILY MEALS*

"Sonja and Alex transform cooking from a mundane necessity into a series of joyful celebrations of togetherness in the kitchen. The recipes are equal parts imaginative and practical, helping you get dinner on the table while enjoying the process. Curated with love, this book proves that life is tastier together!"

—ERIN CLARKE
AUTHOR OF THE BESTSELLING *WELL PLATED COOKBOOK* AND *WELL PLATED EVERY DAY*

"I love the recipes from their blog, *A Couple Cooks*. They have become staples in my kitchen. Whether it's for a dinner party or just my breakfast, Sonja and Alex's food is always delicious. I'm so excited about these new dishes in the book, because eating their tasty, healthy food makes life better."

—HEATHER GRAHAM
ACTRESS AND FILMMAKER

"What I love about this cookbook is how it considers the reader. It goes beyond the vibrant photos and organizes each recipe in a way that thinks about time, effort, dietary restrictions, and even wine pairings and storage. This is truly empathetic cookbook writing that so many authors (including myself) can learn from. Never mind these gorgeous recipes themselves, but *how* it was written and put together will make this book so much more accessible to people. Everyday cooks will impress themselves with this one!"

—JON KUNG
AUTHOR OF *KUNG FOOD*

A COUPLE COOKS

A COUPLE COOKS

100 Recipes to Cook Together

Sonja and Alex Overhiser

Photography by Shelly Westerhausen Worcel

CHRONICLE BOOKS

SAN FRANCISCO

Library of Congress Cataloging-in-Publication Data available.

ISBN 978-1-7972-2299-8

Manufactured in China.

Prop and food styling by Shelly Westerhausen Worcel.
Design by Arsh Raziuddin.
Typesetting by Arsh Raziuddin and Wynne Au-Yeung.

10 9 8 7 6 5 4 3 2 1

Chronicle books and gifts are available at special quantity
discounts to corporations, professional associations, literacy
programs, and other organizations. For details and discount
information, please contact our premiums department at
corporatesales@chroniclebooks.com or at 1-800-759-0190.

Chronicle Books LLC
680 Second Street
San Francisco, California 94107
www.chroniclebooks.com

To Larson and Britta,
our favorite little chefs
and greatest treasures.
May these recipes be
a gateway to a lifetime
of love and laughter.

Contents

Note *from the* Authors

Dear Reader,

Two are better than one, or so the saying goes.

We're Sonja and Alex, a couple of cooks who know that good food is always better with a sprinkle of laughter (and maybe a splash of wine!). We started cooking together shortly after getting married, and we're still at it—all because we've discovered the power of two.

You see, we spent our early years together viewing food as a chore. Getting meals on the table was just one more to-do item on an already long list. Then we realized this:

In our fast-paced, busy lives, feeding ourselves can be easier, more rewarding, and more enjoyable when done together.

That's where this book comes in (and thank you for picking it up, by the way!). This collection is for any pair sharing the kitchen, whether you're newlyweds, partners, couples with kids, empty nesters, family members, or friends. The recipes span all of life's occasions, from a dinner date to an artisan bread-baking project to a big table of friends and family. Each one is designed for two cooks, by two cooks.

Cooking shouldn't be just about getting food on the table. It's about bonding over bubbling pots, chatting over chopping vegetables, and creating memories that last long after the dishes are done.

So grab a partner, crack open a page, and let's get cooking! We can't wait to hear about the laughter, mishaps, and meals that fill your kitchen. After all, life is always tastier together.

Sonja and Alex

Introduction

Our Story

"We're free Saturday night . . . want to ask someone over for dinner?"

That's how it all started. Here we were, Sonja and Alex, college sweethearts who met on the first day of class and ended up married. Neither of us knew quite what to do in the narrow galley kitchen in our pale-green 1920s bungalow. For most of our adult lives we'd survived on packaged or frozen foods, with the occasional pot of overcooked spaghetti.

But now it felt different. Instead of just eating to survive, we wanted to try to spread our wings and do what others had generously done for us: cook an actual dinner. As in, not frozen dinner trays or breakfast cereal!

But where to start? This was 2007, before the internet was the place to turn for recipes. So we maxed out our library card with cookbooks and cooking-show DVDs, and we began figuring out "how to cook."

Our natural culinary instincts surfaced immediately. Sonja, the classically trained musician and journalist of the two of us, set about figuring out the "right" and "most efficient" way to do things. But Alex, the tinkerer and mad scientist, was all about testing unconventional methods and was completely unafraid to fail. It resulted in loads of clashes. But eventually, we started to learn the natural rhythm of our kitchen.

Our first attempts at meals were embarrassingly cute—just thinking about them feels like looking at a photo of your teenage self with braces. There was a blasé rendition of butternut squash soup in a bland same-colored bowl, served with a not-quite-right caprese salad with brown dried basil flakes instead of the bright green fresh herb. There were loads of recipes that didn't work out, but also an occasional win, like a French dinner of lamb and frisée salad cooked from a Julia Child cookbook. Whatever the result, we didn't care. We were having fun, and that was all that mattered.

A few years in, cooking was becoming what we did in our free time, what gave us joy, what made us feel creative. The food tasted more authentic and life-giving than we ever imagined. The best part? It gave true fuel to our relationship. It taught us to listen, to compromise, and to disagree respectfully. And it taught us perseverance. When one of us made something that went straight to the garbage, or caught our dinner on fire in

front of our guests (yes, it happened!), the other would provide encouragement to stay in the game.

This was all before the age of social media, and the place to share online passions was a blog. So in 2010 we decided to start a website devoted to food.

We called it *A Couple Cooks*. We had no idea that it would one day become our profession.

Fast forward: www.acouplecooks.com is now a collection of thousands of recipes with millions of monthly readers. We're proud to have built it into a website offering reliable and delicious recipes that readers make again and again. And the best part is doing it as a husband-and-wife team: creating the recipes together, photographing them (Alex), and writing the posts (Sonja).

In our work as recipe developers, we've had amazing opportunities to write cookbooks, make enchiladas for Al Roker on *The Today Show*, and write for the *Washington Post*. The internet has provided a playground for us to realize our creative dreams. But at the end of the day, it's really just about the thing we fell in love with from the beginning: creating food in the kitchen . . . together.

On a weeknight feeding our family, we might make Pressed Manchego & Prosciutto Sandwiches (page 67) together while jamming to a dance party with our kiddos. Or if we get a quiet night alone (score!), there's nothing better than stirring Risotto with Asparagus, Peas & Pine Nuts (page 95) with a glass of crisp chardonnay or sipping Perfect Margaritas for Two (page 313) on the patio with a bottomless bowl of tortilla chips.

We love baking artisan bread together until it's crispy on the outside with a beautiful tender crumb (see page 245). Each Valentine's Day we make a meal to outdo the last, cooking up Seared New York Strip Steak with Garlic Mushrooms (page 117) or Creamy Scallops with Spinach & Sun-Dried Tomatoes (page 107) and a Chocolate Ganache Tart for Two (page 281). On a lazy weekend morning, we love a stack of Oatmeal Blender Pancakes (page 155), or on holidays we'll indulge in Mini Cardamom Cinnamon Rolls (page 175). We're at our happiest when we've got a big table of friends or family gathered around a Smoky Spinach & Artichoke Lasagna (page 130) or loaded bowls of Hearty Black Bean Chili ("The Chili") (page 123).

Years have passed since those eager young newlyweds posted their first food photos. We're now professional recipe writers and entrepreneurs, and parents to Larson and Britta, both miracle babies who brought us beauty amidst a challenging and painful season. People often ask us, "Do you still love cooking together now that it's your job?" Luckily, we can answer in all honestly, "Absolutely!" It brings us joy in new ways as the years go by.

We hope the pages of this book can bring you the same joy as you cook through it with someone you love. Above all, we hope you'll find these recipes are more than just food: May they become shared stories and strengthened relationships with every bite.

How to Use This Book

This book offers a wide range of recipes, from dishes for everyday meals to special dinner parties, date nights, and cozy breakfasts, to baking projects and cocktails. They are designed for cooking together (not two-serving recipes). Of course, you can make any of the recipes alone at any time—it's just more fun with a partner!

Task symbols for cooking together

Each recipe in this book shows ● *(Cook 1) and* ■ *(Cook 2) symbols next to each step. You can use the symbols to efficiently divide tasks during the cooking process. Or use them as a starting point—feel free to get creative and forge your own path.*

Dinner recipe serving sizes

CHAPTER 1 *offers four-serving dinners designed for everyday meals. If you're a smaller household, leftovers make tomorrow's lunch or dinner.*

CHAPTER 2 *presents two-serving dinners that are perfect for date night or special dinners to cook with a partner.*

CHAPTER 3 *features four- to eight-serving dinners for sharing with friends or family.*

Building the perfect meal

Alongside the recipes, we offer **TIPS** *for side dishes, wine pairings, and more.*

A **DIET** *circle indicates suitable diets, and potential substitutions are suggested above.*

We also created **SAMPLE MENUS** *(page 342) to spark your creativity, made for hosting in any season.*

As you're cooking, we'd love to hear from you! If you have questions or experiences to share, reach out to us at www.acouplecooks.com.

Tips for Cooking as a Team

"How do you do it? I could never work with my partner!" is a common response we get when we tell people we run a business and cook together. After almost two decades of cooking together and over one decade of co-owning a business, we've learned a thing or two!

Cooking together is not for the faint of heart, the hotheaded, or the proud. But if you're open to it, it can be one of the best ways to grow a relationship. Here are our top lessons for working together in the kitchen:

Embrace different work styles. Some people have a linear brain: *This* must happen before *That*. Others have a cloud brain, able to think about multiple layers and workstreams simultaneously. Some cooks are intentionally messy; others embrace the clean-as-you-go method. (If you must know, Alex is linear and clean-as-you-go, and Sonja is cloud brain and messy.) Some people follow a recipe to the letter; others view it as a guide or template to be tweaked and improved upon. Figure out each other's work styles and learn to appreciate them. There is no perfect way to do things! It's all a dance.

Delegate rotating roles of head chef and sous chef. Having two leaders for any project can be challenging. Instead, have one person be the head chef for the recipe and the other be the sous chef. The head chef is responsible for reviewing the recipe and delegating the tasks, taking skills into account—like who's better at chopping, searing meat, or styling a plate. The sous chef is there to take direction and make the meal a success. Rotate these roles for each different recipe and occasion!

Set up separate areas for prep space. This can be challenging, depending on your available kitchen space, but it's important to find a separate space for each of your activities, even if it's a cutting board at the dining table.

Learn to admit when you're wrong (or when you're both right). Humility is by far the most important value we've learned in the kitchen— and in a relationship. Voice your opinion boldly, but then be savvy enough to know when to compromise. Most importantly, don't forget that more salt and hot sauce can be added later, but can never be backed out!

Remember, it's about the relationship, not the food. Above all, cooking together isn't about finishing the recipe in the quickest amount of time. (We're guilty of forgetting that sometimes, even today!) It's about enjoying time together. Even if the lasagna comes out blackened or the freshly baked bread is a little flat, don't worry! The time spent together is worth every second.

Ingredient and Method Notes

Let's start with a few golden rules to follow when cooking these recipes in your kitchen:

A food scale is essential for accurate baking. This is the best way to ensure consistent baked goods (here's where the precise cook wins!).

Flour should be weighed, or spooned and leveled. It's a tricky ingredient to measure; depending on how you pack it, 1 cup of flour can yield different weights. The most accurate way to measure flour is to weigh it. The second most accurate method is to spoon it into a cup, then level it off with a knife.

Using a food thermometer is most precise way to cook meat, fish, and certain sweets. We've provided both visual cues and temperatures in the following recipes, so you can technically get away without it. But a thermometer is the ideal way to make sure meat is cooked through or to make a great lemon curd or caramel.

Unless otherwise stated, all recipes in this book use kosher salt. Its flat granules season food more gently than ordinary table salt. Invest in a big box and use it in all your cooking (store it in a funky salt cellar or salt box on your counter).

Olive oil should be extra-virgin, and make sure it's not labeled "light."

"Neutral oil" is a category term for neutral-tasting oils such as grapeseed, canola, and vegetable oil. Buy organic if possible.

Wash and dry all produce before using it. For leafy greens, a salad spinner is helpful for efficient drying, or use a clean towel to pat them dry.

For best flavor, we recommend maple syrup labeled "Grade A: Dark Color and Robust Taste." We generally prefer it over the lighter flavor of "Grade A: Amber Color and Rich Taste."

Finely zest citrus with a microplane grater to produce light sprinkles that meld right into recipes. Zest directly into the ingredients you're adding to; this will capture the oils as well as the zest.

Fresh herbs are essential! Try not to substitute dried herbs unless they are listed as a substitute in the recipe. See Growing Fresh Herbs, page 228.

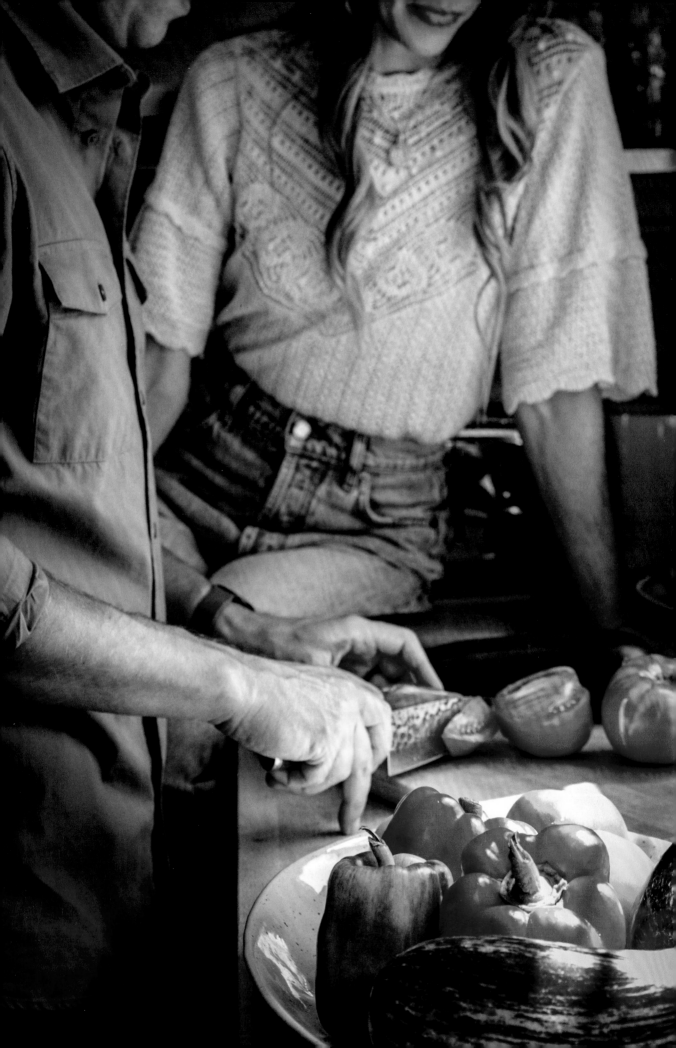

Where to Begin: Ten Recipes

Not sure where to start? We recommend you pick one recipe and just go for it! Don't feel like you have to have it all figured out before you get your hands dirty.

To help, we've picked out ten of our favorite recipes that deliver the biggest bang for the buck. These are reliable, forgiving recipes that cooks of any level can throw together easily for a big impact:

1. Tortellini Vegetable Soup (page 39)
2. Quick & Cozy Chickpea Curry (page 41)
3. Salmon Piccata (page 60)
4. Creamy Mediterranean Chicken Skillet (page 70)
5. Hearty Black Bean Chili ("The Chili") (page 123)
6. Banana Baked Oatmeal with Maple Tahini Drizzle (page 152)
7. Everyday Arugula Salad (page 187)
8. Maple-Glazed Buttermilk Cornbread (page 240)
9. Warm Goat Cheese with Jam (page 263)
10. Glazed Applesauce Spice Cake (page 291)

Chapter 1

EVERYDAY
Dinners

There's cooking for fun, and there's cooking to get food on the table. These recipes are designed to meet at that intersection! If you're anything like us, the majority of meals cooked together are everyday dinners shared with each other at the close of a busy day.

These four-serving recipes are designed to go into your regular rotation, dinners you'll turn to again and again. If you're a two-person household, you're in luck—leftovers make tomorrow's lunch or dinner.

SOME HIGHLIGHTS IN THIS CHAPTER:

Mix up a colorful Harvest Caesar Bowl (page 21).

Simmer a hearty Tortellini Vegetable Soup (page 39) or Quick & Cozy Chickpea Curry (page 41).

Whip up surprisingly simple Seared Tuna Steaks with Chimichurri (page 50).

Opt for sophisticated Salmon Piccata (page 60).

Take the ultra-quick route with Pressed Manchego & Prosciutto Sandwiches (page 67).

Impress everyone with a Creamy Mediterranean Chicken Skillet (page 70) or crunchy, cool Chicken Gyros with Tzatziki (page 77).

Harvest *Caesar* Bowl

SERVES 4

2 lb [910 g] sweet potatoes (about 2 medium), skin on, scrubbed and cut into ¾ in [2 cm] dice

3 Tbsp olive oil

1 tsp garlic powder

1 tsp chili powder

½ tsp Old Bay seasoning (see Tips)

¾ tsp kosher salt

15 oz [430 g] can chickpeas, drained and rinsed, or 1½ cups [240 g] cooked chickpeas

⅛ tsp cumin

Freshly ground black pepper

1 bunch (about 8 oz [230 g]) Tuscan kale, washed, torn into bite-size pieces, and massaged

2 romaine hearts (about 8 oz [230 g]), chopped

2 cups [120 g] chopped red cabbage

¼ cup [18 g] Parmesan cheese shavings

¼ cup [35 g] roasted pepitas (see Tips)

1 recipe Creamy Parmesan Dressing (see page 189) or 1 cup [240 g] store-bought Caesar dressing

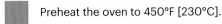 Preheat the oven to 450°F [230°C].

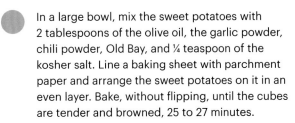 In a large bowl, mix the sweet potatoes with 2 tablespoons of the olive oil, the garlic powder, chili powder, Old Bay, and ¼ teaspoon of the kosher salt. Line a baking sheet with parchment paper and arrange the sweet potatoes on it in an even layer. Bake, without flipping, until the cubes are tender and browned, 25 to 27 minutes.

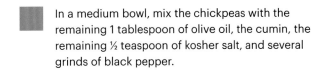 In a medium bowl, mix the chickpeas with the remaining 1 tablespoon of olive oil, the cumin, the remaining ½ teaspoon of kosher salt, and several grinds of black pepper.

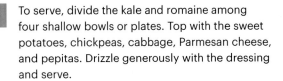 To serve, divide the kale and romaine among four shallow bowls or plates. Top with the sweet potatoes, chickpeas, cabbage, Parmesan cheese, and pepitas. Drizzle generously with the dressing and serve.

COOK 1 ——— • ■ ——— COOK 2

contd.

Here's a bowl that's endlessly customizable—a riff on a dinner we started eating on repeat around the birth of our daughter and still do today! What began as a pregnancy craving for Caesar salad turned into a weeknight main dish with a rotating topping of veggies, chicken, or shrimp. (We'll always remember devouring a takeout version in the hospital room while awaiting the baby's arrival!)

This satisfying combination of roasted sweet potatoes, seasoned chickpeas, and shaved Parmesan cheese is topped with an irresistibly creamy, Greek yogurt–based spin on Caesar (though feel free to use store-bought dressing if you're pressed for time). Customize the bowl by adding cooked chicken or a grain like rice or quinoa, making it a filling meal that never gets old.

Tips

Don't have Old Bay? Substitute ½ teaspoon smoked paprika plus an additional ⅛ teaspoon kosher salt.

If all you can find is raw pepitas, you can toast them yourself in a skillet over medium heat until they start to pop and become golden brown, 3 to 5 minutes.

Cooking Together

While one of you gets the sweet potatoes in the oven and chops the fresh vegetables for the bowl, the other can mix up the chickpeas and the dressing.

For Vegan

Use Lemon Tahini Sauce (see page 189) and omit the Parmesan shavings.

Storage

Leftovers will keep, refrigerated, for up to 3 days.

Diet
Vegetarian, gluten-free, vegan option

Lemony Orzo Skillet with Chickpeas & Broccoli

SERVES 4

3 Tbsp olive oil

2 medium heads (1 lb [455 g]) broccoli, chopped into florets

½ tsp dried thyme

1¼ tsp kosher salt

4 garlic cloves, minced

1 medium shallot, thinly sliced

One 15 oz [430 g] can chickpeas, drained and rinsed, or 1½ cups [240 g] cooked chickpeas

1½ cups (10 oz [280 g]) orzo

Zest of 1 large lemon, plus 2 Tbsp fresh lemon juice

½ tsp onion powder

½ tsp garlic powder

1 tsp dried dill

4 cups [960 ml] vegetable broth

3 cups [90 g] baby or chopped spinach

¼ cup [60 ml] sour cream or cashew cream (see Tip)

Finely chopped parsley or fresh dill, for serving

½ lemon, cut into thin wheels

Grated Parmesan cheese, for serving (optional)

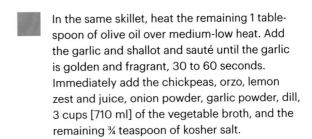

Heat 2 tablespoons of the olive oil in a large skillet over medium heat. Add the broccoli florets and sauté, stirring occasionally, until charred at the edges, 4 to 5 minutes. Stir in the thyme and ½ teaspoon of the kosher salt. Cover and cook an additional 2 to 3 minutes, until the broccoli is tender, bright green, and charred. Transfer to a bowl.

In the same skillet, heat the remaining 1 tablespoon of olive oil over medium-low heat. Add the garlic and shallot and sauté until the garlic is golden and fragrant, 30 to 60 seconds. Immediately add the chickpeas, orzo, lemon zest and juice, onion powder, garlic powder, dill, 3 cups [710 ml] of the vegetable broth, and the remaining ¾ teaspoon of kosher salt.

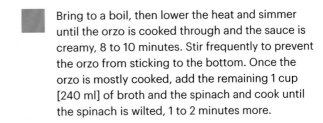

Bring to a boil, then lower the heat and simmer until the orzo is cooked through and the sauce is creamy, 8 to 10 minutes. Stir frequently to prevent the orzo from sticking to the bottom. Once the orzo is mostly cooked, add the remaining 1 cup [240 ml] of broth and the spinach and cook until the spinach is wilted, 1 to 2 minutes more.

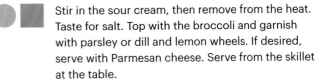

Stir in the sour cream, then remove from the heat. Taste for salt. Top with the broccoli and garnish with parsley or dill and lemon wheels. If desired, serve with Parmesan cheese. Serve from the skillet at the table.

COOK 1

COOK 2

contd.

This one-pan wonder is a creamy skillet of tiny grains of orzo pasta that cook up in a snap, making it a go-to for weeknights. The contrast of the zingy lemon with the earthy thyme-infused charred broccoli creates chef-level depth of flavor in minutes. For an extra touch, garnish with lemon wheels and serve it straight from the skillet at the table. (Then it's front and center for grabbing seconds!)

Serve with a fuss-free side like Everyday Arugula Salad (page 187).

Tip

This one is a breeze to adapt to a vegan diet: Just swap in cashew cream or dairy-free sour cream for the sour cream.

To make cashew cream, place 1 cup [140 g] unsalted cashews (raw or roasted) in a pot and cover with water; boil for 15 minutes to soften. Drain and add the cashews to a blender with ¾ cup [180 ml] water or vegetable broth and ½ teaspoon kosher salt. Blend on high for 1 minute. Stop and scrape, then add additional liquid if necessary to reach a creamy consistency. Blend again until creamy and smooth. It will keep, refrigerated, for up to 1 week.

Wine Pairing

The brightness of a Sancerre beautifully complements this skillet. This crisp, citrusy white wine from France elevates the creamy orzo texture, and its minerality balances the earthy thyme and broccoli.

Cooking Together

One of you can chop the broccoli and start cooking, while the other preps and then cooks the remaining ingredients.

For Vegan

Omit the Parmesan cheese and use cashew cream.

Storage

Leftovers will keep, refrigerated, for up to 3 days.

Diet
Vegetarian, vegan option

Barbecue
Beans & Greens

COOK 2 — COOK 1

SERVES 4

1 cup [200 g] white rice

1¼ tsp kosher salt

1 tsp hot sauce (we like Frank's or Tabasco)

3 Tbsp olive oil

¾ cup [195 g] ketchup

1 Tbsp Dijon mustard

½ Tbsp maple syrup

½ tsp garlic powder

½ tsp smoked paprika

½ tsp chili powder

2 bunches (1 lb [455 g]) rainbow chard, stemmed and chopped

2 garlic cloves, peeled and smashed

Freshly ground black pepper

¼ white onion, minced

Two 15 oz [430 g] cans pinto beans, drained and rinsed

Lemon wedges, for serving

Finely chopped parsley, for garnish (optional)

Rinse the rice in cold water using a fine-mesh strainer, then drain and shake it dry. Add the rice to a saucepan with 1½ cups [360 ml] water and ¼ teaspoon of the kosher salt. Bring it to a boil, then turn down the heat to low. Cover the pot and simmer for 13 to 15 minutes, until the water is completely absorbed (test by pulling back the rice with a fork). Remove from the heat. Cover and rest for 5 minutes. Then stir in the hot sauce, 1 tablespoon of the olive oil, and ¼ teaspoon of the kosher salt.

Meanwhile, mix the sauce for the beans: In a medium bowl combine the ketchup, Dijon mustard, maple syrup, garlic powder, smoked paprika, chili powder, and ¼ teaspoon of the kosher salt. Reserve.

Heat 1 tablespoon of the olive oil in a large skillet over medium heat. Add the chard and smashed garlic cloves and cook, stirring frequently, until wilted and bright green, 3 to 4 minutes. Season with two more pinches of kosher salt and black pepper. Transfer the chard to a bowl, keeping the garlic in the pan.

Heat the remaining 1 tablespoon of olive oil in the skillet over medium heat, then add the onion. Sauté until the onion is translucent, 3 to 4 minutes. Add the pinto beans, the remaining ½ teaspoon of kosher salt, and the sauce and stir. Cook over medium-low heat for 5 minutes.

Serve the beans and greens separately over the rice in shallow bowls or on plates, then squeeze with the juice of a lemon wedge. Garnish with parsley and offer additional hot sauce, if desired.

We adore meals that are nutritious and easy on the wallet, and this dish fits the bill. The zesty barbecue beans are the ideal companion for garlicky greens and fluffy rice seasoned with just a hint of hot sauce, giving it a sparkle without adding heat. Spoon the three components into shallow bowls for a quick and hearty meal.

Tip
Have other types of greens on hand? Feel free to substitute kale or spinach in place of the chard, cooking until wilted.

Cooking Together
Divide and conquer this dish! Have one person make the rice and sauce, while the other cooks the greens and beans.

Storage
Leftovers will keep, refrigerated, for up to 3 days.

Diet
Vegetarian, vegan, gluten-free

Crispy Black Bean Tacos
with Spicy Ranch

MAKES 8 TACOS

Spicy Ranch

½ cup [120 g] Greek yogurt
or sour cream

⅓ cup [80 g] mayonnaise

1½ Tbsp Mexican hot sauce
(like Cholula) (see Tips)

1 tsp apple cider vinegar

½ tsp garlic powder

½ tsp onion powder

½ tsp dried dill

¼ tsp kosher salt

Tacos

3 Tbsp salted butter

1 garlic clove, minced

One 15 oz [430 g] can black
beans, drained, or 1½ cups
[240 g] cooked beans

1 tsp cumin

1 tsp smoked paprika

½ tsp Mexican hot sauce
(like Cholula)

½ tsp kosher salt

8 small flour or corn tortillas
(6 in [15 cm] in diameter)

1½ cups [120 g] shredded
Mexican blend or Cheddar
cheese

1 cup [180 g] pico de gallo

1 cup [30 g] iceberg or romaine
lettuce, shredded

16 tortilla chips

Fresh cilantro, for garnishing
(optional)

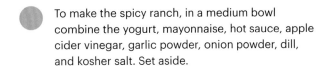 To make the spicy ranch, in a medium bowl combine the yogurt, mayonnaise, hot sauce, apple cider vinegar, garlic powder, onion powder, dill, and kosher salt. Set aside.

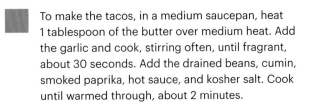 To make the tacos, in a medium saucepan, heat 1 tablespoon of the butter over medium heat. Add the garlic and cook, stirring often, until fragrant, about 30 seconds. Add the drained beans, cumin, smoked paprika, hot sauce, and kosher salt. Cook until warmed through, about 2 minutes.

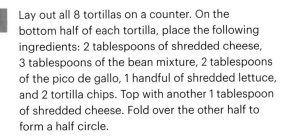 Lay out all 8 tortillas on a counter. On the bottom half of each tortilla, place the following ingredients: 2 tablespoons of shredded cheese, 3 tablespoons of the bean mixture, 2 tablespoons of the pico de gallo, 1 handful of shredded lettuce, and 2 tortilla chips. Top with another 1 tablespoon of shredded cheese. Fold over the other half to form a half circle.

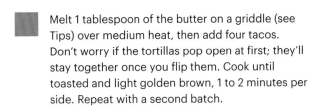 Melt 1 tablespoon of the butter on a griddle (see Tips) over medium heat, then add four tacos. Don't worry if the tortillas pop open at first; they'll stay together once you flip them. Cook until toasted and light golden brown, 1 to 2 minutes per side. Repeat with a second batch.

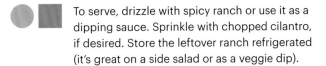 To serve, drizzle with spicy ranch or use it as a dipping sauce. Sprinkle with chopped cilantro, if desired. Store the leftover ranch refrigerated (it's great on a side salad or as a veggie dip).

COOK 1 ——— COOK 2

contd.

These crispy tacos, a delightful mashup of a quesadilla and a taco, have saved many a weeknight dinner at our house. The golden-brown pockets are stuffed with a savory bean filling and drenched in creamy, spicy ranch. For an added crunch, slip in a few tortilla chips if you've got them on hand (so good!).

Tips

Don't feel like you have to make all eight tacos at once. Cook the entire can of beans and fry up as many tacos as you like, then store the leftover bean filling, refrigerated, for up to 3 days. Or, you can refrigerate cooked tacos and reheat them (see the storage instructions).

It's handy to have a double burner griddle that fits all 8 tacos at once (it works for more than just pancakes!).

An ⅛ cup (2 tablespoons) measuring cup is helpful here for portioning out the taco fillings, but you can approximate.

If you prefer mild flavors, omit or use less hot sauce in the ranch dipping sauce: It will still taste great!

Cooking Together

Have one person mince the garlic and make the spicy ranch while the other person makes the beans and cooks the tacos.

For Gluten-Free

Use corn tortillas.

Storage

Leftovers will keep, refrigerated, for up to 3 days. Or wrap leftovers in foil and freeze for up to 3 months (thaw in the microwave for about 1 minute on high before reheating). Leftover ranch will keep 1 week, refrigerated.

To reheat chilled or thawed tacos, add a drizzle of olive oil to a skillet and cook the taco on medium-high heat until crispy, about 1 minute per side.

Diet
Vegetarian,
gluten-free option

Sweet Potato Enchiladas

SERVES 4

Sauce

One 14½ oz [415 g] can diced fire-roasted tomatoes

One 8 oz [230 g] can tomato sauce

1 Tbsp adobo sauce (from 1 can chipotle peppers in adobo sauce) (see Tips)

1 Tbsp apple cider vinegar

1 Tbsp olive oil

1 garlic clove

2 tsp cumin

2 tsp chili powder

1 tsp oregano

1 tsp onion powder

1 tsp sugar

½ tsp kosher salt

Enchiladas

1 lb [455 g] or 1 large or 2 medium sweet potatoes, washed and unpeeled, dark spots removed, diced into ¾ in [2 cm] cubes (3 cups diced)

2 green onions, thinly sliced

One 15 oz [430 g] can black beans, drained and rinsed, or 1½ cups [240 g] cooked beans

One 7 oz [200 g] can mild diced green chiles

2 tsp cumin

1 tsp chili powder

½ tsp garlic powder

contd.

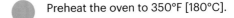 Preheat the oven to 350°F [180°C].

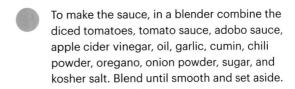 To make the sauce, in a blender combine the diced tomatoes, tomato sauce, adobo sauce, apple cider vinegar, oil, garlic, cumin, chili powder, oregano, onion powder, sugar, and kosher salt. Blend until smooth and set aside.

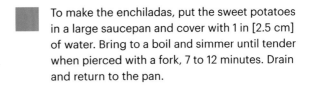 To make the enchiladas, put the sweet potatoes in a large saucepan and cover with 1 in [2.5 cm] of water. Bring to a boil and simmer until tender when pierced with a fork, 7 to 12 minutes. Drain and return to the pan.

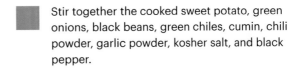 Stir together the cooked sweet potato, green onions, black beans, green chiles, cumin, chili powder, garlic powder, kosher salt, and black pepper.

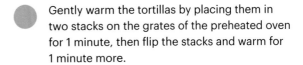 Gently warm the tortillas by placing them in two stacks on the grates of the preheated oven for 1 minute, then flip the stacks and warm for 1 minute more.

contd.

¾ tsp kosher salt

Freshly ground black pepper

Eight 8 in [20 cm] flour tortillas

8 oz [230 g] Colby Jack cheese, shredded (2 cups)

Sour cream, chopped cilantro, pico de gallo, cotija or feta cheese crumbles, Pickled Red Onions (page 128), pickled jalapeños, for topping

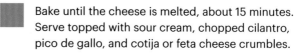

In a 9 x 13 in [23 x 33 cm] or larger baking dish, spread 1 cup [240 ml] of the sauce. Fill each tortilla with a ½ cup [108 g] scoop of the sweet potato mixture, add 1 small handful of the cheese (be sure to leave enough for topping), and roll it up. Place each tortilla seam side down in the baking dish. Repeat for the remaining tortillas, scooping any remaining filling into the ends of the rolls if desired. Pour the remaining sauce over the top and use a spatula to smooth it. Sprinkle the top with the remaining cheese.

Bake until the cheese is melted, about 15 minutes. Serve topped with sour cream, chopped cilantro, pico de gallo, and cotija or feta cheese crumbles.

A COUPLE COOKS

These enchiladas are a spin on one of the early recipes we published on *A Couple Cooks* back in 2012. We had just discovered how deliciously satisfying meatless meals can be, and we eagerly shared this sweet and savory enchilada filling with our readers. It spiraled into a fan-favorite recipe, and we still get rave reviews from readers.

The original recipe uses salsa verde to make green enchiladas, but here we've revamped it with a new homemade red sauce. Either works! You'll love the way the bold sauce and gooey cheese highlight the hearty filling.

Tips

The heat level of the enchilada sauce is mild, with a subtle back-end heat. If you are cooking for people sensitive to spice, use half the quantity of adobo sauce.

Make green enchiladas instead! Substitute 2 cups [480 ml] store-bought salsa verde for the enchilada sauce.

Cooking Together

This recipe is simple to prepare with two people: Have one person make the enchilada sauce while the other preps the filling.

For Vegan

Add a line of guacamole to the inside of each enchilada instead of the cheese, and omit the cheese topping or use a quality plant-based cheese.

For Gluten-Free

We prefer flour tortillas for enchiladas because they're easier to roll, but you can use corn tortillas for a gluten-free dish. To prevent breakage, buy a best-quality corn tortilla brand. Before assembling, brush each tortilla lightly with oil and heat it in a skillet for 15 seconds per side.

Storage

Make the Enchilada Sauce in advance and refrigerate until serving, up to 5 days. You can also make the entire pan the night before and refrigerate before baking. Straight from the refrigerator, bake for 20 to 30 minutes total.

Diet
Vegetarian, vegan option, gluten-free option

Lentil Soup
with Tarragon

COOK 2

COOK 1

SERVES 6

¼ cup [60 ml] olive oil

1 small yellow onion, small diced

2 medium carrots, peeled
and small diced

2 celery ribs, small diced

1 fennel bulb, small diced

4 medium garlic cloves, minced

1¾ cups (12 oz [340 g]) dried
brown lentils

8 cups (2 quarts [1.9 L])
vegetable broth (see Tips)

½ Tbsp cumin

2 Tbsp dried tarragon (see Tips)

½ Tbsp lemon zest

1 tsp kosher salt

Freshly ground black pepper

Fresh tarragon, for garnishing
(optional)

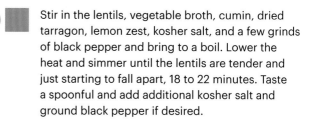

In a large pot or Dutch oven, heat the olive oil over medium heat. Add the onion, carrots, celery, fennel, and garlic and sauté, stirring occasionally, until the onion is translucent, 5 to 6 minutes.

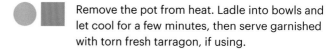

Stir in the lentils, vegetable broth, cumin, dried tarragon, lemon zest, kosher salt, and a few grinds of black pepper and bring to a boil. Lower the heat and simmer until the lentils are tender and just starting to fall apart, 18 to 22 minutes. Taste a spoonful and add additional kosher salt and ground black pepper if desired.

Remove the pot from heat. Ladle into bowls and let cool for a few minutes, then serve garnished with torn fresh tarragon, if using.

This hearty soup has been a regular in our kitchen for years (one January we ate it for four weeks straight). Tarragon adds an herby elegance, making this humble weeknight meal transport you right to a French bistro. Leftovers save well, so it's great for preparing a big pot to eat from all week.

Lentils are a powerhouse ingredient. They're shelf stable for 2 to 3 years and add a hefty dose of plant-based protein to soups and stews. Here they make a satisfying vegan dish with no meat or dairy—though we admit, we do love it finishing it off with a grating of Parmesan or pecorino romano cheese!

Tips

Tarragon is the star in this recipe, so make sure your dried tarragon is high quality. It should be bright green and have a pungent anise aroma. Using fresh tarragon for garnish adds a delicate freshness.

We always use regular broth for our recipes. If you choose to use low-sodium broth, the soup can taste bland; make sure to adjust the seasoning accordingly.

Cooking Together

This soup comes together easily once the chopping is done. Get out two cutting boards and do the dicing together.

Storage

Leftovers will keep, refrigerated, for up to 5 days.

Diet
Vegetarian, vegan, gluten-free

Tortellini Vegetable Soup

SERVES 4

2 Tbsp olive oil

1 small yellow onion, small diced

1 medium carrot, peeled and small diced

4 garlic cloves, minced

1 tsp dried fennel seed

One 28 oz [800 g] can diced fire-roasted tomatoes

One 15 oz [430 g] can crushed tomatoes

3 cups [720 ml] vegetable broth

½ cup [15 g] grated Parmesan cheese, plus more for garnishing

1 tsp dried oregano

1 tsp garlic powder

½ tsp dried sage

1 tsp kosher salt

1 Tbsp soy sauce or tamari

9 oz [265 g] refrigerated cheese tortellini or tortelloni

4 cups [80 g] baby spinach or 1 bunch Tuscan kale, chopped into bite-size pieces

Freshly ground black pepper

 In a large pot or Dutch oven, heat the olive oil over medium heat. Add the onion and carrot and cook, stirring occasionally, until the onion is translucent and the carrot is tender, 5 to 7 minutes. Add the garlic and fennel seed, lightly crushing the seeds with your fingers as you add them, and cook until fragrant, 30 to 60 seconds.

 Immediately add the diced tomatoes with their juices, crushed tomatoes, vegetable broth, Parmesan cheese, oregano, garlic powder, sage, kosher salt, and soy sauce. Bring to a simmer, then cook for 10 minutes.

 Add the tortellini or tortelloni and baby spinach and cook until the spinach is wilted, 2 to 3 minutes (or according to package directions). Season with black pepper. Ladle into bowls and garnish with Parmesan cheese.

COOK 1 ── ● ■ ── COOK 2

contd.

When you serve a recipe to someone and all they can do is keep exclaiming how tasty it is, you know it's a keeper. That's always the case with this tortellini soup (and we hope it will be for you, too). The broth is vibrant and rich, with sage and fennel lending complex, earthy notes. Plump tortellini float in a sea of vegetables, adding a chewy punch to each mouthful.

We love serving this soup with a hunk of crusty bread or Pressed Manchego & Prosciutto Sandwiches (page 67). For a meatless pairing, swap out the sandwich's prosciutto for a handful of shredded mozzarella, provolone, or Gouda cheese.

Tips

Leftovers store well but the tortellini will soak up a bit of the broth. If your broth came in a 1 quart (4 cup [960 ml]) container, save the extra for leftovers and add a splash when reheating.

Use refrigerated tortellini or tortelloni, which is fresh pasta that cooks quickly. Avoid substituting dried or frozen. Tortelloni are large tortellini with a filled center; tortellini are smaller and have a hole in the center.

Cooking Together

Tackle the chopping together, then one of you can sauté and stir while the other cleans up and makes a side dish.

Storage

Leftovers will keep, refrigerated, for up to 2 days.

Diet
Vegetarian

Quick & Cozy
Chickpea Curry

SERVES 4

1 Tbsp olive oil

1 sweet yellow onion, finely chopped

1 large garlic clove, minced

1 tsp peeled and grated fresh ginger

6 cups (5 oz [120 g]) baby spinach leaves or chopped spinach (see Tips)

One 14½ oz [415 g] can crushed fire-roasted tomatoes (see Tips)

One 15 oz [430 g] can chickpeas, drained and rinsed, or 1½ cups [240 g] cooked chickpeas

1 Tbsp curry powder

1 tsp cumin

½ tsp coriander

¾ tsp kosher salt

Freshly ground black pepper

½ cup [120 ml] unsweetened canned full-fat coconut milk

Cooked white basmati rice and naan, for serving

Fresh cilantro, for garnish (optional)

In a large skillet, heat the olive oil over medium-high heat. Add the onion and cook, stirring often, until translucent, 4 to 5 minutes. Add the garlic, ginger, and spinach and cook until the spinach is wilted, 1 to 2 minutes.

Lower the heat to medium and carefully pour in the crushed tomatoes. Add the chickpeas, curry powder, cumin, coriander, kosher salt, and a few grinds of black pepper. Cook until bubbly, 3 to 4 minutes. Stir in the coconut milk and simmer for 1 minute, then remove from the heat. Serve with basmati rice and naan and garnish with chopped cilantro, if using.

COOK 1

COOK 2

contd.

Our best friends have had this much-loved recipe from our website on their regular rotation for years, and here's why: It's incredibly quick to prepare, nutritious, brimming with flavor, and chock-full of vegetables. Keep this page handy for when you need a quick answer to that age-old question, "What's for dinner?"

The key to speed here? Fire-roasted tomatoes are sweet and smoky right out of the can, requiring less simmering time than standard canned tomatoes. Serve with rice for a hearty meal.

Tips

Fire-roasted tomatoes let you get away with a short cook time because they taste complex and developed right out of the can. Can't find them? Use the best-quality canned tomatoes you can find, stir in 1 pinch of sugar and ½ teaspoon of smoked paprika, and simmer the sauce for an extra 5 minutes.

This recipe is a simple way to load up on leafy greens. The fresh spinach quantity might feel like too much, but it wilts down quickly. If desired, substitute kale, chard, collards, or other leafy greens. Add a few extra minutes to the cook time for tougher greens such as kale.

Cooking Together

One cook tackles the chopping while the other cleans the spinach and preps the spices.

Storage

Leftovers will keep, refrigerated, for up to 3 days or frozen for up to 3 months.

Diet
Vegetarian, vegan, gluten-free

Coconut Tofu Curry
with Green Beans

COOK 2 —————— COOK 1

SERVES 4

One 14 oz [400 g] block extra-firm tofu

¼ cup [60 ml] neutral oil

¾ teaspoon kosher salt

1 medium yellow onion, finely chopped

1 red bell pepper, diced

6 oz [170 g] French green beans (haricots verts), trimmed and halved (about 2 cups)

2 garlic cloves, minced

1 tablespoon peeled and grated fresh ginger

½ cup [70 g] canned bamboo shoots, drained

3 Tbsp [45 g] Thai red curry paste (see Tips)

One 13.6 oz [403 ml] can unsweetened full-fat coconut milk

1 Tbsp brown sugar

2 Tbsp soy sauce or tamari

1 Tbsp fresh lime juice

½ Tbsp sambal oelek, plus more to taste

Cooked jasmine rice, for serving

Torn cilantro or Thai basil, for garnish

Pat the tofu dry with a towel and cut it into cubes, about 1 x ¾ in [2.5 x 2 cm].

Add 2 tablespoons of the oil to a large, cold nonstick skillet. Add the tofu cubes (starting them in cold oil helps avoid spattering) and sprinkle with ¼ teaspoon of the kosher salt. Cook over medium heat until the tofu is lightly browned on the bottom, 5 to 6 minutes. Briefly remove the pan from the heat (to reduce spitting oil) and flip the tofu with tongs. Return to medium heat and cook until browned, another 5 to 6 minutes. Transfer the tofu to a bowl and set aside.

In a large Dutch oven over medium heat, heat the remaining 2 tablespoons of oil. Add the onion and cook, stirring often, until translucent, about 5 minutes. Add the red pepper and green beans and cook for 2 minutes, stirring occasionally. Then add the garlic and ginger and cook for 3 minutes, stirring occasionally.

Add the bamboo shoots, red curry paste, coconut milk, brown sugar, soy sauce, lime juice, and sambal oelek. Turn down the heat to medium-low, then add the tofu and the remaining ½ teaspoon of kosher salt. Simmer until the sauce is slightly thickened and the green beans are tender, 5 to 8 minutes. Taste and add additional sambal oelek to taste. Serve over jasmine rice and garnish with torn cilantro or Thai basil.

contd.

This warm, comforting curry is inspired by a dish we had one rainy evening from a local Thai restaurant: The bright red broth was just the antidote we needed for the dreary weather! The combination of green beans, tangy bamboo shoots, and chewy pillows of tofu make it near impossible to stop shoveling in bites. Serve it up with aromatic jasmine rice, and it's sunshine in a bowl.

Tips

This curry is mild-to-medium spicy using the widely available Thai Kitchen brand curry paste, which is very mild. Taste your curry paste before using: The heat level varies widely based on brand. If your curry paste tastes very spicy, use less than specified in the recipe, then add more to taste.

Sambal oelek is an Indonesian chili sauce made of chiles, garlic, ginger, and lime. It adds a depth and heat here that makes it worth seeking out.

Cooking Together

This dish gets on the table much more quickly with two cooks! One of you can focus on browning the tofu while the other gets to work on chopping the vegetables for the curry.

For Gluten-Free

Use gluten-free soy sauce or tamari.

Storage

Leftovers will keep, refrigerated, for up to 3 days.

Diet
Vegetarian, vegan, gluten-free option

Sticky Orange Tofu & Broccoli

SERVES 4

½ cup freshly squeezed orange juice (about two navel oranges)

1 tsp orange zest

¼ cup [60 ml] soy sauce or tamari

¼ cup [50 g] granulated sugar

2 Tbsp [30 ml] rice vinegar

2 garlic cloves, grated

1 tsp peeled and grated fresh ginger (see Tip)

¼ cup plus 2 Tbsp [55 g] cornstarch

One 14 oz [400 g] block extra-firm tofu, cut into ¾ in [2 cm] pieces

½ tsp kosher salt

¼ cup [60 ml] sesame oil or neutral oil

6 cups broccoli florets (about 1½ lb [680 g])

3 green onions, white and green parts thinly sliced

Sesame seeds, for garnishing

Rice or quinoa, for serving

In a medium bowl, whisk together the orange juice and zest, soy sauce, sugar, rice vinegar, garlic, ginger, and the 2 tablespoons [20 g] of cornstarch until the cornstarch is fully dissolved. Set aside.

Lay out the tofu cubes on a clean dish towel, then gently pat with a second towel to remove excess moisture. In a small bowl, mix the ¼ cup [35 g] of the cornstarch and ¼ teaspoon of the kosher salt. Put the tofu cubes in a large bowl and slowly sprinkle half of the cornstarch mixture onto the tofu, using your hands to gently turn the cubes to coat. Sprinkle in the remaining cornstarch mixture and mix gently to coat.

In a 10 or 12 in [25 or 30 cm] nonstick skillet over medium-high heat, warm 3 tablespoons of the sesame oil until shimmering. Add the tofu and cook until light golden brown, 7 to 9 minutes, using a small spatula or spatula tongs to flip the pieces once. (It's okay if the pieces of tofu stick to each other; it helps them flip.) Transfer to a plate and allow the cubes to rest; they will crisp up as you make the remainder of the recipe.

In the same skillet, heat the remaining 1 table-spoon of sesame oil over medium heat. Add the broccoli florets and the remaining ¼ teaspoon of kosher salt and cook for 3 minutes, stirring occasionally. Add 1 tablespoon of water and continue cooking until crisp-tender and just starting to brown on the edges, 2 to 3 minutes. Turn off the heat and transfer the broccoli to a bowl.

Add the reserved sauce to the same skillet and cook over medium heat, stirring constantly, until it starts to thicken, for 30 seconds to 1 minute. Remove from the heat and continue to stir until the sauce is thick and glossy. Add the tofu to the pan, breaking up any stuck pieces, and stir gently until coated in the sauce. Once the tofu is coated, stir in the broccoli and the green onions. Garnish with sesame seeds and serve over rice or quinoa.

COOK 1 ——————— COOK 2

contd.

Here's a match made in heaven: crisp-on-the-outside, tender-on-the-inside tofu pillows and a tangy citrus-sweet glaze. This is just the dish to make a tofu lover out of any skeptic (promise!). Of course, we're unabashed lovers of the stuff, especially when topped with a gooey, sticky sauce like this one.

Leftovers hold up well, and it's just as craveable for lunch the next day. Serve with rice or quinoa, and, if you like a little heat, drizzle with chili garlic sauce or sriracha.

Tip

In a pinch, substitute ½ teaspoon of ground ginger for the fresh ginger.

Cooking Together

It's nice to have a partner to speed up prep time. Have one of you start cooking the tofu while the other chops the broccoli and preps the sauce ingredients.

For Gluten-Free

Use gluten-free soy sauce or tamari.

Storage

Leftovers will keep, refrigerated, for up to 3 days.

Diet
Vegetarian, vegan, gluten-free option

Seared Tuna Steaks
with Chimichurri

SERVES 4

Tuna Steaks

16 oz [455 g] high-quality
ahi tuna steak (2 to 4 steaks)
(see Tips)

1 tsp kosher salt

Freshly ground black pepper

1 Tbsp neutral oil

Chimichurri

½ cup [25 g] very finely
chopped Italian parsley

¼ cup [15 g] very finely chopped
cilantro (see Tips)

2 garlic cloves, minced

¼ tsp red pepper flakes or
1 teaspoon finely minced Fresno
pepper (seeds removed)
(see Tips)

1½ Tbsp red wine vinegar

¼ cup olive oil

½ tsp kosher salt

COOK 2

COOK 1

Allow the tuna steaks to stand at room temperature while preparing the chimichurri.

To make the chimichurri, in a medium bowl, stir together the parsley, cilantro, garlic, red pepper flakes, red wine vinegar, olive oil, and kosher salt. Stir in 2 tablespoons of warm water until a loose sauce forms.

To prepare the steaks, pat the tuna steaks dry. Sprinkle with the kosher salt and black pepper evenly on both sides.

Heat the neutral oil in a medium stainless steel or cast-iron skillet over medium-high heat. Add the tuna steaks and cook until lightly browned on the outside but pink on the inside, about 2 minutes per side. Remove from the heat and let cool for 2 minutes (the tuna will continue cooking while sitting). Then slice the tuna against the grain into ½ in [13 mm] slices. Arrange the slices on individual plates or a serving platter and drizzle with the chimichurri. Serve immediately.

contd.

Ahi tuna is our secret weapon. It's fancy enough for dazzling guests or a Friday date night, but it takes only minutes to put together. It tastes more like steak than fish, making it the perfect gateway dish for anyone who's on the fence about seafood.

Drizzle it with zingy, garlicky chimichurri, a rustic Argentinian sauce that adds a sparkle to everything it touches. Pair with Herby Quinoa (page 226) or Lemon Pepper Broccolini (page 219).

Tips

Ahi tuna steak should be available at your local fish counter or frozen. Tuna marked as "sushi" or "sashimi grade" is top quality.

The cooking instructions are for a rare tuna steak. If you prefer a medium tuna steak that's fully cooked through, remove from the heat when the internal temperature is 140°F [60°C] when measured with a food thermometer at the thickest point.

Don't love cilantro? Substitute more parsley or fresh oregano instead.

Sensitive to spice? Customize the heat level in the chimichurri to your own tastes.

Try leftover chimichurri on eggs, on baked or grilled salmon, with chicken, or swirled into pasta.

Wine Pairing

A dry French rosé is ideal. This crisp, refreshing wine has notes of fruit, citrus, and minerality that complement the tuna's delicate texture and balance the zesty chimichurri sauce.

Cooking Together

Make your sides and chimichurri together while the tuna sits at room temperature, then cook and plate the tuna.

Storage

Leftover seared tuna will keep, refrigerated, for up to 2 days. Leftover chimichurri will keep, refrigerated, for 2 to 3 weeks: the oil solidifies when cold, so bring to room temperature before serving.

Diet
Pescatarian,
gluten-free,
dairy-free

Baked Tilapia *with Feta, Olives & Cherry Tomatoes*

SERVES 4

1½ lb [680 g] tilapia fillets
(see Tips)

1 pint [320 g] cherry tomatoes,
sliced in half

1 large shallot, thinly sliced

3 garlic cloves, minced

¼ cup [35 g] ripe green olives
(such as Castelvetrano), pitted
and halved (see Tips)

2 Tbsp olive oil

½ cup (2 oz [60 g]) feta cheese
crumbles

1 tsp lemon zest

¾ tsp kosher salt

Freshly ground black pepper

3 Tbsp fresh lemon juice

1 Tbsp Italian seasoning

½ tsp smoked paprika or paprika

2 Tbsp capers, drained

Chopped fresh parsley,
for garnishing

Preheat the oven to 425°F [220°C]. Let the fish rest at room temperature while chopping the vegetables.

Put the tomatoes, shallot, garlic, and olives in a 9 x 13 in [23 x 33 cm] baking dish. Stir in 1 tablespoon of the olive oil, the feta cheese crumbles, lemon zest, ¼ teaspoon of the kosher salt, and black pepper.

Place the fillets on top of the vegetable mixture in the baking dish. Season them with the remaining 1 tablespoon of olive oil and ½ teaspoon of kosher salt, divided evenly between the fillets, using the back of a spoon to distribute the olive oil. Drizzle with the lemon juice. Sprinkle with the Italian seasoning, smoked paprika, and more grinds of black pepper, then sprinkle the capers over the top.

Bake until the fish is flaky and the internal temperature is 140°F [60°C], 15 to 20 minutes. Garnish with chopped parsley and serve, adding a few spoonfuls of vegetables with each serving of fish.

COOK 1 ———

——— COOK 2

contd.

Here are all our favorite Mediterranean flavor secrets in one recipe (a.k.a. "how to make fish taste incredible"). Olives and capers add a salty, briny punch, fresh lemon gives a citrusy pop, and feta crumbles seal the deal with salty richness. Like Seared Tuna Steaks with Chimichurri (page 50), this moist baked fish will make a seafood lover out of anyone.

We stumbled across this dish years ago, and to this day it's a staple in our regular meal rotation. It comes together simply, making it great for weeknights or when your in-laws or friends drop by for a visit.

Tips

Look for ripe green olives or the Italian variety Castelvetrano, a green olive that tastes mild and buttery. Halve them with a knife or tear them into pieces with your fingers.

When purchasing the fish, shop for sustainable tilapia. Ask at your fish counter, read the packaging, and check www.seafoodwatch.org for guidance on seafood purchases.

This recipe works well with other white fish, such as cod or mahi mahi. Adjust the bake time to the thickness of your fish.

Cooking Together

This one comes together quickly! One of you can grab all the ingredients from the refrigerator and pantry while the other chops and assembles them in the baking dish.

Storage

Leftovers will keep, refrigerated, for up to 2 days.

Diet
Pescatarian, gluten-free

Crispy Fish
with Remoulade

SERVES 4

Crispy Fish

1½ lb [680 g] tilapia

1 cup [80 g] panko

1 Tbsp olive oil

½ cup [15 g] shredded Parmesan cheese

1 tsp garlic powder

1 tsp onion powder

1 tsp smoked paprika

¾ tsp kosher salt, plus more for sprinkling

2 eggs

Remoulade

½ cup [120 g] mayonnaise

2 Tbsp drained capers, finely chopped

1 green onion, minced

1 Tbsp Dijon mustard

2 tsp Cajun seasoning

1 tsp white wine vinegar

½ tsp sugar

COOK 2

COOK 1

To prepare the fish, preheat the oven to 425°F [220°C]. Bring the fish to room temperature and cut it into 4 fillets (or pieces).

In a medium bowl, mix the panko with the olive oil. Pour it onto a rimmed baking sheet in an even layer and bake until lightly browned, 4 to 5 minutes. Pour the toasted bread crumbs into a shallow bowl and let cool for 1 minute. Add the Parmesan cheese, garlic powder, onion powder, smoked paprika, and kosher salt.

In another shallow bowl, whisk the eggs.

When the baking sheet is cool, wipe out any remaining crumbs and line it with parchment paper.

Working with each fish fillet, dredge in the eggs and tap off any excess liquid. Set it in the breadcrumb mixture and toss until fully coated. Arrange the fillets on the lined baking sheet. When all of the fillets are breaded, sprinkle them with a few more pinches of kosher salt.

Bake until the outside is golden brown, the flesh is flaky, and the internal temperature measures 140°F [60°C] at the thickest point, 11 to 15 minutes depending on the thickness of the fillets.

To make the remoulade sauce, in a medium bowl, combine all the ingredients.

When the fish is done, serve immediately, topped with remoulade.

We can't resist a piece of good crispy fish, but frying it at home can be tricky and rather messy. So here's a baked fish recipe that's easier to pull off and just as tasty as fried. Each bite pairs a seasoned, crispy exterior with a buttery, moist interior. (Our son goes crazy over it, so it's a hit with kids, too.)

The creamy remoulade for dipping is an absolute must! This luscious sauce originated in France and is commonly served with fish in Cajun and Creole cuisine. Its blend of bright, creamy, and savory is pure bliss—and it's equally great with fries or Crispy Potato Wedges (page 221).

Tips

We recommend tilapia because it's easier to find in thinner fillets. Cod or other white fish also work, though cod is generally thicker so it will need a few minutes longer cook time.

This also makes a great fish sandwich! Serve on a bun with lettuce and remoulade sauce.

Even with the Cajun seasoning, the remoulade is mild and works for serving to spice-sensitive eaters.

Cooking Together

One cook makes the remoulade while the other seasons and dredges the fish.

For Gluten-Free

Use gluten-free panko.

Storage

Leftovers will keep, refrigerated, for 1 day; rewarm them in a 375°F [190°C] oven.

Diet
Pescatarian,
gluten-free option

Salmon Piccata

COOK 2 —————— COOK 1

SERVES 4

Four 6 oz [170 g] salmon fillets, skin on

¾ tsp kosher salt

Freshly ground black pepper

½ cup [70 g] all-purpose flour

3 Tbsp [45 g] unsalted butter

1 Tbsp olive oil

1 medium shallot, minced

½ cup [120 ml] vegetable broth

¼ cup [60 ml] fresh lemon juice

½ Tbsp lemon zest

3 Tbsp [45 g] capers, drained

Lemon wheels, for garnishing

Finely chopped parsley, for garnishing

Allow the salmon to come to room temperature. Season the fillets with the kosher salt and plenty of black pepper. Spread the flour on a plate and dredge each fillet until lightly coated with flour on all sides.

In a large skillet over medium-high heat, heat 1 tablespoon of the butter and the olive oil. When the butter is melted, add the salmon, skin side up. Cook until the bottom is browned, 3 to 4 minutes. Flip and cook skin side down until browned, 1 to 2 minutes—watch to make sure the flour doesn't burn. Transfer the salmon to a plate and turn down the heat to low.

Add another tablespoon of the butter to the same pan; when it melts, add the shallot and cook, stirring frequently, until transparent and fragrant, about 1 minute. Add the remaining 1 tablespoon of butter and the vegetable broth, lemon juice and zest, and capers, scraping up the browned bits from the bottom of the pan. Add the salmon to the pan, skin side down. Bring to a simmer and cook, occasionally spooning the sauce over the fish, until the fish is fully cooked, about 5 minutes. For a medium salmon, cook until the internal temperature reaches at least 130°F [55°C] when measured with a food thermometer at the thickest point.

To serve, garnish the salmon with lemon wheels and chopped parsley. Drizzle a few spoonfuls of sauce over each fillet and serve.

Here's how to make salmon sing: Pair it with butter, lemon, and capers in a move that's genius in its simplicity. Swapping fish for chicken in this classic Italian American dish makes it (dare we say?) even more irresistible than the original. The salmon turns moist and tender in the buttery sauce, and the light breading gives a satisfying texture to each bite.

This one never fails to get big wows around our table, and we hope it will do the same for you! Serve with rice or orzo, Everyday Arugula Salad (page 187), Blistered Green Beans Almondine (page 217), or Lemon Asparagus with Crispy Prosciutto (page 211).

Tips

Make chicken piccata using the same method: Use two boneless skinless chicken breasts or 4 cutlets (about 1½ lbs [680 g]). Pat the chicken dry with a paper towel. If using breasts, slice them in half horizontally (if you bought cutlets, skip this step). Then follow the steps in this recipe, using 1 teaspoon kosher salt to season the chicken.

A food thermometer is the best way to measure the internal temperature of fish. The temperature of 130°F [55°C] makes for moist, tender salmon. Feel free to cook up to 140°F [60°C] if you prefer a more well-done piece of fish.

Wine Pairing

Pair this dish with a pinot noir. This red wine is known for its bright acidity, medium body, and fruity flavors, making it a perfect companion for the rich and flavorful salmon dish. We love the light and bright flavor of a pinot noir from Oregon.

Cooking Together

Assign the fish prep to one of you! That person can season and dredge the fish while the other prepares the remaining ingredients.

For Gluten-Free

Omit the flour or use gluten-free flour.

For Dairy-Free

Use vegan butter.

Storage

Leftover salmon will keep, refrigerated, for up to 3 days.

Diet
Pescatarian, gluten-free option, dairy-free option

Blackened Shrimp Tacos
with Avocado Lime Sauce

**MAKES 8 TACOS
(4 SERVINGS)**

Blackened Shrimp

1 lb [455 g] medium shrimp, deveined (tail on or peeled) (see Tips)

1 Tbsp smoked paprika

1 tsp onion powder

1 tsp garlic powder

1 tsp oregano

¼ tsp celery seed

⅛ tsp cayenne (optional)

½ tsp kosher salt

2 Tbsp extra-virgin olive oil

Eight 6 in [15 cm] corn or flour tortillas

Feta or cotija cheese crumbles, for garnishing

Fresh cilantro leaves, torn, for garnishing

Avocado Lime Sauce

1 ripe avocado

⅓ cup [80 g] sour cream

2 Tbsp mayonnaise

3 Tbsp [45 ml] fresh lime juice, plus zest of ½ lime

⅛ tsp grated garlic

½ tsp kosher salt

Quick Slaw

2 cups [110 g] shredded red cabbage

1 Tbsp apple cider vinegar

¼ tsp cumin

¼ tsp sugar, or honey

¼ tsp kosher salt

To make the blackened shrimp, allow the shrimp to come to room temperature.

Meanwhile, to make the avocado lime sauce, scoop the avocado flesh into a food processor or small blender. Add the sour cream, mayonnaise, lime juice and zest, garlic, and kosher salt. Blend until smooth, stopping to scrape down the sides as necessary.

In a medium bowl, make the quick slaw by combining the cabbage, apple cider vinegar, cumin, sugar, and kosher salt. Set aside.

Pat the shrimp dry with a clean towel or paper towel, then put it in a bowl. Add the smoked paprika, onion powder, garlic powder, oregano, celery seed, cayenne, and kosher salt and mix to combine.

Heat the olive oil over high heat in a large cast-iron or stainless steel skillet. Add the shrimp in a single layer. Cook on one side until lightly charred, 1 to 2 minutes, then turn with tongs and cook until opaque throughout, another 20 to 30 seconds.

Warm and char the tortillas by placing them on an open gas flame on medium until they are slightly blackened and warm, flipping with tongs, a few seconds per side. Alternatively, place the tortillas in foil and warm them in a preheated 300°F [150°C] oven for about 10 minutes.

To serve, place a scoop of slaw in a tortilla, then top with 3 to 4 shrimp and the avocado lime sauce. Sprinkle with feta cheese crumbles and torn cilantro leaves and serve.

COOK 2

COOK 1

Who can resist a good shrimp taco? (We certainly can't.) The combination of charred juicy seafood, crunchy slaw, and zingy avocado lime sauce hits the spot every time. This one is easy for a pair of cooks to make: The separate components make it easy to divide tasks, so you can chat away as you slice and sauté.

Blackening is a technique in Cajun cuisine where meat or fish is cooked in a skillet with a spice blend until the outside is lightly charred. Each chef has a custom mix of spices that make "blackening seasoning"; ours is a simplified riff that still achieves big flavor. Serve up the tacos with chips and Corn & Feta Salad (page 199), Charred Corn Guacamole (see page 258), or Cilantro Lime Chopped Salad (see page 193).

Tips

Avoid small shrimp here. We like 21- to 25-count for medium-size, juicy shrimp; 26- to 30-count also works well.

For a different serving spin, the Blackened Shrimp is tasty served on a bed of rice with a side of pico de gallo. Serve with the tangy avocado lime sauce for dipping; if you're not serving with the sauce, make sure to spritz the shrimp liberally with fresh lime juice.

Alternative grilled method: Preheat a grill to medium-high heat (375°F to 450°F [190°C to 230°C]). Put the shrimp directly on the grates and grill until opaque and cooked through, 1 to 2 minutes per side.

If you're a taco lover, a tortilla warmer is worth the purchase! It's inexpensive and effective at keeping those tortillas soft and warm.

To speed up prep, make the avocado lime sauce and quick slaw in advance and refrigerate until serving.

Cooking Together

Divide and conquer! Have one of you take on the sauce and the shrimp, while the other preps the slaw and the tortillas.

For Gluten-Free

Use corn tortillas.

For Dairy-Free

Substitute vegan sour cream in the avocado sauce.

Storage

Leftover shrimp will keep, refrigerated, for 2 to 3 days. The avocado lime sauce will keep (and stay green), refrigerated, for up to 5 days.

Diet
Pescatarian,
gluten-free option,
dairy-free option

Pasta al Limone *with Shrimp*

SERVES 3 TO 4

8 oz [230 g] spaghetti
or bucatini

1 lb [455 g] medium shrimp,
deveined (tail on or peeled)

¾ tsp kosher salt

Freshly ground black pepper

2 Tbsp olive oil

6 garlic cloves, finely minced

4 Tbsp [55 g] salted butter

¼ cup [60 ml] fresh lemon juice

Zest of 1 large or 2 small lemons

¼ cup [8 g] grated Parmesan
cheese, plus more for
garnishing

1 Tbsp heavy cream

Finely minced parsley,
for garnishing

Lemon wheels or wedges,
for garnishing (optional)

Bring a pot of salted water to a boil. Add the pasta and boil until al dente. Reserve ½ cup [120 ml] of the pasta water. Drain the pasta, then toss it with a drizzle of olive oil to prevent sticking.

Meanwhile, pat the shrimp dry. Place them in a medium bowl and stir together with ½ teaspoon of the kosher salt and the black pepper.

In a very large skillet, heat the olive oil over medium heat. Add the garlic and cook for 30 seconds. Add the shrimp in a single layer and cook, turning halfway through, until just cooked, about 3 minutes total. Transfer the shrimp to a bowl.

In the same skillet over medium-low heat, combine the butter, lemon juice, lemon zest, Parmesan cheese, heavy cream, the remaining ¼ teaspoon of kosher salt, and ¼ cup [60 ml] of the reserved pasta water. Simmer until slightly thickened, about 2 minutes. Remove from the heat. Add the shrimp and pasta to the skillet and toss with the warm sauce (add a splash more pasta water if you'd like a thinner sauce).

Garnish with parsley and more Parmesan cheese, plus lemon wheels or wedges, if desired. Serve immediately.

COOK 1 ———— COOK 2

contd.

This one is an ode to the Amalfi Coast of Italy, a region abundant with citrus and seafood. We fell in love with simple pastas like this one while honeymooning there, marveling at the impossibly blue Mediterranean Sea and lemon groves clinging to the cliffs. This recipe, pairing bright lemon with garlic and juicy shrimp, takes us right back to those days. It's one of those meals that tastes much greater than the sum of its parts. One bite and you'll be a believer.

Tip

The pasta becomes drier as it sits. If necessary, reheat the skillet and add another few splashes of pasta water or a spritz of lemon juice.

Wine Pairing

Enhance the experience with a white Italian table wine (ask for a recommendation at your local wine store). Whether a pinot grigio or a blend, Italian whites offer crisp and fruity notes that go hand in hand with this pasta.

Cooking Together

One of you can start the pasta and mise-en-place the sauce ingredients while the other starts cooking the shrimp.

Storage

The pasta is best the day it is made. Leftovers will keep, refrigerated, for 1 day.

Diet
Pescatarian

Pressed Manchego & Prosciutto Sandwiches

**MAKES 4 SMALL OR
2 LARGE SANDWICHES**

8 slices sourdough bread or
one 14 in [35 cm] artisan loaf
(like a French bâtard, ciabatta,
or Cuban loaf)

4 oz [115 g] Manchego cheese,
sliced, rind removed

4 slices (2 oz [60 g]) prosciutto
or jamón serrano

4 small handfuls baby arugula

2 Tbsp mayonnaise

1 Tbsp Dijon mustard

⅛ tsp dried dill

2 Tbsp salted butter

Slice the sourdough into eight ¾ in [2 cm]
thick slices or slice the large artisan loaf in half
lengthwise and in half widthwise.

On each bottom slice of bread, place the
Manchego cheese slices, then add a slice of
prosciutto and a small handful of baby arugula.

In a small bowl, mix the mayonnaise, Dijon
mustard, and dried dill. Spread on each top slice
and place it on top of the arugula.

In a large skillet, melt the butter over medium
heat. Add the sandwiches and cook until golden
brown, 2 to 3 minutes, pressing down with the
bottom of another skillet several times throughout
the cooking time to flatten the sandwiches. Flip
and cook the other side until golden brown and
the cheese is soft and the bread toasted, another
2 to 3 minutes, again pressing down with the
skillet several times. Serve immediately.

COOK 1 ———— COOK 2

This sandwich is a play on one we once shared at Spanish restaurant
Jaleo by José Andrés. The intense crunch of the bread, the smoky
cured ham, and the buttery Manchego cheese are pure bliss.

Tips
Make this a gourmet grilled cheese:
Replace the prosciutto with a few
handfuls of shredded mozzarella,
provolone, or gouda cheese.

Another variation: Go savory-sweet!
Add a slather of fig jam or other fruity
preserves in place of the Dijon dill
spread.

Chicken Cutlets *with* Honey Mustard Pan Sauce

COOK 2

COOK 1

SERVES 4

Chicken Cutlets

½ cup [70 g] all-purpose flour

1 Tbsp paprika

1 Tbsp garlic powder

1 Tbsp onion powder

1 lb [455 g] chicken cutlets,
or 2 chicken breasts, sliced in
half horizontally (see Tip)

1 tsp kosher salt

2 Tbsp olive oil

Honey Mustard Pan Sauce

¼ cup [60 g] yellow mustard

¼ cup [85 g] honey

1 Tbsp Dijon mustard

Zest of ½ lemon

½ tsp Worcestershire sauce

¼ tsp kosher salt

⅛ tsp dried thyme

Finely chopped Italian parsley,
for garnishing (optional)

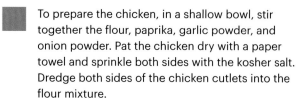

To prepare the chicken, in a shallow bowl, stir together the flour, paprika, garlic powder, and onion powder. Pat the chicken dry with a paper towel and sprinkle both sides with the kosher salt. Dredge both sides of the chicken cutlets into the flour mixture.

To make the honey mustard pan sauce, combine all the sauce ingredients in a medium bowl.

In a stainless steel or cast-iron skillet, heat the olive oil over medium-high heat. Cook the chicken, turning with tongs, until browned and the internal temperature reaches 165°F [75°C], 2 to 3 minutes per side. Transfer the cutlets to a plate.

Turn the heat to low and add the honey mustard pan sauce to the same pan. Cook, scraping the brown bits off the bottom of the pan, until the sauce just starts to thicken and deepen slightly in color, 1 to 2 minutes.

Pour the sauce over the chicken, sprinkle with parsley, if using, and serve.

Here's the kind of dish we love to prepare on a time-stressed weeknight; sharing the cooking tasks, we can get it on the table in 20 minutes. The tender, thin chicken cutlets are pan-fried in a coating of spices, then tossed in a rich, sweet, and tangy brown pan sauce. It's elevated and sophisticated without being fussy, which makes this a star recipe for us.

Pair this one with Herby Quinoa or Rice (page 226), then add a salad or green vegetable such as Lemon Pepper Broccolini (page 219).

Tip

Chicken cutlets are chicken breasts that are cut horizontally, making two thinner pieces. If you can't find cutlets of "thin sliced" chicken breasts at the store, simply slice the breasts in half horizontally with a sharp knife.

Cooking Together

One of you can mix up the sauce, while the other dredges and cooks the chicken.

For Gluten-Free

Use gluten-free flour.

Storage

Leftovers will keep, refrigerated, for up to 3 days.

Diet
Dairy-free,
gluten-free option

Creamy Mediterranean Chicken Skillet

COOK 2 ──────── COOK 1

SERVES 4

2 boneless, skinless chicken breasts (1 lb [455 g]), sliced lengthwise (butterflied) into 4 cutlets (see Tips)

1 tsp kosher salt

Freshly ground black pepper

½ tsp garlic powder

2 Tbsp olive oil

2 Tbsp salted butter

2 garlic cloves, minced

1 tsp dried oregano

1 tsp fresh thyme leaves (see Tips)

1 Tbsp capers, drained

¾ cup [180 ml] heavy cream

2 cups [80 g] roughly chopped fresh spinach, loosely packed

6 small lemon wedges

1 Tbsp grated Parmesan or pecorino romano cheese

Pat the chicken dry with a paper towel. Season both sides of the chicken with the kosher salt, black pepper, and garlic powder.

In a large skillet, heat the olive oil over medium heat. Add the chicken and cook until browned on both sides and the internal temperature is 165°F (74°C), or the center is no longer pink, 3 to 5 minutes per side. Transfer to a plate and set aside.

In the same pan over medium-low heat, melt the butter. Add the garlic, oregano, and thyme and cook until the garlic is lightly browned and fragrant, 30 seconds to 1 minute. Add the capers and cream and simmer for 2 minutes, stirring occasionally and scraping the brown bits off the bottom of the pan. Add the spinach and cook until wilted, about 1 minute, then return the chicken to the pan and warm it for 2 minutes, spooning some of the sauce over the chicken.

Squeeze the lemon wedges onto the chicken and add them to the pan. Top with a sprinkle of Parmesan cheese. Serve warm, with a spoonful of sauce.

contd.

When it comes to picking favorites in this book, this recipe holds a special place in our hearts. Trust us, everyone at the table will be smitten (as in, sneaking extra bites straight from the skillet). The succulent chicken, cozied up in a luscious sauce of cream, spinach, garlic, and herbs, melts in your mouth.

To make it a meal, pair with Herby Quinoa or Rice (page 226). It's fun alongside Crunchy Green Panzanella (page 208), but if you're short on time, stick with Everyday Arugula Salad (page 187).

Tips

Chicken breasts cook up more tender and juicy with the butterflying technique.

If you have time, allow the chicken to stand at room temperature for 30 minutes before cooking; this makes for the most evenly cooked meat.

The fresh thyme makes this dish; if you're not already growing some, it's worth seeking out and paying a little extra at the store.

Wine Pairing

This skillet pairs well with a muscadet from the Loire Valley in France. Its crisp acidity, light body, and minerality complement the rich, creamy sauce.

Storage

Leftovers will keep, refrigerated, for up to 3 days.

Diet
Gluten-free

Mango Chicken Bowls
with Peanut Sauce

SERVES 4

Chicken

2 boneless skinless chicken breasts (1 lb [455 g]), sliced lengthwise (butterflied) into 4 cutlets

1 tsp kosher salt

1 Tbsp olive oil

Zest of 1 lime

1 tsp peeled and grated fresh ginger

Freshly ground black pepper

Mango Salad

1 ripe mango, diced (see Tips)

1 red bell pepper, diced

½ English cucumber, diced

¼ red onion, thinly sliced

3 Tbsp [8 g] roughly chopped cilantro, plus more for serving

3 Tbsp [45 ml] fresh lime juice (2 small or 1 large lime)

1 Tbsp olive oil

½ Tbsp honey

¼ tsp kosher salt

Peanut Sauce

¼ cup [65 g] unsweetened creamy peanut butter

3 Tbsp [45 ml] fresh lime juice (2 small or 1 large lime)

2 Tbsp soy sauce or tamari

2 Tbsp honey

1 tsp peeled and grated fresh ginger

1 medium garlic clove, grated

Cooked white jasmine rice, for serving (see Tips)

Crushed peanuts, for serving

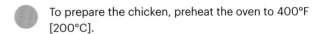 To prepare the chicken, preheat the oven to 400°F [200°C].

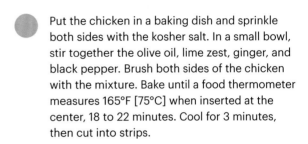 Put the chicken in a baking dish and sprinkle both sides with the kosher salt. In a small bowl, stir together the olive oil, lime zest, ginger, and black pepper. Brush both sides of the chicken with the mixture. Bake until a food thermometer measures 165°F [75°C] when inserted at the center, 18 to 22 minutes. Cool for 3 minutes, then cut into strips.

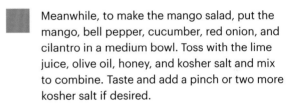 Meanwhile, to make the mango salad, put the mango, bell pepper, cucumber, red onion, and cilantro in a medium bowl. Toss with the lime juice, olive oil, honey, and kosher salt and mix to combine. Taste and add a pinch or two more kosher salt if desired.

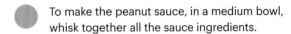 To make the peanut sauce, in a medium bowl, whisk together all the sauce ingredients.

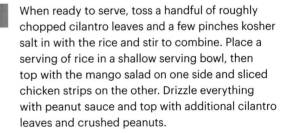 When ready to serve, toss a handful of roughly chopped cilantro leaves and a few pinches kosher salt in with the rice and stir to combine. Place a serving of rice in a shallow serving bowl, then top with the mango salad on one side and sliced chicken strips on the other. Drizzle everything with peanut sauce and top with additional cilantro leaves and crushed peanuts.

COOK 1

COOK 2

contd.

A good peanut sauce is the perfect balance of all five flavors on your tongue: sweet, salty, sour, bitter, and umami. Here's a colorful bowl meal we designed around our favorite one. Drizzle it over juicy chicken strips and a fresh salad of mango, red pepper, and cucumber, garnish with crunchy peanuts and fresh cilantro, and it's *chef's kiss*.

Make it vegetarian or vegan by replacing the chicken with tofu, like the pan-fried tofu from the Coconut Tofu Curry with Green Beans (page 44).

Tips

Jasmine rice tastes uniquely nutty and aromatic; it's worth seeking out for this recipe. You can make it up to 5 days in advance; before serving, reheat on the stovetop with a splash of water until heated through.

Look for a mango that is still firm but indents slightly when pressed with your thumb.

Cooking Together

Have one person start the chicken and make the peanut sauce while the other preps the mango salad.

For Vegetarian or Vegan

Use cooked tofu instead of chicken (cook it as directed in Coconut Tofu Curry with Green Beans, page 44, but use ½ teaspoon of kosher salt). Use agave syrup instead of honey.

For Gluten-Free

Use gluten-free soy sauce or tamari.

Storage

Leftovers will keep, refrigerated, for up to 2 days; refrigerate all components separately.

Diet
Vegetarian option,
vegan option,
gluten-free option

Chicken Gyros
with Tzatziki

MAKES 4 LARGE GYROS

Tzatziki

1 cup [150 g] peeled and grated English cucumber (about ½ large cucumber)

1 small garlic clove, grated

2 Tbsp fresh lemon juice

1 cup [240 g] full-fat Greek yogurt

1 Tbsp olive oil

2 Tbsp fresh dill, plus more for serving

½ tsp kosher salt

Chicken

2 large chicken breasts (1 to 1½ lb [455 to 680 g]), cut in half horizontally and cubed

2 tsp dried oregano

1 tsp kosher salt

½ tsp freshly ground black pepper

1 Tbsp olive oil

¼ cup [35 g] minced onion

2 garlic cloves, minced

4 pita breads

1 romaine heart, chopped

1 cup [110 g] English cucumber, sliced into half-moons

1 cup [150 g] cherry tomatoes, quartered

1 recipe Pickled Red Onions (page 128) or 1 handful sliced red onion

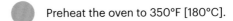 Preheat the oven to 350°F [180°C].

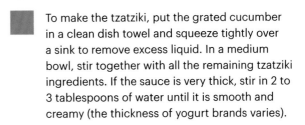 To make the tzatziki, put the grated cucumber in a clean dish towel and squeeze tightly over a sink to remove excess liquid. In a medium bowl, stir together with all the remaining tzatziki ingredients. If the sauce is very thick, stir in 2 to 3 tablespoons of water until it is smooth and creamy (the thickness of yogurt brands varies).

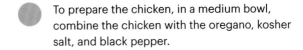 To prepare the chicken, in a medium bowl, combine the chicken with the oregano, kosher salt, and black pepper.

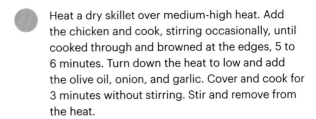 Heat a dry skillet over medium-high heat. Add the chicken and cook, stirring occasionally, until cooked through and browned at the edges, 5 to 6 minutes. Turn down the heat to low and add the olive oil, onion, and garlic. Cover and cook for 3 minutes without stirring. Stir and remove from the heat.

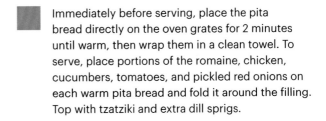 Immediately before serving, place the pita bread directly on the oven grates for 2 minutes until warm, then wrap them in a clean towel. To serve, place portions of the romaine, chicken, cucumbers, tomatoes, and pickled red onions on each warm pita bread and fold it around the filling. Top with tzatziki and extra dill sprigs.

COOK 1 —————— COOK 2

contd.

Greek gyros are in our personal hall of fame of favorite foods, especially after trying them years ago on the sun-drenched island of Santorini. This chicken version is fun to whip up and comes out brilliantly, with pillowy soft pita and crunchy veggies all drenched in a cool tzatziki. They're similar to the takeout we occasionally get from our local corner gyro joint, but when we have time, we whip up this homemade version. It's a total hit on our dinner playlist!

Tips

Make sure to wrap the pita bread around the gyros filling instead of stuffing the pita pocket.

The pickled red onions and tzatziki develop in flavor over time! Make them the day before and refrigerate if you have time. Use leftover tzatziki as a dip for veggies or a sauce for grain bowls. Pickled red onions are also great on Kale Salad with Creamy Parmesan Dressing (page 189), Nacho-Loaded Sweet Potato Bar (page 125), and Sweet Potato Enchiladas (page 31).

Cooking Together

Divvy it up! Have one person make the pickled red onions while the other makes the tzatziki. Then have one person cook the chicken while the other preps the vegetables and pita bread.

Storage

The tzatziki will keep, refrigerated, for up to 1 week; the chicken and vegetables, for up to 3 days.

Meatballs *with* Fire-Roasted Marinara

SERVES 4

Marinara Sauce

2 Tbsp olive oil

One 14½ oz [415 g] can crushed fire-roasted tomatoes (see Tips)

2 handfuls fresh basil, roughly torn, plus more for garnishing

¼ tsp dried thyme

¼ tsp dried rosemary

½ tsp kosher salt

1 pinch red pepper flakes

Meatballs

½ cup [40 g] panko

½ cup [15 g] grated Parmesan cheese, plus more for garnishing

2 garlic cloves, grated

2 tsp dried oregano

1 tsp kosher salt

Freshly ground black pepper

1 lb [455 g] ground beef or plant-based ground beef

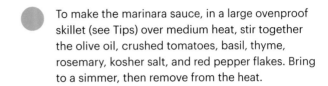 Preheat the oven to 450°F [230°C].

To make the marinara sauce, in a large ovenproof skillet (see Tips) over medium heat, stir together the olive oil, crushed tomatoes, basil, thyme, rosemary, kosher salt, and red pepper flakes. Bring to a simmer, then remove from the heat.

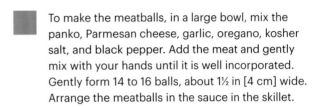 To make the meatballs, in a large bowl, mix the panko, Parmesan cheese, garlic, oregano, kosher salt, and black pepper. Add the meat and gently mix with your hands until it is well incorporated. Gently form 14 to 16 balls, about 1½ in [4 cm] wide. Arrange the meatballs in the sauce in the skillet.

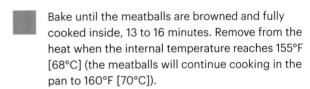 Bake until the meatballs are browned and fully cooked inside, 13 to 16 minutes. Remove from the heat when the internal temperature reaches 155°F [68°C] (the meatballs will continue cooking in the pan to 160°F [70°C]).

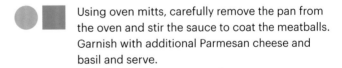 Using oven mitts, carefully remove the pan from the oven and stir the sauce to coat the meatballs. Garnish with additional Parmesan cheese and basil and serve.

COOK 1 ——————————————— COOK 2

contd.

This skillet of bold red sauce comes together in minutes for a dinner that will make you feel like a rock star. Canned fire-roasted tomatoes are the trick to the developed, cozy undertones in this sauce. Roasted over an open flame, they have a sweet flavor that saves you precious minutes of simmering time. Serve with pasta (with double the sauce) or in shallow bowls with Lemon Pepper Broccolini (page 219) and Heart-Melting Garlicky Greens (page 214).

These meatballs work with plant-based meat crumbles, too. Look for any plant-based ground beef or sausage (and dairy-free Parmesan if desired).

Tips

If you're planning to serve this as a sauce to cover pasta, double the marinara sauce ingredients.

Avoid using a cast-iron skillet for this recipe. The acid in the tomatoes can make it impart a metallic aftertaste to the dish.

Can't find fire-roasted tomatoes? Use the best-quality canned crushed tomatoes you can find, add 1 pinch of sugar, and simmer for 15 minutes before adding the meatballs.

Repurpose leftovers as a meatball sandwich! Place crusty sub or hoagie rolls on a baking sheet, brush with olive oil, and season with kosher salt. Broil for 1 minute, then add the meatballs (reheated) and a sprinkle of shredded mozzarella cheese. Broil until the cheese melts, 1 to 2 minutes. Top with chopped Italian parsley or basil.

Wine Pairing

Go bold with a California zinfandel. This red wine, known for its fruitiness and spicy undertones, enhances the richness of the meatballs and the sweet, smoky flavor of the sauce.

Cooking Together

One of you can make the marinara while the other forms the meatballs. Toss them together and get a side ready while they bake.

For Vegetarian

Use plant-based meat crumbles.

For Vegan

Use plant-based meat crumbles and dairy-free Parmesan.

For Gluten-Free

Use gluten-free panko.

Storage

Meatballs will keep, refrigerated, for up to 3 days.

Diet
Vegetarian option, vegan option, gluten-free option

Tips for a Date Night In

We love a good evening out, with white napkins and attentively murmuring servers. But when it comes to date night, often we'd rather pour our own bottle of wine, put on some good tunes, and cook up dinner together.

Actually, that's how the two of us fell in love with cooking in the first place! Our initial cooking dates were pretty basic. But after we honeymooned in Italy, food started to captivate us in a new way—especially pizza.

That started our pizza Friday tradition, each week trying to make an artisan pie that outshone the pizza from the week before. Sure, there were mistakes and spills and the occasional blackened crust. But there were also laughs, inside jokes, and new memories made together.

Want to have an epic date night in? Here a few pointers to set yourself up for success:

- **Set the mood with music.** Use a playlist of your favorite tunes to get the party started.

- **Open a bottle of wine or make a signature beverage.** We've sprinkled some wine pairing suggestions throughout the book, or go with cocktails for two, like the Perfect Margaritas for Two (page 313) or Amaretto Whiskey Sours (page 333).

- **Put out a few easy snacks to nosh on while cooking.** Avoid getting hangry—that's hungry plus angry—the worst way to start a date night! Think mini-charcuterie: a gourmet cheese with crackers, a bowl of nuts, veggies and hummus, and so on.

- **Appreciate each person's work style.** Different approaches can be tricky to manage: clean-as-you go versus make-a-big-mess, the follow-the-recipe-exactly cook versus the free-styler. Before you start, take time to read our Tips for Cooking as a Team (page 14).

- **Take your time.** Focus on the fun in the process, not the end goal.

- **Go simple on dessert.** With a full meal to cook together, dessert can sometimes feel overly ambitious. Buy a bar of fancy chocolate, or whip up a Chocolate Ganache Tart for Two (page 281) and let it refrigerate while cooking. In summer, serve homemade Whipped Cream (page 303) with fresh berries and mint, or simply pour hot espresso over vanilla ice cream to make the simplest Italian dessert, affogato.

- **One last tip:** If young kids are in the picture, date nights can be tricky. Once we had children, it was much more difficult to find time for cooking together as a date. With very young kiddos, sometimes it can work to have a late dinner date after the kids are in bed. With school-age kids, try setting them up with a movie and pizza while the two of you commandeer the kitchen.

Chapter 2

JUST FOR
Two

These two-serving recipes are just the thing for a special evening for two, whether it's a cozy night with your sweetheart, a catch-up with your bestie, or a cooking date with a family member. They're fancy enough to wow, but practical enough that you won't spend three hours making four sauces and end up exhausted before you take the first bite!

So grab a partner, roll up your sleeves, and let's get cooking.

SOME HIGHLIGHTS IN THIS CHAPTER:

Bake up a Date-Night Pizza for a cozy night in (page 88).

Escape to Italy with a fancy Truffle Pasta with Mixed Mushrooms & Goat Cheese (page 93).

Try seasonal Risotto with Asparagus, Peas & Pine Nuts in spring (page 95) or Grilled Eggplant Parmesan with Burrata in summer (page 99).

Opt for simple but elegant Pecorino Shrimp & Grits that's ready in 15 minutes (page 105).

Spice up your relationship with Sweet Heat Salmon (page 110).

Cook up a sumptuous Seared New York Strip Steak with Garlic Mushrooms (page 117).

Date-Night Pizza

MAKES 1 LARGE PIZZA

Pizza Dough

2 cups [280 g] Tipo 00
or bread flour

½ Tbsp active dry yeast

1 tsp kosher salt

¾ cup [180 ml] warm water

½ Tbsp olive oil

Sauce

½ cup [140 g] crushed fire-
roasted tomatoes, or best-
quality crushed tomatoes

1 tsp olive oil

½ small garlic clove, grated

¼ tsp dried oregano

Heaping ⅛ tsp kosher salt

¾ cup [90 g] shredded whole-
milk mozzarella cheese

¼ cup [20 g] grated pecorino
romano cheese

1 handful sliced red onion

1 handful sliced, jarred
pepperoncini

1½ Tbsp Italian seasoned panko
(optional)

1 handful fresh basil, some
finely chopped and some small
whole leaves

COOK 2

COOK 1

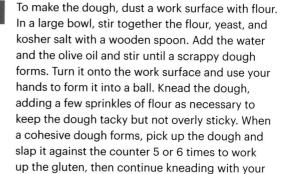

To make the dough, dust a work surface with flour. In a large bowl, stir together the flour, yeast, and kosher salt with a wooden spoon. Add the water and the olive oil and stir until a scrappy dough forms. Turn it onto the work surface and use your hands to form it into a ball. Knead the dough, adding a few sprinkles of flour as necessary to keep the dough tacky but not overly sticky. When a cohesive dough forms, pick up the dough and slap it against the counter 5 or 6 times to work up the gluten, then continue kneading with your hands until the dough is very smooth, pillowy, and just a bit tacky, 7 to 8 minutes. (Alternatively, attach the dough hook to a stand mixer and knead on low speed for 7 to 8 minutes.)

On a work surface, form the dough into a boule by stretching and folding it under itself several times until the top is taut and smooth like a ball. Cut a 12 in [30.5 cm] square of parchment paper and set the boule in the center. Rub the top of the boule with a drizzle of olive oil. Cover it with a clean damp towel and let rest until doubled in size, 45 minutes to 1 hour.

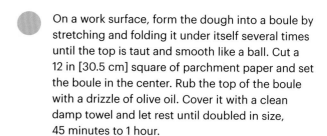

Meanwhile, to make the pizza sauce, in a small bowl, mix the crushed tomatoes, olive oil, garlic, oregano, and kosher salt.

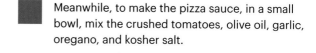

At least 30 minutes before baking, set a pizza stone on the middle rack of the oven and preheat to 475°F [246°C].

When ready to bake the pizza, remove the towel and press the dough lightly into a circle. Carefully pick it up and drape it over your knuckles to stretch it slightly, then return it to the parchment paper and form into an 11 in [28 cm] round. Create the crust by gently pressing your fingers into the dough about 1 in [2.5 cm] from the edge all the way around the crust. Brush the edge of the crust lightly with olive oil.

A COUPLE COOKS

■ Cut off any parchment paper that extends more than 1 in [2.5 cm] beyond the crust. Spread the pizza sauce evenly onto the dough with the back of a spoon. Top with the mozzarella, pecorino romano, red onion, pepperoncini, and panko, if using.

● ■ Slide an unrimmed baking sheet under the pizza and parchment paper. Open the oven and carefully use the baking sheet to slide the pizza and parchment paper onto the hot pizza stone.

● ■ Bake until the cheese is melted and slightly browned, 7 to 10 minutes. To remove from the oven, transfer the pizza to the baking sheet and set it on a cutting board. Top with the basil and let cool for 2 minutes. Slice and serve.

COOK 1 ──────── ● ■ ──────── COOK 2

contd.

Our honeymoon took us to Italy, where we hoped to soak in the history, dip our toes in the Mediterranean, and most importantly, eat all the pizza. And it was pizza as we'd never experienced before: supple, lightly charred dough; sweet, garlicky tomatoes; and gooey, rich mozzarella. On the plane ride home, we asked ourselves: How can we re-create this at home? Our pizza date-night tradition was born.

Homemade pizza is the ideal cooking date for two: It's hands-on, the pacing is perfect for conversation, and there's something *oh-so-satisfying* about creating an artisan pie that will rival any from your favorite pizzeria. Like the good Italian pizzas, this recipe is an exercise in simplicity and letting quality ingredients shine. It's hearty and satisfying enough for any eater, though meat lovers may want to add cooked sausage or torn slices of prosciutto.

So here's to pizza night! Throw on some good tunes, grab a bottle of wine, and make the dough together. While the dough rests, clean up and make an Everyday Arugula Salad (page 187) or a Big Chopped Salad (page 193), and maybe some Tiramisu Sundaes (page 306) before baking the pizza together. Buon appetito!

Tips

A pizza stone is key for achieving a crisp-on-the-outside, soft-on-the-inside crust.

Don't have a pizza stone? Substitute a very large cast-iron pan, at least 12 inches [30 cm] in diameter, turned upside down in the oven. Place a baking sheet underneath to catch any drips. If all you have is a smaller cast-iron pan, divide the dough into 2 smaller pizzas and bake them separately.

We recommend using a food scale to weigh the flour in grams for the dough. This provides the most precision when baking.

Tipo 00 flour is finely ground Italian flour that Neapolitan pizza restaurants use to make a supple, fluffy dough; it's available at some grocery stores or online. Bread flour also makes a top-notch dough. We recommend either of these over all-purpose flour (though in a pinch, that also works).

For the toppings, fire-roasted tomatoes are key to the no-cook sauce; their flavor is sweet and developed right out of the can. Whole-milk, low-moisture shredded mozzarella cheese is also worth seeking out here. It has a rich flavor and melts and stretches better than part-skim mozzarella

To take it over the top, use a culinary torch to simulate the char of a wood-fired pizza oven. After baking, torch the crust in several spots until small black char marks appear.

A drizzle of hot honey also makes this pizza shine. Mix 2 tablespoons of honey with 1 teaspoon of chopped Calabrian chili peppers or 1 teaspoon of hot sauce.

The dough and pizza sauce are easy to double if you'd like to make this for a double date or dinner party. If making 2 pizzas at once, rise the first dough for 45 minutes and bake it, then bake the second dough after proofing for 1 hour. If the dough rises more than 1 hour, reform it into a boule and let it rest for 15 minutes before stretching.

Wine Pairing

Opt for a bottle of Côtes du Rhône. Pairing a French wine with Italian pizza might seem unexpected, but this red wine has berry undertones and a hint of spiciness, which accentuate the variety of flavors on this pie. Enjoy it while you're cooking and with the meal!

Cooking Together

Mix up the dough together and take turns kneading (if you're doing it by hand). While the dough rises, share the tasks of preparing the toppings. Then have one person shape the dough and the other top the pizza. Clean up as you go, and you'll be able to enjoy a clean kitchen after dinner!

Storage

Leftover pizza will keep, refrigerated, for 2 days.

Diet
Vegetarian

Truffle Pasta *with* Mixed Mushrooms & Goat Cheese

SERVES 2

4 oz [115 g] dried tagliatelle pasta, linguine, fettuccine, or 6 oz [170 g] fresh pasta

2 Tbsp olive oil

8 oz [230 g] cremini (a.k.a. baby bella) mushrooms, brushed clean and sliced

4 oz [115 g] oyster, maitake, or shiitake mushrooms, cleaned and stems removed (see Tips)

¾ tsp kosher salt

1 garlic clove, minced

1 Tbsp fresh sage, minced

1 tsp to 1 Tbsp natural truffle oil (see Tips)

¼ cup [60 ml] heavy cream

2 oz [55 g] soft goat cheese, crumbled

Freshly ground black pepper

Fresh grated Parmesan cheese, for garnishing

Bring a pot of salted water to a boil. Once you start cooking the mushrooms (in the following step), add the pasta and boil until al dente (see Tips). Reserve ½ cup [120 ml] of the pasta water.

In a large cast-iron or stainless steel skillet, heat the olive oil over medium-high heat. Add the mushrooms and ½ teaspoon of the kosher salt and cook for 3 minutes, stirring occasionally. Lower the heat to medium and cook until the mushrooms are tender and golden brown, another 4 to 5 minutes.

Turn the heat down to low, add the garlic and 2 teaspoons of the sage, and cook until the garlic is starting to turn golden, about 1 minute. Add the truffle oil and cream to the skillet and stir until a sauce forms, then remove from the heat.

Take the pasta out of the water with tongs and add it to the mushrooms. Stir in the goat cheese, the remaining ¼ teaspoon of kosher salt, and black pepper to taste. Add a splash of the reserved pasta water to loosen the sauce. Taste and add more truffle oil to taste (see Tips). Serve immediately, garnished with the remaining sage and Parmesan cheese.

COOK 1 —— COOK 2

contd.

What's better than two plates piled high with elegant long noodles to twirl alongside glasses of crisp wine? We created this one for special celebrations like birthdays, anniversaries, or Valentine's Day. It's especially memorable paired with a Chocolate Ganache Tart for Two (page 281).

This pasta for two brings in one of our favorite flavor tricks: black truffles. The earthy, pungent notes of this notoriously expensive fungus take the dish to gourmet status. Look for natural truffle oil (not synthetic), which tastes delicate and authentic. Of course, if you're feeling extra fancy, top it off with real shaved black truffles.

Tips

This recipe is timed so the pasta finishes just after the mushrooms are cooked. If the pasta finishes first, reserve the ½ cup [120 ml] of pasta water, then drain. Return the pasta to the pot, toss with a little olive oil, and reserve until the mushrooms are cooked.

For oyster mushrooms, slice off the bottom stem to separate the individual caps. For maitake mushrooms, use your fingers to pull them into bite-size segments. For shiitake mushrooms, remove the stems and slice any larger caps into bite-size pieces. To clean the mushrooms, give them a quick rinse if you see dirt, and pat them dry (don't soak).

Our favorite brand of truffle oil (TRUFF) tastes great with 1 tablespoon in this recipe, but each brand is different, so adjust to taste. Avoid using synthetic truffle oil if possible. If that's all you can find, start with half of the amount listed (or less).

If you have access to real black truffles, grate them over the top of this pasta in place of truffle oil. We've also found canned truffles and mushrooms (by the brand Urbani) that work well here; stir in 1 to 2 tablespoons of the paste to taste.

Other ways to use truffle oil once you have a bottle? Drizzle on pizza, pasta, sandwiches, risotto, or scrambled eggs, or toss with french fries.

Wine Pairing

We recommend serving with a chilled Albariño wine from Spain. The bright, citrusy notes help to cut through the richness of the creamy goat cheese and complement the earthy truffles and mushrooms.

Cooking Together

Chop the ingredients together, then have one person cook the mushrooms and sauce while the other cooks the pasta.

Diet
Vegetarian

Risotto *with Asparagus, Peas & Pine Nuts*

SERVES 2

4 cups [960 ml] water

¼ cup [60 g] light miso (white or yellow)

4 sprigs rosemary

1½ tsp kosher salt

Freshly ground black pepper

½ lb [230 g] thin asparagus spears, trimmed and cut into 3 in [7.5 cm] pieces

2½ Tbsp extra-virgin olive oil

½ cup [70 g] finely chopped sweet yellow onion

2 garlic cloves, minced

1 cup [200 g] white arborio rice

½ cup [120 ml] dry white wine, such as a pinot grigio or unoaked chardonnay

2 Tbsp pine nuts

1 Tbsp refined coconut oil (see Tips)

½ cup [60 g] frozen peas, warmed under hot water

¼ tsp granulated sugar

Zest of ½ lemon, plus more for garnishing

Flaky smoked salt, for garnishing (optional)

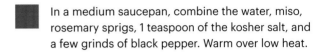 Preheat the oven to 425°F [220°C].

In a medium saucepan, combine the water, miso, rosemary sprigs, 1 teaspoon of the kosher salt, and a few grinds of black pepper. Warm over low heat.

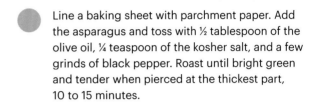 Line a baking sheet with parchment paper. Add the asparagus and toss with ½ tablespoon of the olive oil, ¼ teaspoon of the kosher salt, and a few grinds of black pepper. Roast until bright green and tender when pierced at the thickest part, 10 to 15 minutes.

In a medium skillet over medium heat, heat the remaining 2 tablespoons of olive oil. Add the onion and sauté until tender, 4 to 5 minutes. Add the garlic and rice and cook, stirring occasionally, until the rice starts to turn light brown, about 2 minutes. Add the wine and stir until the liquid is fully absorbed.

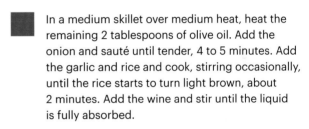 Turn down the heat to medium-low and add one ladle of the hot miso broth to the pan. Cook on a low simmer, stirring occasionally, until the liquid is fully absorbed, then add another ladle of broth. Cook in this manner for 18 minutes, then taste. If the rice is creamy but still al dente in the center, move to the next step. If the rice is still crunchy, continue to cook, adding broth and tasting every few minutes until it is creamy and al dente.

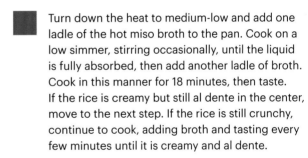 While the rice is cooking, add the pine nuts to a small dry skillet. Toast over medium heat, stirring, until golden, about 3 minutes. Set aside.

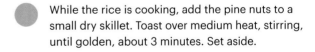 Once the rice is al dente, turn down the heat to low. Add one more ladle of broth, the coconut oil, and a few grinds of black pepper. Stir vigorously for 1 to 2 minutes, until the risotto becomes very creamy. Then stir in the peas, asparagus, sugar, lemon zest, and the remaining ¼ teaspoon of kosher salt. Top with the pine nuts and lemon zest and garnish with a hint of flaky smoked salt, if desired. Serve immediately.

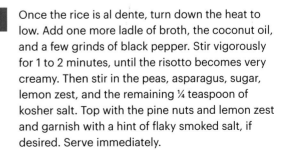

COOK 1

COOK 2

contd.

Risotto is a recipe practically built for two! Turn on some tunes and cook the dish together, toasting with a glass from that open bottle of white wine.

The ingredients absolutely sing—creamy rice, bright green veggies, and a burst of citrus combine with the buttery richness of toasted pine nuts. In a departure from the classic Italian risotto, we've swapped out Parmesan cheese for a surprise element: a miso-rosemary broth. The savoriness it imparts proves there's no need for cheese. In fact, we prefer it this way.

Tips

Don't eat strictly vegan? Use butter in place of the coconut oil and garnish with Parmesan cheese shavings.

Look for packages marked light miso (yellow or white), which has a shorter fermenting time and milder taste. Avoid red or dark miso here, as it is much too strong and salty. Use up leftover miso in Brown Butter–Miso Chocolate Chip Cookie Bars (page 279) or Ginger Miso Dressing (page 194).

We prefer using refined coconut oil, as it imparts richness without a strong coconut flavor. If desired, substitute vegan butter.

Wine Pairing

Celebrate this dish with an organic pinot grigio from Italy. Its crisp, light notes balance the savory essence of the miso-rosemary broth and highlight the zesty lemon.

Cooking Together

One of you can roast the asparagus and toast the pine nuts while the other starts the broth and cooks the risotto. Complete the final few minutes of cooking the risotto together.

Storage

Risotto is best served immediately. However, leftovers will keep refrigerated for up to 2 days. Reheat on the stovetop and add a little extra broth and a few pinches of salt to taste.

Diet
Vegetarian, vegan, gluten-free

Grilled Eggplant
Parmesan with Burrata

SERVES 2

1 medium eggplant (about 1 lb [455 g])

1 tsp kosher salt

⅓ cup [45 g] all-purpose flour

2 eggs

½ cup [15 g] grated Parmesan cheese

½ cup [40 g] panko

½ Tbsp dried oregano

One 14½ oz [415 g] can crushed fire-roasted tomatoes

1 garlic clove, grated

1 handful fresh basil, chopped, plus more, for garnishing

1 Tbsp olive oil

½ cup [40 g] shredded whole-milk mozzarella cheese

One 4 oz [115 g] ball burrata cheese

Heat a grill to medium heat, 350°F to 375°F [180°C to 190°C] (or preheat the oven; see Tips for baking instructions).

Cut off the ends of the eggplant and cut it into ½ in [13 mm] slices (to make approximately 9 slices). Sprinkle the slices with a scant ½ teaspoon of the kosher salt and allow them to sit for 10 minutes while preparing the breading ingredients. (Don't wipe off any salt or extra moisture.)

Spread the flour on a plate. Whisk the eggs in a shallow bowl. In another shallow bowl, combine the Parmesan cheese, panko, 1 teaspoon of the oregano, and ¼ teaspoon of the kosher salt.

Dip both sides of each eggplant slice into the flour, then the eggs, then the Parmesan cheese mixture. Place each slice on a baking sheet. When all slices are breaded, discard any remaining breading ingredients.

To make the sauce, in a small saucepan over medium-low heat, combine the crushed tomatoes, garlic, basil, olive oil, the remaining ½ teaspoon of oregano, and a scant ½ teaspoon of the kosher salt. Mix well and warm for at least 5 minutes.

Brush the grates of a grill with neutral oil. Place the breaded eggplant slices on the grates and cook until the bottoms are golden, 5 to 6 minutes. Flip and top each slice with a sprinkle of mozzarella cheese. Continue cooking until the grilled surface is golden and the cheese is melted, 5 to 6 minutes. Slide a knife tip into a slice to make sure the inside is tender; if not, cook a few minutes more.

When the eggplant is done, arrange the slices on a platter or divide between two plates. Top with the warm tomato sauce and torn pieces of burrata cheese. Garnish with basil and serve.

COOK 1 — ● ■ — **COOK 2**

contd.

There's something endlessly satisfying about juicy breaded eggplant rounds drowned in tangy marinara sauce and stretchy cheese. This grilled spin on the Italian classic is *the* warm-weather date-night dinner, in our opinion.

Burrata—fresh mozzarella with gooey cream inside—is our addition to the dish, which takes it over the top (has anyone ever complained about adding burrata?). Add two glasses of wine and you're set! Serve with pasta or a few summer salads.

Tips

To bake, preheat the oven to 425°F [220°C]. Line two baking sheets with parchment paper. Prepare the eggplant as for grilling, placing the rounds on the lined baking sheets. Bake for 10 minutes, then flip, top with the cheese, and bake until tender and golden brown, 10 to 15 minutes more.

Can't find fire-roasted tomatoes? Use best-quality canned crushed tomatoes, add 1 pinch of sugar, and simmer for 15 minutes (San Marzanos are a good substitution).

This recipe is easy to double and make for four if you've got dinner guests.

Wine Pairing

Look for a Montepulciano d'Abruzzo from Italy. This deep red wine is full-bodied and has a bright peppery and berry flavor profile. It's a beautiful complement to the creamy burrata and tangy marinara sauce.

Cooking Together

Choose one person to preheat the grill and make the sauce, while the other cuts and dredges the eggplant slices.

For Gluten-Free

Omit the all-purpose flour dredging step, and substitute almond flour for the panko.

Storage

The dish is best eaten immediately. Leftovers will keep, refrigerated, for up to 2 days.

Diet
Vegetarian, gluten-free option

Gambas al Ajillo
with Crusty Bread

SERVES 2

¾ lb [340 g] medium shrimp, deveined (tail on or peeled) (see Tips)

½ tsp kosher salt, plus more to taste

½ tsp smoked paprika

¼ tsp red pepper flakes

1½ Tbsp dry sherry, or brandy or dry white wine

½ Tbsp fresh lemon juice

½ baguette, for serving

¼ cup [60 ml] olive oil

4 garlic cloves, thinly sliced

Fresh parsley, for garnishing

Lemon wedges, for garnishing

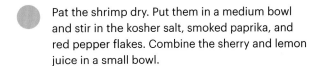 Preheat the oven to 350°F [180°C].

Pat the shrimp dry. Put them in a medium bowl and stir in the kosher salt, smoked paprika, and red pepper flakes. Combine the sherry and lemon juice in a small bowl.

Slice the bread into ¾ in [2 cm] slices and arrange on a baking sheet. Bake until just crisp on the outside and chewy in the middle, about 5 minutes.

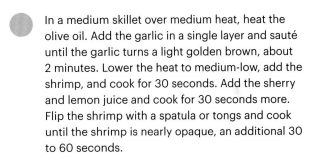 In a medium skillet over medium heat, heat the olive oil. Add the garlic in a single layer and sauté until the garlic turns a light golden brown, about 2 minutes. Lower the heat to medium-low, add the shrimp, and cook for 30 seconds. Add the sherry and lemon juice and cook for 30 seconds more. Flip the shrimp with a spatula or tongs and cook until the shrimp is nearly opaque, an additional 30 to 60 seconds.

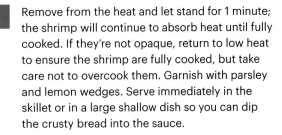 Remove from the heat and let stand for 1 minute; the shrimp will continue to absorb heat until fully cooked. If they're not opaque, return to low heat to ensure the shrimp are fully cooked, but take care not to overcook them. Garnish with parsley and lemon wedges. Serve immediately in the skillet or in a large shallow dish so you can dip the crusty bread into the sauce.

COOK 1

COOK 2

contd.

Gambas al ajillo (shrimp with garlic) is a traditional tapa we discovered together in Spain. Tender shrimp is cooked in garlic-infused olive oil, then tossed with a splash of dry sherry and lemon juice. It takes just a few minutes to make at home, and the flavors are unreal.

While it's typically served as a small plate, we like to eat this dish right out of the skillet as a light date-night meal, paired with a salad (like Sunshine Citrus Salad with Orange & Fennel, page 197). Cozy up with your partner and use chunks of crusty bread to soak up that liquid gold sauce.

Tips

We like using 21- to 25-count shrimp in this recipe for larger, juicer bites, but 26- to 30-count also works.

Dry sherry is best here, but you can substitute brandy or a dry white wine if desired.

Drink Pairing

Don't waste the bottle of sherry! Pair this meal with our Sherry Negroni. Fill a rocks glass with ice and add 1 ounce [30 ml] each of dry sherry, sweet vermouth, and Campari. Stir gently to combine. Use a knife to remove a 1 in [2.5 cm] wide strip of an orange peel, then squeeze it into the drink to release the oils. Gently run the peel around the edge of the glass, then place it in the glass.

Cooking Together

One person can slice and toast the bread and prep ingredients while the other cooks the shrimp. Bring it together, and boom: You've got dinner.

Diet
Pescatarian,
dairy-free

Pecorino Shrimp & Grits

SERVES 2

Pecorino Grits

2 cups [240 ml] water

½ cup [120 ml] milk

½ cup [70 g] medium- or coarse-grind cornmeal or grits

¼ tsp kosher salt

⅓ cup [20 g] grated pecorino romano cheese, plus more for garnishing (see Tip)

Freshly ground black pepper

2 Tbsp heavy cream, plus more if needed

Shrimp

½ lb [230 g] shrimp, peeled and deveined (tail on optional)

1 tsp Old Bay seasoning

1 tsp smoked paprika

¼ tsp kosher salt

2 Tbsp salted butter

½ green bell pepper, finely diced

2 green onions, thinly sliced

2 garlic cloves, minced

Zest and juice of ½ lemon

1 Tbsp heavy cream

Finely chopped Italian parsley, for garnishing

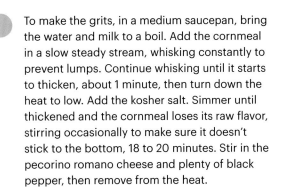 To make the grits, in a medium saucepan, bring the water and milk to a boil. Add the cornmeal in a slow steady stream, whisking constantly to prevent lumps. Continue whisking until it starts to thicken, about 1 minute, then turn down the heat to low. Add the kosher salt. Simmer until thickened and the cornmeal loses its raw flavor, stirring occasionally to make sure it doesn't stick to the bottom, 18 to 20 minutes. Stir in the pecorino romano cheese and plenty of black pepper, then remove from the heat.

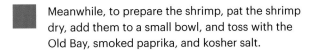 Meanwhile, to prepare the shrimp, pat the shrimp dry, add them to a small bowl, and toss with the Old Bay, smoked paprika, and kosher salt.

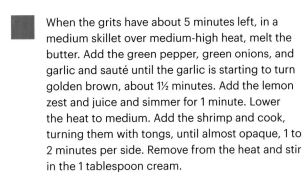 When the grits have about 5 minutes left, in a medium skillet over medium-high heat, melt the butter. Add the green pepper, green onions, and garlic and sauté until the garlic is starting to turn golden brown, about 1½ minutes. Add the lemon zest and juice and simmer for 1 minute. Lower the heat to medium. Add the shrimp and cook, turning them with tongs, until almost opaque, 1 to 2 minutes per side. Remove from the heat and stir in the 1 tablespoon cream.

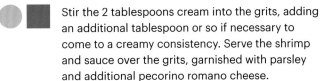 Stir the 2 tablespoons cream into the grits, adding an additional tablespoon or so if necessary to come to a creamy consistency. Serve the shrimp and sauce over the grits, garnished with parsley and additional pecorino romano cheese.

COOK 1 ———— COOK 2

contd.

Close your eyes, and this cozy dish transports you out to an intimate table for two—minus the server, of course! This fusion-style recipe combines Roman *cacio e pepe* pasta with Southern-style shrimp and grits, and you'll be tempted to lick the skillet clean (a perk of cooking it at home).

We learned to make shrimp and grits from our chef friend Tanorria Askew, author of the cookbook *Staples +5*. Her famous recipe won over chef Gordon Ramsay himself when she competed on *MasterChef*! She shared a custom version of her recipe on our website, swapping out the traditional bacon for Old Bay and smoked paprika. Here we've riffed on it even further, making a two-serving version with ingredients from our favorite Italian pasta.

Tip

It's worth seeking out pecorino romano cheese for this recipe. It's a very sharp, aged cheese similar to Parmesan but with a saltier, deeper flavor that adds the magic to Italian cacio e pepe.

Wine Pairing

Grab a bottle of an unfiltered orange wine, which gets its signature hue from fermentation with the grape skins and seeds. A balanced wine with subtle tannins, it cuts through the creaminess of the grits without overpowering the spiced shrimp.

Cooking Together

This recipe divides easily: One person can make the grits while the other prepares and cooks the shrimp.

Storage

Leftovers will keep, refrigerated, for up to 3 days; reheat on the stovetop over low heat.

Diet

Pescatarian, gluten-free

Creamy Scallops with Spinach & Sun-Dried Tomatoes

SERVES 2

Kosher salt, for brining and seasoning

½ lb [230 g] sea scallops (see Tips)

1½ Tbsp neutral oil

1 Tbsp salted butter

2 garlic cloves, minced

1 tsp dried oregano

¼ cup [60 ml] milk

¼ cup [60 ml] heavy cream

2 Tbsp grated Parmesan cheese

2 cups [80 g] chopped fresh spinach

¼ cup [60 g] chopped sun-dried tomatoes (packed in oil)

○ In a shallow dish, mix 2 cups [475 ml] of room-temperature water and 1 tablespoon of kosher salt. Add the scallops and let soak in the brine for 10 minutes. Remove the scallops and dry as thoroughly as possible (any extra water causes the pan to spit when searing). Lightly season the scallops with 1 generous pinch of kosher salt.

■ In a medium stainless or cast-iron skillet, heat the oil over high heat. Carefully add the scallops and cook without turning until an even brown crust forms on the bottom, 1 to 3 minutes depending on how high a heat your range provides. Flip the scallops using a fish spatula and cook on the other side until a crust just forms on bottom and the center of the scallop is almost opaque, 1 to 2 minutes. Remove from the heat and transfer the scallops to a plate, leaving the juices in the pan.

○■ Add the butter to the pan and melt it over medium-low heat. Add the garlic and oregano and cook until the garlic is lightly browned and fragrant, about 30 seconds. Add the milk, heavy cream, and Parmesan cheese and simmer for 2 minutes, stirring occasionally and gently scraping the brown bits off the bottom of the pan. Add the spinach, sun-dried tomatoes, and ¼ teaspoon of kosher salt and cook until the spinach is wilted, about 2 minutes. Return the scallops to the pan and warm for 30 seconds, spooning the sauce over the top. Serve immediately.

COOK 1 ———————————— COOK 2

contd.

Buttery-sweet seared scallops are a favorite to order when we're out for a fancy dinner, and it turns out they're surprisingly easy to make at home. We like pairing them with a lusciously creamy sauce and chewy sun-dried tomatoes, which add a bacon-like flair.

Make sure to use a neutral oil for high-heat cooking, since butter or olive oil will smoke. A stainless or cast-iron skillet is essential to forming that golden-brown seared crust on the outside. Don't worry if you don't get the perfect sear the first time—just another reason to make this recipe again for more practice! Serve with rice, quinoa, or couscous.

Tips

Sea scallops are large, with a sweet, buttery texture. Avoid bay scallops, which are very small.

Brining the scallops in a solution of salt water for 10 minutes evens out the flavor and helps to season the scallops before cooking. Make sure to pat them fully dry before searing.

Use either fresh or frozen scallops; we prefer fresh. To thaw frozen, refrigerate the bag overnight. For a quicker thaw, keep the scallops in the package and place it in a large bowl of cold water for 30 minutes.

Wine Pairing

Pair with a French white wine, such as a chardonnay from the Burgundy region (white Burgundy). The green apple, citrus, and pear notes balance the creamy sauce and enhance the natural sweetness of the scallops.

Cooking Together

This recipe comes together quickly, so it's important to measure out your ingredients (mise en place) before cooking. Get everything prepped together—one of you handles the scallops while the other gathers ingredients—then choose one person to manage the skillet.

Diet
Pescatarian,
gluten-free

Sweet Heat Salmon

COOK 2 — COOK 1

SERVES 2

Two 6 oz [170 g] salmon fillets, skin on, about 1½ in [4 cm] thick

2 Tbsp salted butter

½ Tbsp Louisiana- or picante-style hot sauce (such as Valentina, Cholula, Tabasco, or Frank's) (see Tips)

½ Tbsp sriracha

2 tsp honey

½ tsp soy sauce or tamari

Minced chives, or green onion tops, for garnishing

Allow the salmon to come to room temperature, about 20 minutes (see Tips).

In a small saucepan, melt the butter, then stir in the hot sauce, sriracha, honey, and soy sauce. Taste and add additional hot sauce if desired. Pour half of the sauce into a small bowl.

Preheat the broiler to high.

Line a baking sheet with aluminum foil and lightly oil it. Put the salmon on the foil skin side down and sprinkle it with several pinches of kosher salt. Brush the top and sides of the salmon with half of the glaze.

Broil the salmon until just tender and pink at the center, 7 to 10 minutes (thinner salmon will need only 4 to 5 minutes). The internal temperature should reach at least 125°F to 130°F [50°C to 55°C] when measured with a food thermometer at the thickest point.

Remove from the oven and brush with the reserved half of the glaze. Garnish with chives and serve.

contd.

A COUPLE COOKS

One taste of this thick, glossy sauce and you'll want to drizzle it on everything. This quick salmon is great for spicing up date night—although we make it on the regular because it's just that good. Stir up the sauce, pop the salmon in the broiler for 10 minutes, then brush with more of that luscious glaze before serving.

If you can handle the heat, feel free to add more hot sauce; this recipe comes out mildly spicy as written. Serve with Lemon Asparagus with Crispy Prosciutto (page 211), Ginger Miso Chopped Salad (page 193), or Everyday Arugula Salad (page 187).

Tips

This recipe has a mild-to-medium heat level; increase the hot sauce to your liking to make a spicier dish. Keep in mind that the final dish will taste less spicy than a taste of the sauce directly from a spoon.

It's important to bring the salmon to room temperature for even cooking in the broiler. If the fish is too cold, it can blacken on the outside without fully cooking through on the inside.

Repurpose this dish as a salmon salad: Flake the cooked salmon and use it to top chopped romaine with tomatoes, croutons, and Creamy Parmesan Dressing (see page 189).

Wine Pairing

A dry Riesling is the perfect match for this dish. Its crisp acidity and subtle minerality balance the spicy sweetness of the sauce. For a nonalcoholic pairing, try a zero-proof Riesling (we like Leitz Eins Zwei Zero Riesling).

Cooking Together

Make a side dish together while the salmon comes to room temperature, then one of you can whip up the sauce while the other prepares and broils the salmon.

For Gluten-Free

Use gluten-free soy sauce or tamari.

For Dairy-Free

Use vegan or dairy-free butter.

Storage

Leftovers will keep, refrigerated, for up to 3 days.

Diet
Pescatarian, gluten-free option, dairy-free option

Prosciutto Chicken Roulade *with Salmoriglio*

SERVES 2

¼ cup [60 g] cream cheese spread, or plain cream cheese at room temperature (see Tips)

1 garlic clove, minced

1 tsp Italian seasoning

1 boneless, skinless chicken breast (8 oz [230 g])

½ tsp kosher salt

Freshly ground black pepper

3 prosciutto slices

¼ cup [3 g] Italian parsley leaves, loosely packed

1 Tbsp olive oil

Salmoriglio

¼ cup [10 g] very finely chopped Italian parsley

1 tsp dried oregano

1 garlic clove, minced

2 Tbsp fresh lemon juice

2 Tbsp olive oil

1 Tbsp water

¼ tsp kosher salt

Freshly ground black pepper

Preheat the oven to 425°F [220°C].

In a small bowl, use a spatula to stir together the cream cheese spread, garlic, and Italian seasoning. Set aside.

Use a sharp knife to butterfly the chicken breast: Slice it in half horizontally, keeping the halves attached. Open the chicken breast flat and lay it on a cutting board. Lay a piece of plastic wrap over the chicken and gently pound it with a rolling pin until it is thin and about doubled in surface area. Discard the plastic wrap.

Sprinkle the top of the chicken with the kosher salt and a few grinds of black pepper. Add a layer of prosciutto slices, covering all of the chicken. Spread the cream cheese mixture over the prosciutto with a spatula. Add the parsley.

Tightly roll the chicken and filling into a log, using 3 toothpicks to temporarily hold it together. Use kitchen twine to tie the roll tightly three times around, then remove the toothpicks (see Tips). Season the outside of the roll with salt.

In a medium ovenproof skillet, heat the olive oil over medium-high heat. Cook the chicken roll until it is browned on all sides, turning with tongs, 6 to 8 minutes total. Transfer the pan to the oven and bake until the chicken reaches an internal temperature of 165°F [75°C] at the thickest point, 12 to 16 minutes. Transfer the chicken to a cutting board and allow it to rest for 5 minutes.

Meanwhile, to make the salmoriglio, in a small bowl, stir together the parsley, oregano, garlic, lemon juice, olive oil, water, kosher salt, and black pepper.

Remove the twine from the roulade, then slice it into ¾ in [2 cm] rounds. Drizzle the sauce over the top and serve.

COOK 1

COOK 2

contd.

This masterpiece Alex whipped up for us one evening was so special, we had to immortalize it here. Roulade comes from the French word "to roll" and can describe anything from meat to a cake roll. Here juicy, tender chicken breasts are rolled around a creamy cheese and prosciutto filling. It looks fancy without much effort, though the rolling and tying is easiest with a partner.

The roulade is even better drowned in salmoriglio, an Italian green sauce made with garlic and parsley. Similar to the Argentine classic chimichurri (page 50), it adds a bright pop to each bite.

Tips

Cream cheese spread is cream cheese mixed with cream so it's easier to spread; it's sold in round containers. You can substitute regular cream cheese at room temperature (let it sit on the counter for 1 hour, or microwave a block for a few seconds at a time until it is room temperature).

If you don't have kitchen twine, you can secure the roulade with several toothpicks during cooking. Just be gentle when pan frying so that the roll stays together.

Cooking Together

While one of you butterflies the chicken, the other can prep the filling mixture and prosciutto. Roll it up together: Four hands make easy work of the tying!

Storage

Leftover chicken will keep, refrigerated, for 3 days. Leftover salmoriglio will keep, refrigerated, for 2 weeks; bring to room temperature (about 10 minutes) before serving.

Diet
Gluten-free

Seared New York Strip Steak *with Garlic Mushrooms*

SERVES 2

Steak

One 8 oz [230 g] New York strip steak, about 1½ in [4 cm] thick, trimmed of excess fat

1½ tsp kosher salt

Freshly ground black pepper

1 Tbsp salted butter

Garlic Mushrooms

2 Tbsp salted butter

8 oz [230 g] cremini (a.k.a. baby bella) mushrooms, cleaned and sliced

1 Tbsp chopped fresh thyme, plus more for garnishing (optional)

¼ tsp kosher salt

Freshly ground black pepper

2 garlic cloves, minced

1 Tbsp fresh lemon juice

Preheat the oven to 325°F [165°C].

Line a baking sheet with parchment paper and lay the steak on top. Season with the kosher salt and plenty of black pepper on all sides.

Bake until the internal temperature measures 95°F [35°C], 10 to 12 minutes (see Tips). (Steaks can vary in thickness, so check with a food thermometer.)

Meanwhile, prepare the garlic mushrooms. In a stainless steel or cast-iron skillet, heat 2 tablespoons of the butter over medium-high heat. Add the mushrooms and cook for 2 minutes, stirring often. Add the thyme, kosher salt, and a few grinds of black pepper and cook, stirring frequently, until most of the liquid is cooked out and the mushrooms are tender and golden brown, 3 to 5 minutes. Turn off the heat and transfer the mushrooms to a bowl.

When the steak is ready to sear, melt the butter in the same skillet over medium-high heat. Turn on your stove's vent, as the steak will smoke while cooking. Add the steak and cook, turning every minute, until it is browned on both sides and the internal temperature is 130°F [55°C], 4 to 5 minutes. Turn off the heat and add the mushrooms to the pan, along with the garlic and lemon juice, taking care as the pan will steam. Stir constantly for 1 minute to cook the garlic with the residual heat from the pan.

Let rest 5 minutes on a carving board or serving plate before serving. Garnish with additional sprigs of thyme, if desired. Slice into strips before serving.

contd.

Here's a secret for you: You can whip up a restaurant-quality steak at home for a fraction of the cost. Using a "reverse sear" technique, you'll bake the steak in the oven first to warm the center, then sear it in a pan to get those brown, crisp edges.

Possibly even better than that steak are those garlic mushrooms (sounds a little backward, but trust us). They're the jewel in the crown of this recipe, infused with punchy flavor from butter, lemon juice, and fresh thyme. Pour some glasses of full-bodied red wine, and it's got Saturday night written all over it.

Tips

For a steak that is closer to 1 in [2.5 cm] thick, cook it in the oven for 8 to 10 minutes and then sear in the skillet for 2 to 3 minutes.

For best results, seek out a high-quality NY strip steak from a reputable butcher. Opt for prime and organic or grass-fed for the ultimate tenderness and flavor, and look for marbling for maximum juiciness.

Cook to a sizzling medium-rare at 130°F [55°C], or cook to your liking, with rare at 125°F [52°C] or medium at 140°F [60°C]. In our opinion, a well-done steak is a waste of this luscious cut.

Wine Pairing

Try this dish with an Argentinian malbec. Its full-bodied nature, fruity flavors, and moderate tannins enhance the steak's richness without overwhelming the herby mushrooms. Look for a well-balanced malbec from the Mendoza region.

Cooking Together

Choose one person to get the steak in the oven while the other cooks the mushrooms. Then choose one person to sear the steak while the other assists, glass of wine in hand!

Storage

Leftovers will keep, refrigerated, for up to 3 days.

Diet
Gluten-free

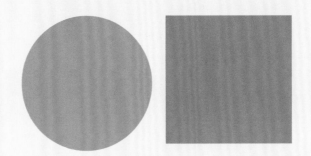

Chapter 3

GATHERINGS

This chapter is your guide to foolproof entertaining, from intimate dinner parties to big, festive gatherings. Each recipe concept is scalable and flexible for different diets and occasions, guaranteed to make you the heroes of the night!

The recipes in this chapter range from 4 to 8 servings, and are big on both impact (drool-worthy flavors) and function (reliable results every time).

Hearty Black Bean Chili
("The Chili")

SERVES 6 TO 8

2 Tbsp olive oil

1 medium yellow onion, diced

4 garlic cloves, minced

Three 15 oz [430 g] cans black beans, drained, or 4½ cups [720 g] cooked beans

Two 28 oz [800 g] cans diced fire-roasted tomatoes and their juices

One 15 oz [430 g] can corn

¼ cup [45 g] dry quinoa

¼ cup [65 g] ketchup

3 Tbsp [45 g] salted butter

2 Tbsp Worcestershire sauce

2 Tbsp chili powder

1 Tbsp dried oregano

1 Tbsp garlic powder

1 Tbsp cumin

½ Tbsp kosher salt

1 Tbsp smoked paprika (optional)

Shredded cheese, sour cream, sliced green onion, torn cilantro, pickled jalapeños, crushed tortilla chips, for topping (optional)

In a large pot or Dutch oven, heat the olive oil over medium heat. Add the onion and garlic and cook, stirring occasionally, until translucent, 5 to 7 minutes.

Add the black beans, tomatoes, corn, quinoa, ketchup, butter, Worcestershire sauce, chili powder, oregano, garlic powder, cumin, kosher salt, and 1 cup [240 ml] of water. Make sure to add the juices of the tomatoes, because they form the broth. Simmer for 25 minutes, stirring occasionally. Remove from the heat and stir in the smoked paprika. Serve immediately with toppings of your choice.

COOK 1

COOK 2

contd.

When our friends request that we make "the chili," this is the recipe we pull out. We started making it on fall evenings in a cast-iron pot directly over our campfire. Maybe it was the flannel blankets and the chirping crickets, but this chili seems to have a bit of magic when eaten outdoors.

Here we've modified the recipe for the stovetop while keeping its rustic preparation. It's ideal for serving a crowd—even the kids in our lives inhale their bowl. You'll find that it pleases all types of eaters, no matter their diet. A few of this chili's flavor secrets are butter for richness, ketchup for brightness, and smoked paprika as an ode to its fireside origins.

Tip

Love cooking outdoors? Turn this into campfire chili! This method is optimized for "dump and stir" campfire cooking. For smooth prep, cut the onion and garlic in advance and pack in a sealed container; refrigerate until cooking time. Mix the spices and store in a container until cooking.

Cooking Together

Have one person assemble and prep all of the ingredients, while the other sautés the onion and garlic and gets everything to a simmer.

For Vegan

Use vegan butter and vegan Worcestershire sauce.

Storage

Leftovers will keep, refrigerated, for up to 3 days, or frozen for up to 3 months. Leftovers become very thick, so add a splash of water and a pinch of kosher salt when reheating.

Diet

Vegetarian, gluten-free, vegan option

Nacho-Loaded Sweet Potato Bar

SERVES 8

8 medium sweet potatoes (about 10 to 12 oz [280 to 340 g] each)

1 Tbsp olive oil, plus more for rubbing

1½ lb [680 g] ground beef or plant-based crumbles

1 Tbsp cumin

1 Tbsp chili powder

½ Tbsp smoked paprika

½ Tbsp onion powder

½ Tbsp garlic powder

½ tsp kosher salt

One 15 oz [430 g] can refried beans

Toppings

Pickled Red Onions (recipe follows)

Lime Crema (recipe follows) or sour cream

Pico de gallo (see Tips)

Shredded cheese

Guacamole

Iceberg lettuce, chopped

Green onions, thinly sliced

Cilantro, roughly chopped

Jarred pickled jalapeño peppers

Canned corn, drained

Crushed tortilla chips

Preheat the oven to 425°F [220°C].

Line a baking sheet with foil or parchment paper. Scrub and dry the sweet potatoes, then prick them all over with a fork. Rub each potato lightly with olive oil and place it on the baking sheet.

Bake for 30 minutes, then flip with tongs. Bake until a fork can easily pierce the sweet potato to the center, an additional 20 to 30 minutes. If it is not tender, continue baking. Most medium sweet potatoes take 45 minutes; large sweet potatoes take 1 hour. Remove from the oven to cool slightly.

In a large skillet over medium heat, heat the 1 tablespoon of olive oil. Add the ground beef or plant-based crumbles and the cumin, chili powder, smoked paprika, onion powder, garlic powder, and kosher salt. Cook, breaking the meat into crumbles, about 2 to 3 minutes for plant-based and about 8 minutes for ground beef (drain any excess fat from the ground beef after cooking).

In a small saucepan over low heat, warm the refried beans, adding a few pinches of kosher salt.

Assemble the toppings (see Tips).

When the sweet potatoes are done, slice them in half and sprinkle with kosher salt. Set up a buffet spread with the toppings in small bowls and allow each eater to top their own potato.

COOK 1 ———— COOK 2

contd.

Lime Crema

MAKES 1 CUP [240 ML]

1 cup [240 g] sour cream, or ¾ cup [180 g] Greek yogurt plus ¼ cup [60 g] mayonnaise

2 Tbsp fresh lime juice

Zest of ½ lime

¼ tsp granulated sugar

¼ tsp garlic powder

¼ tsp kosher salt

Stir together all the ingredients. The crema will keep, refrigerated, for up to 2 weeks.

Pickled Red Onions

MAKES 2 CUPS [480 G]

3 cups thinly sliced red onion (1 medium onion, 10 to 12 oz [280 to 340 g])

¾ cup [180 ml] white vinegar

¼ cup [50 g] granulated sugar

2 tsp kosher salt

Put the red onion slices in a medium bowl. In a small saucepan over high heat, heat the white vinegar, ¾ cup [180 ml] of water, the sugar, and kosher salt. Whisk until the sugar and salt are dissolved and the mixture starts to simmer, 2 to 3 minutes. Pour the brine over the onion slices and allow it to sit for 30 minutes. Transfer the onions and brine to a covered jar. Makes 1 pint (2 cups); it will keep, refrigerated, for up to 1 month.

Here's a fun concept for serving a crowd where everyone always leaves satisfied! It's an ode to Alex's mom, who has this talent for feeding large numbers of people with different diets and preferences. She somehow magically always has enough food for everyone, even when unexpected guests drop by!

Let each eater go crazy with the toppings of their choice. The key is to have a nice mix of crunchy, fresh textures to contrast with the soft sweet potato. Homemade components like Pickled Red Onions and Lime Crema are easily made ahead for a big payoff in punchy, zingy pops of flavor.

Tips

Don't have store-bought pico de gallo? Chop some fresh tomatoes, add minced red onion and chopped cilantro, and toss with a squeeze of lime juice and a pinch of kosher salt.

This recipe has endless riffs: It works with russet potatoes, which have a similar bake time. Or ditch the potatoes entirely for a taco salad or loaded nachos.

If you're making the pickled red onions and lime crema just for this dish, start them when the sweet potatoes go into the oven.

Cooking Together

Get the sweet potatoes into the oven quickly, then make a list of your favorite toppings and knock them out together!

For Vegetarian

Use a quality brand of plant-based crumbles. Or substitute drained black beans, mixed with a drizzle of olive oil and spices similar to the crumbles filling.

For Vegan

Use plant-based crumbles, omit the cheese, and use guacamole or cashew cream instead of sour cream.

Storage

Leftover potatoes will keep, refrigerated, for up to 3 days.

Diet
Gluten-free, vegetarian option, vegan option

Smoky Spinach & Artichoke Lasagna

COOK 2

COOK 1

SERVES 9 TO 12

3 Tbsp olive oil

4 garlic cloves, minced

One 28 oz [800 g] can crushed fire-roasted tomatoes

One 15 oz [430 g] can tomato sauce

1 tsp dried oregano

1¾ tsp kosher salt

Freshly ground black pepper

9 to 12 lasagna noodles (8 oz [230 g]) (see Tips)

10 oz [280 g] frozen spinach, thawed

One 14 oz [400 g] can artichoke hearts, chopped (8½ oz [240 g] drained weight)

1 cup [240 g] sour cream

8 oz [230 g] smoked mozzarella, provolone, or Gouda cheese, grated (see Tips)

¾ cup [25 g] shredded Parmesan or pecorino romano cheese (see Tips)

¼ tsp garlic powder

1 cup (8 oz [230 g]) shredded whole-milk mozzarella cheese

Chopped fresh parsley, for garnishing (optional)

Preheat the oven to 375°F [190°C].

To make the tomato sauce, heat the olive oil in a saucepan over medium heat. Add the garlic and sauté, stirring, until fragrant, about 1 minute. Lower the heat and carefully add the crushed tomatoes, tomato sauce, oregano, ¾ teaspoon of the kosher salt, and several grinds of black pepper. Simmer on low heat while making the rest of the recipe, for at least 15 minutes.

Bring a large pot of salted water to a boil. Boil the noodles, stirring often, until just before al dente, then drain. Drizzle a baking sheet with a bit of olive oil. Lay each noodle flat on the sheet, turning them over to coat with the oil.

Squeeze all the moisture out of the thawed spinach with your hands. In a medium bowl, mix the artichokes and spinach with the sour cream, the smoked mozzarella, ½ cup [15 g] of the Parmesan cheese, the garlic powder, the remaining 1 teaspoon of kosher salt, and several grinds of black pepper. Stir until fully combined.

In a 9 x 13 in [23 x 33 cm] baking dish, spread ½ cup [120 ml] of the hot tomato sauce over the bottom. Top with a layer of noodles, half of the artichoke filling, and 1 cup [225 g] of tomato sauce, then repeat for another layer of noodles, the remaining half of the spinach-artichoke filling, and 1 cup [225 g] more of the tomato sauce. Top with the remaining noodles and remaining tomato sauce. Sprinkle the top with the whole-milk mozzarella and the remaining ¼ cup [10 g] of Parmesan cheese.

Cover the pan with aluminum foil and bake for 30 minutes. Carefully remove the foil and bake until bubbly and golden brown on top, another 20 to 25 minutes. Let stand for 15 minutes before serving (this sets the texture). Garnish with chopped parsley, if desired, cut into pieces, and serve.

contd.

You'll want to dive right into this cozy, cheesy pan. It's a play on everyone's favorite party dip, with pops of tangy artichokes, rich sour cream, and savory Parmesan. But the real star here is the smoked cheese, which makes it nearly impossible to put down your fork.

Make it for a wintry dinner party with a crowd of friends, served with a crisp salad and hunks of crusty bread. Or bake up a pan for new parents for a gift that keeps on giving with leftovers!

Tips

The number of noodles needed varies based on the pan size and noodle brand. Some noodles are long enough to fit the entire length of a 9 x 13 in [23 x 33 cm] pan; shorter noodles require using more and cutting the noodles to fit the pan. We like to cook a few extra noodles to make sure we have enough.

It can be hard to find smoked mozzarella; smoked provolone or Gouda work well as a substitute. Check your local cheese counter.

Use grated or shredded pecorino romano cheese instead of Parmesan cheese for an even more savory, satiating result.

This lasagna freezes and reheats well. Stash it in the freezer to share as a gift for new parents or a friend healing from surgery.

Wine Pairing

Reach for a California chardonnay, specifically from the Sonoma region. This region's chardonnays have a buttery undertone and subtle oakiness, which offer a delightful counterpoint to the smoked cheese and tangy artichokes.

Cooking Together

Make the dish as a team of two! Have one person make the tomato sauce and boil the noodles and the other make the filling, then layer the lasagna together.

Storage

Leftovers will keep, refrigerated, for up to 4 days; reheat in a 375°F [190°C] oven for 15 to 20 minutes, until warmed through. Freezer instructions: Make the entire recipe in a metal pan and bake it. Let cool to room temperature, then wrap in foil and freeze. To reheat, bake the frozen lasagna in a 375°F [190°C] oven until warmed through and the cheese is melted, about 40 minutes.

Diet
Vegetarian

Cozy Vegetable
Pot Pie

SERVES 6 TO 8

¼ cup [60 ml] olive oil

2 large portobello mushroom caps, diced

1 medium yellow onion, sliced

2 large or 4 small carrots, peeled and sliced into rounds or half-circles

1 large Yukon gold, yellow, or red potato (12 oz [340 g]), cut into ¼ in [6 mm] cubes

1 tsp kosher salt

4 garlic cloves, minced

3 Tbsp all-purpose flour

1 tsp whole fennel seeds

1 Tbsp dried sage

1 tsp smoked paprika

1 tsp garlic powder

2½ cups [600 ml] vegetable broth

1 cup [120 g] frozen peas

One 15 oz [430 g] can lentils, drained, or 1½ cups [340 g] cooked lentils

2 Tbsp light miso (yellow or white) (see Tips)

1 sheet refrigerated puff pastry (vegan, if desired) (see Tips)

1 Tbsp milk of choice

Preheat the oven to 400°F [200°C].

In a large pot over medium-high heat, heat 2 tablespoons of the olive oil. Add the mushrooms and sauté until golden and tender, about 5 minutes. Lower the heat to medium and add the remaining 2 tablespoons of olive oil and the onion, carrots, and potato. Sprinkle with ½ teaspoon of the kosher salt and cook until the onion is tender, 5 to 7 minutes. Add the garlic and cook until fragrant, about 30 seconds.

Turn down the heat to medium-low. Stir in the flour, fennel seeds, sage, smoked paprika, and garlic powder and cook for 1 minute. Add the vegetable broth, peas, lentils, miso, and the remaining ½ teaspoon of kosher salt. Increase the heat to medium and bring to a simmer; cook for 5 to 7 minutes, until the broth is thick and the vegetables are heated through, stirring occasionally.

Pour the filling into a 9 x 13 in [23 x 33 cm] baking dish. Roll out the puff pastry sheet to be ½ in [13 mm] wider than the baking dish on all sides. Gently roll it up onto a rolling pin and carefully transfer it to the top of the baking dish. Press the pastry down over the filling, letting excess pastry come up the sides of the dish (it will puff up around the edges). Cut four 4 in [10 cm] slits across the center of the pastry. Brush the top with milk and sprinkle with salt and pepper.

Bake until the pastry is golden brown, 23 to 26 minutes. Let rest for at least 10 minutes before serving (the flavor gets even better the longer it sits).

COOK 1 — ● ■ — COOK 2

contd.

Who would turn down pie for dinner? Our friends and family rave about this veggie-filled spin on classic comfort food; even meat lovers can't resist it. The flaky pastry and creamy gravy make a fast fan out of just about anyone.

Don't be fooled by its showy appearance; this pot pie is fairly simple to put together. Canned or precooked lentils cut down on kitchen time, and store-bought puff pastry makes a quick and easy crust. Make a big pan for the week or share this homey, comforting meal with a table of friends.

Tips

Several puff pastry brands are vegan even if they are not labeled as such; review the ingredient list when shopping.

If you can't find miso, substitute 1 tablespoon full-sodium soy sauce or tamari.

Cooking Together

Chop the ingredients together, then have one person sauté the vegetables while the other cleans up and gathers the remaining ingredients. Join forces to assemble the pot pie as a team.

For Vegan

Use vegan puff pastry and nondairy milk.

Storage

Leftover pot pie will keep, refrigerated, for up to 3 days; reheat in a 375°F [190°C] oven for 15 to 20 minutes, until warmed through.

Diet
Vegetarian,
vegan option

Rigatoni
with Fennel & Pancetta

COOK 2 ———— COOK 1

SERVES 6 TO 8

3 Tbsp olive oil

1 large fennel bulb, thinly sliced (about 2 cups [200 g])

4 oz [115 g] pancetta, cut into ¼ in [6 mm] cubes

4 garlic cloves, minced

One 28 oz [800 g] and one 14½ oz [411 g] can high-quality crushed tomatoes (see Tips)

1 Tbsp tomato paste concentrate or 2 Tbsp tomato paste

1½ tsp kosher salt, plus more for the pasta water

Freshly ground black pepper

1 lb [454 g] rigatoni, or calamarata, bucatini, or any other pasta shape

Grated pecorino romano cheese, for garnishing

Finely chopped parsley, for garnishing (optional)

Heat the olive oil in a large skillet or Dutch oven over medium heat. Add the fennel and cook until tender and starting to brown at the edges, about 5 minutes. Add the pancetta and cook until it starts to brown, 3 to 4 minutes. Add the garlic and cook until it turns golden, about 2 minutes. Add the crushed tomatoes, tomato paste, kosher salt, and black pepper. Simmer uncovered for 25 minutes. Taste and adjust the salt and pepper as desired.

Meanwhile, bring a large pot of water to a boil. Stir in 1 tablespoon kosher salt. Boil the pasta until it is al dente. Drain the pasta and return it to the pot (if the sauce is not yet done, stir in a drizzle of olive oil to keep the pasta from sticking). Immediately toss the pasta with the sauce.

Serve topped with pecorino romano cheese and finely chopped parsley, if desired.

contd.

We stumbled upon a pasta like this one in a busy restaurant in the winding, narrow streets of Rome's vibrant Trastevere district. Here it's reborn as a big, beautiful platter of pasta for a crowd, simply put together with a bold, aromatic sauce scented with garlic and fennel. Pancetta infuses a smoky richness throughout the dish, proving that often, a little bit of meat can go a long way.

You can whip up this one with any type of pasta. We like it with rigatoni or calamarata (a very large tubular pasta), but it works just as well with long noodles like bucatini.

Tips

Use the highest-quality brand of canned tomatoes you can find. Look for San Marzano or fire-roasted tomatoes.

Spice up your pasta by stirring in a dollop of fiery jarred Calabrian chiles to the sauce. (See more on page 270.)

Wine Pairing

Pair this rich and flavorful pasta with a Barbera d'Asti red wine from the Piedmont region of Italy. Its bright acidity and vibrant red fruit flavors make an ideal complement. Serve slightly chilled for best flavor.

Storage

This dish is best eaten the day it's made, but leftovers will keep, refrigerated, for up to 2 days. Reheat on the stovetop.

Curry Salmon Burgers
with Cilantro Chutney

MAKES 6 BURGERS

24 oz [680 g] salmon, skin and bones removed

¼ cup [3 g] loosely packed fresh cilantro leaves and stems

2 tsp curry powder

2 tsp cumin

¾ tsp kosher salt

Freshly ground black pepper

1 cup [80 g] panko

3 Tbsp mayonnaise

2 Tbsp Dijon mustard

Olive oil, for cooking

6 burger buns or artisan rolls (optional)

Leafy lettuce, for serving

Quick-Pickled Cucumbers and Onions (recipe follows)

Cilantro Chutney

2 cups [25 g] loosely packed fresh cilantro leaves and stems

¼ cup [40 g] chopped golden raisins

2 Tbsp white wine vinegar

2 Tbsp olive oil

½ tsp kosher salt

Cut the salmon into chunks. Add it to the bowl of a food processor with the cilantro, curry powder, cumin, kosher salt, and several grinds of black pepper. Pulse 12 to 15 times until roughly chopped. (Alternatively, chop everything with a large chef's knife until it has a uniformly roughly chopped texture.) Add the panko, mayonnaise, and Dijon mustard and pulse 4 or 5 more times, then stir with a spatula until fully combined.

Form the mixture into 6 burger shapes about ¾ in [2 cm] thick (4 oz [115 g] each). Refrigerate the burgers for 30 minutes to firm up the texture. (Or refrigerate the burgers for up to 24 hours. If chilling for more than 1 hour, allow the burgers to stand at room temperature for 15 minutes prior to cooking.)

Meanwhile, make the cilantro chutney. Clean the food processor and add the cilantro, golden raisins, white wine vinegar, olive oil, 2 tablespoons of water, and the kosher salt. Process into a thick, smooth sauce. (Alternatively, chop the cilantro and raisins as finely as possible, then mix with the remaining ingredients.)

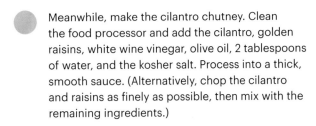

When ready to cook, preheat a grill to medium-high heat. Cook the burgers until browned on each side and the inside registers 130°F [55°C] on a food thermometer, 5 to 8 minutes total. Alternatively, lightly coat the bottom of a large skillet, grill pan, or griddle with olive oil and heat over medium-high heat. Add the burgers and cook until browned on each side and the internal temperature is 130°F [55°C], 4 to 5 minutes total.

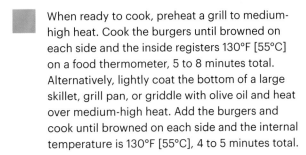

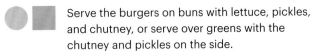

Serve the burgers on buns with lettuce, pickles, and chutney, or serve over greens with the chutney and pickles on the side.

COOK 1 ———— COOK 2

contd.

Quick-Pickled Cucumbers and Onions

MAKES 3 CUPS [375 G]

2 cups [250 g] thinly sliced English cucumber, sliced diagonally

½ medium red onion, thinly sliced

¾ cup [180 ml] white vinegar

¼ cup [50 g] granulated sugar

2 tsp kosher salt

1 tsp peeled and grated fresh ginger

1 tsp coriander seed

Put the cucumber and onions in a medium glass or metal bowl.

In a small saucepan over high heat, heat ¾ cup [180 ml] of water with the white vinegar, sugar, kosher salt, ginger, and coriander seed. Whisk until the sugar and salt are dissolved and the mixture starts to simmer, about 2 minutes.

Pour the mixture into the bowl with the vegetables and let cool to room temperature (about 30 minutes). If desired, transfer the pickles and brine to a covered jar and store, refrigerated, for up to 1 month.

Inspired by the layers of flavor in Indian cuisine, these patties are infused with warm curry powder and cumin, then topped with tangy, gingery pickled cucumbers and onions.

The icing on the cake? A sweet-tart emerald-green cilantro chutney. We couldn't resist riffing on the popular chutney from our first cookbook, *Pretty Simple Cooking*. For a fun spin, ditch the bun and serve the burgers over greens with pickles on the side and the sauce drizzled over the top.

Tips

For a vegetarian option, make the Falafel Burgers on www.acouplecooks.com and substitute curry powder for the ground coriander.

Want to simplify prep? Use a store-bought jarred mango chutney instead of the cilantro chutney.

Make the Quick-Pickled Cucumbers and Onions (facing page) and allow them to stand while making the burgers (or make them up to 1 month in advance).

Consider making a double batch of the pickles to store refrigerated and use as a condiment for bowl meals and sandwiches.

These burgers are great to make ahead. Refrigerate for up to 24 hours before cooking or freeze them uncooked. Wrap each burger in plastic wrap, then wrap them all in aluminum foil. Freeze for up to 3 months. Defrost in the refrigerator the night before, then let stand at room temperature for 15 minutes before cooking.

Wine Pairing

Serve with a Torrontés white wine, an Argentinian wine known for its aromatic allure. The light floral and fruity undertones provide a refreshing contrast to the rich flavors of curry and cumin.

Cooking Together

Have one person make the pickles and chutney while the other makes and grills the salmon burgers.

For Gluten-Free

Use gluten-free panko, omit the bun, and serve over leafy greens.

Storage

Leftover cooked burgers will keep, refrigerated, for up to 2 days.

Diet
Pescatarian,
gluten-free option

One-Pan Roast Chicken & Herby Veggies

COOK 2 ─── COOK 1

SERVES 4

1½ Tbsp plus ¾ tsp kosher salt

1 tsp garlic powder

1 tsp onion powder

1 tsp smoked paprika

1 whole chicken (4 to 5 lb [1.8 to 2.3 kg]), thawed if frozen

3 Tbsp olive oil

1 Tbsp salted butter, cut into 4 thin pats

Freshly ground black pepper

1 yellow onion, sliced

1 red onion, sliced

2 lb [910 g] baby or fingerling potatoes (slice fingerlings in half)

4 medium carrots, peeled and sliced into rounds

2 celery ribs, sliced

4 garlic cloves, smashed

½ Tbsp dried oregano

½ Tbsp dried thyme

½ Tbsp dried tarragon or rosemary

2 Tbsp balsamic vinegar

Preheat the oven to 425°F [220°C]. Set an oven rack in the lower third of the oven.

In a small bowl, mix the 1½ tablespoons kosher salt with the garlic powder, onion powder, and smoked paprika.

Set the chicken on a cutting board and pat it dry with a paper towel. Rub it with 1 tablespoon of the olive oil. Generously sprinkle the salt mixture over all sides of the chicken and rub it around the surface. Use your fingers to lift the skin from the chicken breast and the edge of the drumsticks and season under the skin as well. Tuck the pats of butter under the skin.

Use one piece of kitchen twine to tie the legs together with a knot. Wrap a second piece of twine around the other end of the chicken and tie another knot to secure the wings to the body (see Tips). Top the chicken with a few grinds of black pepper. Allow the chicken to rest on the cutting board for 15 minutes while preparing the vegetables.

Add the remaining 2 tablespoons of olive oil to a large ovenproof skillet (see Tips) and heat over medium-high heat. Add the onions, potatoes, carrots, celery, and garlic and sprinkle with the oregano, thyme, tarragon, and the remaining ¾ teaspoon kosher salt. Cook until the onions are tender, stirring frequently, about 5 minutes. Remove from the heat and stir in the balsamic vinegar.

Place the chicken on top of the vegetables. Roast for 55 minutes, then check the temperature and continue roasting until cooked through, 10 to 15 minutes. The internal temperature should read 170° to 175°F [77° to 80°C] at the thighs and 155° to 165°F [68° to 74°C] at the breast.

Gently tip the chicken to let the juices run out into the pan. Allow the chicken to rest on a cutting board for 10 to 15 minutes before carving. Toss the vegetables with the chicken juices before serving.

contd.

This foolproof method for roasting chicken will become your go-to for Sunday dinners, special occasions, and holiday celebrations. It makes a succulent, juicy bird, with a layer of veggies cooked underneath that absorb all of its delicious juices. You'll never need another method!

Many roast chicken recipes come out dry or underseasoned. Here you'll rub salt and spices over and under the skin, tucking in a few pats of butter for rich, moist flesh. The irresistible flavor will have you singing its praises.

Tips

Don't have an ovenproof skillet? Sauté the vegetables in your largest skillet, then transfer them to a rimmed baking sheet or roasting pan and place the chicken on top.

This method for tying the chicken is easy to master, but you can skip it in a pinch. Tying simply helps the chicken keep its shape and cook evenly.

If you haven't carved a chicken before, watch a video online. Learning several simple slicing techniques will result in a beautifully plated platter of chicken.

Once the meat has been stripped from the bones, don't toss them! It's easy to transform them into a deeply flavorful broth that you can use for soups or stews or just sip on its own. Simply place the bones in a pot and cover with water, add 1 to 2 teaspoons of salt, and throw in some sliced onion and celery if you have it. Simmer for 1 to 2 hours. Strain out any solids—and get ready to be blown away by how good homemade chicken broth can be.

Wine Pairing

An unoaked chardonnay is our choice to complement this meal. The wine's light, refreshing mouthfeel balances the buttery succulence and earthy herbs of this dish.

Cooking Together

One person can season and tie the chicken while the other chops and cooks the vegetables. Get the chicken in the oven and while it roasts, make a salad or dessert together.

For Dairy-Free

Use vegan butter.

Storage

Leftovers will keep, refrigerated, for up to 3 days.

Diet
Gluten-free,
dairy-free option

Spice-Rubbed Surf & Turf

SERVES 4 TO 6

2 Tbsp olive oil

1 lime, zested

3 garlic cloves, grated

2 tsp smoked paprika

2 tsp dried oregano (see Tips)

1 tsp garlic powder

1 tsp onion powder

½ tsp ground black pepper

2 tsp brown sugar

2 tsp kosher salt

1½ lb [680 g] flank steak, cut into 3 pieces

1 lb [455 g] medium shrimp, tails on and deveined

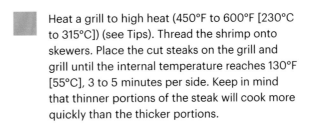 In a large container or bowl, stir together the olive oil, lime zest, garlic, smoked paprika, oregano, garlic powder, onion powder, black pepper, brown sugar, and kosher salt. Add the steak and shrimp and mix until fully coated with the spice rub. Cover and let rest for 30 minutes, or refrigerate for up to 24 hours, then rest at room temperature 30 minutes before serving.

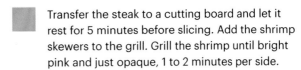 Heat a grill to high heat (450°F to 600°F [230°C to 315°C]) (see Tips). Thread the shrimp onto skewers. Place the cut steaks on the grill and grill until the internal temperature reaches 130°F [55°C], 3 to 5 minutes per side. Keep in mind that thinner portions of the steak will cook more quickly than the thicker portions.

Transfer the steak to a cutting board and let it rest for 5 minutes before slicing. Add the shrimp skewers to the grill. Grill the shrimp until bright pink and just opaque, 1 to 2 minutes per side.

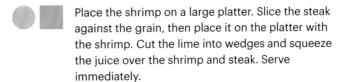 Place the shrimp on a large platter. Slice the steak against the grain, then place it on the platter with the shrimp. Cut the lime into wedges and squeeze the juice over the shrimp and steak. Serve immediately.

COOK 1 —————— ● ■ —————— COOK 2

contd.

Picture this: an outdoor dinner party, your friends gathered around, and laughter echoing in the air as the sun lowers in the sky. This prep-ahead number's got punchy, bold flavors and that effortlessly chic vibe you need without being too fussy.

Pairing steak and shrimp looks impressive and luxurious, presented at the table on a large platter. But this one doesn't even break the bank, using economical flank steak, marinated in a zingy spice rub with garlic and lime. Both of the proteins come out unbelievably juicy and tender.

Tips

If you have an herb garden, substitute a handful of fresh oregano, thyme, or basil for the dried oregano.

Stovetop instructions: Prepare the dish using the same steps, but use a stainless steel or cast-iron skillet. Cook the steak and shrimp separately over high heat, covered with the lid slightly ajar. Flip the steak several times until it reaches the specified internal temperature. Expect some smoke when cooking the steak, so be sure to turn on your oven vent.

Wine Pairing

We recommend serving with a chilled New Zealand sauvignon blanc. The crisp, lively character of the wine balances the richness of the steak while enhancing the tangy, garlicky shrimp.

Storage

Leftovers will keep, refrigerated, for up to 3 days.

Diet
Gluten-free, dairy-free

Dinner Party Planning

The reason we started cooking in the first place? We wanted to have people over for dinner. Newly married, we knew our repertoire of frozen and convenience foods wouldn't quite do for guests. For our initial attempt at a "fancy" dinner, we paged for hours through a borrowed Julia Child cookbook and put together an ambitious rendition of roasted lamb, frisée salad, and peach crêpes.

That beginner's luck gave us a taste of success, and it fueled our love of gathering over a home-cooked meal. Want to plan an epic gathering or an intimate dinner party? Here are a few tips for effortless entertaining:

- **Plan the menu and general theme.** Think about pairing dishes that fit the season and theme and have a cohesive vibe. Play up color and texture contrasts, like a brightly colored citrus salad with a rich cheesy lasagna. Surround a main dish protein with vegetable-filled appetizers and side dishes. Get started with our Sample Menus (see page 342).

- **Ask in advance if your guests have special diets, allergies, or dislikes.** Use this to guide your planning. This book contains recipes for a variety of diets that are marked throughout the book.

- **Serve a signature drink.** This sets the tone of the meal, whether it's a simple bottle of wine or a cocktail. For a crowd, try Party Mojitos (page 327) or Red Wine Sangria (page 319). Or go for alcohol-free options like Sangria Mocktail (page 321) or a Mocktail Gin & Tonic (page 314).

- **Pick a few super-easy items to pair with recipes that involve more prep time.** Try the Everyday Arugula Salad (page 187) or the free-form Lillet Spritzer (page 316). Or go for non-recipe ideas like a cheese board or easy crostini. It's also helpful to combine things you've made before with new recipes. Avoid being overly ambitious, so you can focus on the people, not just the food!

- **Set the stage in advance.** Before your guests arrive, make sure the dishwasher and/or kitchen sink are empty so you can get ahead of the mess at the end of the party. Set the table well in advance so you don't have to rush (see page 273). Then set the mood with twinkle lights, candles, and some party background music.

- **Decide which of you will answer the door and pour drinks for guests.** Meanwhile, the other partner can put the finishing touches on the food. It can get stressful if people arrive when you're still trying to finish up! It's nice to designate one person to greet guests.

- **Set house rules for the cleanup.** At our place, guests aren't allowed to do dishes! Our philosophy is to let our hospitality extend to the cleanup. (Of course, you can set your own house rules!)

Chapter 4

MORNINGS

Imagine slanting morning light, the smell of coffee brewing, and a lazy morning with your partner. (Sure, that doesn't often happen if kids are in the picture, but let's just pretend!) Regular mornings might be rushed, but when it comes to the weekend, there's room for a little more fun.

How about a date for breakfast or brunch? Make up a recipe while you're still in your PJs, draining endless mugs of coffee and jamming to your favorite playlist. Or make it a party: Invite some friends or family over for a fun brunch to nosh on together.

SOME HIGHLIGHTS IN THIS CHAPTER:

Bake up a warm-spiced pan of Banana Baked Oatmeal with Maple Tahini Drizzle (page 152).

Share a plate of fluffy French Toast Waffles (page 158).

Mix up a Sheet-Pan Egg Bake for a crowd of friends (page 161).

Create a new holiday or weekend tradition with Mini Cardamom Cinnamon Rolls (page 175).

Banana Baked Oatmeal
with Maple Tahini Drizzle

SERVES 8

2 cups [200 g] old-fashioned rolled oats

½ cup [60 g] chopped walnuts

1 tsp baking powder

1½ tsp cinnamon

½ tsp ground ginger

½ tsp allspice

½ tsp kosher salt

¾ cup [180 g] mashed banana (from 1 large or 2 medium very ripe bananas), plus additional banana slices for serving

1¾ cups [415 ml] milk of choice

¼ cup [60 ml] maple syrup

2 tsp vanilla extract

Maple Tahini Drizzle (optional)

¼ cup [60 ml] maple syrup

2 Tbsp tahini

¼ tsp cinnamon

2 pinches kosher salt

Preheat the oven to 375°F [190°C]. Grease a 9 x 9 in [23 x 23 cm] or medium baking dish (about 7 x 11 in [18 x 28 cm]).

In a large bowl, mix the rolled oats, walnuts, baking powder, cinnamon, ginger, allspice, and kosher salt.

In a separate bowl, whisk together the mashed banana, milk, maple syrup, and vanilla extract. Pour into the bowl with the dry ingredients and mix to combine. Then pour into the prepared pan in an even layer.

Bake until the top is golden and set, 40 to 45 minutes. Remove from the oven and let cool for at least 10 minutes.

Meanwhile, to make the maple tahini drizzle, stir together the maple syrup, tahini, cinnamon, and kosher salt in a small bowl until smooth.

Slice the baked oatmeal into pieces or scoop it into bowls, then top with fruit slices and the maple tahini drizzle, if desired, or maple syrup.

COOK 2

COOK 1

contd.

This big pan of baked oatmeal will be equally loved by your mother-in-law and your hip vegan friends. The moist oats are infused with cinnamon, vanilla, ginger, and the fruity essence of banana. Don't miss the maple tahini drizzle, which adds salted caramel decadence to each bite. This one is a standby from our website we use for fancy brunch or regular weekdays. Refrigerate the pan for snacks and breakfasts all week long.

Tips

Most maple syrup has been labeled "Grade A" since a change in 2014 that absorbed the old Grade B. We recommend Grade A with the descriptor "Dark Color and Robust Taste."

Get creative with toppings. Add fresh fruit like strawberries, blueberries, or blackberries, or a slather of almond butter.

Cooking Together

Split up mixing the wet and dry ingredients, then have one person mix and bake while the other prepares the drizzle.

Storage

Leftover oatmeal will keep, refrigerated, for up to 1 week and leftover drizzle, refrigerated separately, for up to 2 weeks. Eat cold or reheat in a 300°F [150°C] oven or the microwave until warm.

Diet
Vegetarian, vegan, gluten-free

Oatmeal Blender Pancakes

MAKES 9 MEDIUM PANCAKES

2 cups [200 g] old-fashioned rolled oats

2 large eggs

¾ cup [180 ml] milk of choice

2 Tbsp maple syrup, plus more for serving

2 Tbsp neutral oil

½ Tbsp vanilla extract

1 tsp apple cider vinegar

½ Tbsp baking powder

¼ tsp cinnamon

½ tsp kosher salt

For serving

Maple syrup

Fresh fruit, nut butter, and powdered sugar (optional)

Put the oats in a blender and blend on high power until very fine (see Tip). Add the eggs, milk, maple syrup, oil, vanilla extract, apple cider vinegar, baking powder, cinnamon, and kosher salt. Blend until a smooth batter forms, stopping once to scrape down the sides.

Allow the batter to stand and thicken for 5 minutes while you preheat a large skillet or griddle over medium heat.

Lightly grease the skillet or griddle and wipe off excess with a paper towel. Pour the thickened batter into 4 in [10 cm] circles. Cook the pancakes until bubbles rise to the surface and pop and the bottoms are golden, then flip and cook until golden on the other side.

Cook the remaining batter, adjusting the heat as necessary. Place the cooked pancakes under an inverted bowl to keep them warm. Serve immediately with maple syrup, and if desired, fresh fruit, nut butter, and powdered sugar.

COOK 1

COOK 2

contd.

Typically we're not huge on breakfast, heading straight from the second cup of coffee to mid-morning snack. But it's a different story on weekends, and when we decide to cook breakfast, it's often these satisfyingly hearty, wholesome flapjacks—as filling as a bowl of oatmeal, but loads more fun!

The blender magically turns rolled oats into flour for fluffy pancakes, and makes for one slick and easy-to-clean method. We make these together on Saturday mornings (and eat as leftovers for snacks). Add a slather of nut butter before drowning them in syrup.

Tip

It's important to grind the oats into oat flour before adding the remaining ingredients. In a high-speed blender this takes just a few seconds, but it may take longer in a standard blender.

Cooking Together

Designate a griddle master to cook and flip while the partner cleans up and preps pancake toppings. The first pancake is never perfect—and that's okay!

Storage

Leftover pancakes will keep, refrigerated, for up to 5 days or frozen for up to 3 months (freeze in a single layer on a baking sheet for 30 minutes before placing in a freezer-safe container). Reheat on a skillet or griddle before serving.

Diet
Vegetarian,
gluten-free

French Toast Waffles

MAKES 4 STANDARD WAFFLES OR 2 LARGE BELGIAN WAFFLES

1 cup [226 g] small-curd cottage cheese

3 eggs

¼ cup [60 ml] milk of choice

3 Tbsp maple syrup

1 tsp vanilla extract

1 cup [140 g] all-purpose flour

1 tsp baking powder

¼ tsp kosher salt

Fresh fruit, for serving (optional)

Cinnamon Maple Syrup

¼ cup [60 ml] maple syrup

⅛ tsp cinnamon

Preheat a waffle iron to the high-heat setting. Grease a baking sheet or line it with parchment paper.

In a blender (see Tips), blend the cottage cheese, eggs, milk, maple syrup, and vanilla extract until smooth. Add the flour, baking powder, and kosher salt and pulse until incorporated into a thick batter.

Grease the waffle iron with baking spray. Add batter to the center of the waffle iron (about a heaping 1 cup [240 ml] for a Belgian waffle maker or a heaping ½ cup [120 ml] for a standard waffle maker, but all makers vary). Cook according to the waffle iron instructions until golden brown, checking often, as the color can quickly change from golden to dark brown.

Put the cooked waffles on the prepared baking sheet without stacking. If desired, place the cooked waffles in a preheated 250°F [120°C] oven to keep warm.

For the cinnamon maple syrup, combine the maple syrup and cinnamon in a small saucepan over medium heat and cook, stirring, until the cinnamon is incorporated, about 1 minute.

Serve the waffles topped with cinnamon maple syrup.

contd.

Cottage cheese is an unconventional ingredient here, but never fear! It makes waffles that are both tender and fluffy, reminiscent of the charm of French toast. Plus, they're packed with protein, so you'll be fueled up and ready to conquer the day. Drizzle them with cinnamon maple syrup for the ultimate French toast–inspired experience.

Tips

Don't want to pull out the blender? This works with a whisk, too. Be sure to use small-curd cottage cheese, which allows the cheese texture to melt into the waffle. Whisk together the cottage cheese, eggs, milk, maple syrup, and vanilla extract, breaking up any large clumps of cheese with the whisk. Combine the dry ingredients in a separate bowl. Add them to the egg mixture and stir with a spatula until all the flour is incorporated.

Baking spray makes for cleaner cooking than butter with a waffle maker, but either works.

Cooking Together

Mix up the batter together, then have one person cook the waffles while the other cleans and makes the cinnamon maple syrup.

Storage

Waffles will keep, refrigerated, for up to 5 days or frozen for 3 months. To freeze, first cool to room temperature. Place in a ziplock bag and remove the remaining air with a straw before sealing, or place in a sealable container. To reheat, defrost in the refrigerator overnight or at room temperature before lightly toasting in a toaster.

Diet
Vegetarian

Sheet-Pan *Egg* Bake

SERVES 8

1 Tbsp olive oil

½ medium red onion, thinly sliced

2 cups [150 g] very small broccoli florets

1 medium red pepper, small diced

1½ tsp kosher salt

Freshly ground black pepper

12 eggs

1 cup [240 ml] milk

1 cup [240 ml] half-and-half

1 Tbsp Dijon mustard

1 tsp dried oregano

1 tsp garlic powder

1 tsp onion powder

½ tsp dried dill

4 cups [150 g] crusty artisan or sourdough bread, cut into 1 in [2.5 cm] cubes

1½ cups [120 g] shredded Cheddar cheese

For the pistou

1 small garlic clove, finely minced

1½ Tbsp very finely chopped basil leaves (about 5 large leaves)

2 Tbsp olive oil

2 pinches kosher salt

Preheat the oven to 375°F [190°C]. Grease a 15 x 10 in [38 x 25 cm] jelly roll pan.

Heat the olive oil in a large skillet over medium heat. Add the onion, broccoli, red pepper, ½ teaspoon of the kosher salt, and black pepper. Sauté until tender, 7 to 8 minutes.

Meanwhile, whisk together the eggs with the milk, half-and-half, Dijon mustard, oregano, garlic powder, onion powder, dill, and the remaining 1 teaspoon of kosher salt. Pour the egg mixture into the prepared pan. Add the bread cubes, pushing the tops down into the eggs with a spoon so they are fully submerged. Sprinkle with 1¼ cups [100 g] of the Cheddar cheese. Top with the vegetables, then sprinkle on the remaining ¼ cup [20 g] of Cheddar cheese.

Bake until the egg mixture is set, about 30 minutes.

Mix the pistou ingredients in a small bowl and add a light drizzle of pistou to the top of the egg bake. Slice into pieces and serve.

COOK 1 ———— ● ■ ———— COOK 2

contd.

A good egg bake was often on the table at special occasions growing up, so this veggie-packed rendition goes out to Sonja's mom, a skilled host whose egg bakes always are a hit at holiday brunch. This one bakes up in a jelly roll pan, perfect for family and friends elbow-to-elbow around the table. It's also great for batch cooking breakfast for the week, or enjoying as a quick vegetarian dinner (add a whole grain and a pile of fresh greens).

The sparkling green pistou, a French spin on pesto, adds just the right bright, herby notes to take it over the top.

Tip

This is a fun way to use up extra homemade Crusty Rosemary Artisan Bread (page 245), but any store-bought artisan loaf will do.

Cooking Together

Have one person sauté the veggies while the other whisks up the egg mixture. Then designate one person to clean while the other makes the pistou.

Storage

Leftovers will keep, refrigerated, for up to 4 days and frozen for up to 3 months.

Diet
Vegetarian

Pesto Omelet
Breakfast Bagels

COOK 1 ———————— COOK 2

MAKES 2 SANDWICHES

2 bagels, sliced, or bread of choice

2 slices mild Cheddar cheese

4 eggs

¼ tsp dried oregano

¼ tsp kosher salt

Freshly ground black pepper

1 Tbsp salted butter

2 oz [55 g] lox smoked salmon (optional)

2 Tbsp mayonnaise

½ Tbsp jarred basil pesto or basil paste (see Tips)

Toast the bagels. Place the cheese between the two halves to melt while making the omelets.

Crack the eggs into a small bowl. With a fork, whisk them vigorously with 1 teaspoon of water and the oregano, kosher salt, and a few grinds of black pepper.

Heat a medium nonstick skillet over high heat, with the pan handle facing toward you. Add the butter and swirl the pan to fully coat. Wait until the butter starts to become foamy with large bubbles but is not yet browned, then pour in the eggs.

Cook the omelet for about 20 seconds, until a skin just starts to form on the bottom. Use a spatula to scrape the cooked eggs into one half of the pan so the uncooked portion can run out and continue to cook. As the eggs cook, use the spatula to gently roll the egg so that it covers half the pan. Cook for another 10 to 15 seconds until the eggs are just set; the outside should be pale golden and the inside soft and creamy (the total cooking time is about 1 minute).

Gently roll the omelet onto a plate and slice it into two pieces. Open the bagels and place a half omelet on top of the melted cheese on each bagel. Top with the smoked salmon. Stir together the mayonnaise and pesto, then spread it on the top bagel slice. Assemble the sandwich and serve immediately.

On those rare delightful occasions when we get to eat out for breakfast, we always lean savory over sweet. This hearty breakfast sandwich is one we'd order in a heartbeat. It's over-the-top tasty, with simple ingredients: a quick and easy omelet, a few slices of smoked salmon, and a rich, creamy pesto mayo. The smoky cured salmon takes it to all-star status, though you can omit it for a nearly as good vegetarian rendition.

It's best with a good everything bagel, if you can find one. Make these up for two and add a steaming cup of coffee for a lazy weekend morning.

Tips

Using jarred pesto makes this sandwich quick and easy, but the flavor can vary based on the brand. Basil paste is our preferred option; it's sold in the refrigerated section and has a fresher flavor. If you have homemade pesto on hand, use 2 tablespoons pesto without the mayo.

Feel free to throw a handful of baby arugula or fresh basil into the sandwich if you have them on hand.

Cooking Together

One person can cook the omelet while the other toasts the bagels and stirs together the mayo and pesto.

For Vegetarian

Omit the smoked salmon (consider adding tomato or avocado).

Storage

These sandwiches are best consumed on the spot—no leftovers!

Diet
Pescatarian,
vegetarian option

Spinach & Sun-Dried Tomato Crustless Quiche

SERVES 6 TO 8

10 oz [280 g] frozen spinach, thawed

6 eggs

1 cup [226 g] cottage cheese

¼ cup [8 g] grated Parmesan cheese

6 tablespoons [90 g] roughly chopped sun-dried tomatoes, packed in oil

½ tsp Italian seasoning or dried oregano

¼ tsp garlic powder

½ tsp kosher salt

Freshly ground black pepper

3 tablespoons [20 g] feta cheese crumbles

COOK 2

COOK 1

● Preheat the oven to 375°F [190°C]. Grease a 9 in [23 cm] round pie dish.

● Use your hands to squeeze out as much excess liquid as you can from the thawed spinach, then break it into small pieces.

■ In a large bowl, whisk the eggs. Stir in the spinach, cottage cheese, Parmesan cheese, 4 tablespoons of the sun-dried tomatoes, Italian seasoning, garlic powder, kosher salt, and a few grinds of black pepper.

■ Pour the egg mixture into the prepared dish. Sprinkle the top with the remaining sun-dried tomatoes and the feta cheese crumbles.

● ■ Bake the quiche until set in the center and golden around the edges, 28 to 30 minutes. Let rest for at least 15 minutes before cutting into pieces and serving.

contd.

This crustless quiche is quite the heavy lifter; it works just as well at big family brunches as for make-ahead weekday breakfasts. The savory egg custard is baked without the traditional pastry shell, making it much simpler to whip up. Cottage cheese adds a boost of protein, and the custard is packed with nutrient-dense spinach.

Tips

Leftover quiche keeps well, and you can eat leftovers cold, at room temperature, or warm. Try it on a sandwich; it's especially good on bread spread with the Dijon dill spread (see page 67).

If possible, look for bagged frozen spinach rather than boxed. It thaws easily in a colander under warm water.

Storage

Leftovers will keep, refrigerated, for up to 5 days.

Diet
Vegetarian, gluten-free

Power Couple Bars

MAKES 8 BARS

1¼ cups [125 g] old-fashioned rolled oats

¼ cup [45 g] raw quinoa

½ cup [125 g] creamy peanut butter

¼ cup [85 g] honey, agave, or brown rice syrup

2 Tbsp hot water

1 tsp vanilla extract

¾ tsp cinnamon

¼ tsp kosher salt

¾ cup [13 g] puffed rice

⅓ cup [45 g] finely chopped nuts (pistachios, almonds, or pecans), plus more for topping

2 Tbsp chopped dried fruit (dried cranberries or cherries, raisins, blueberries, or other), plus more for topping

2 Tbsp chocolate chips

½ tsp coconut oil

Flaky sea salt, for topping

Coconut flakes, for topping (optional)

Preheat the oven to 350°F [180°C]. Spread the oats and quinoa in a single layer on a baking sheet. Bake for 10 minutes.

In a small bowl, whisk together the peanut butter, honey, hot water, vanilla extract, cinnamon, and kosher salt until combined. Transfer the baked oats and quinoa to a large bowl and add the puffed rice, nuts, and dried fruit. Pour the wet mixture over the dry and stir until well combined.

Line a 9 x 5 in [23 x 13 cm] loaf pan with a sheet of parchment paper, letting the edges drape over the sides (if you'd like, use clips to hold the edges in place on the sides of the pan). Scrape out the mixture into the pan and press it firmly in an even layer with your fingers or a bench scraper (for a smooth surface on the bars, roll a small shot glass over the top). Sprinkle with additional chopped nuts and dried fruit.

Melt the chocolate and coconut oil over low heat in a small saucepan; remove from the heat when the chocolate starts to melt, and stir until smooth (see Tips). Drizzle the bars with the chocolate using a small spatula. Sprinkle the top with flaky sea salt and a handful of coconut flakes, if using.

Freeze the bars for 1 hour.

Use the parchment paper to lift the bars out of the pan. Use a sharp knife to cut them into 8 bars widthwise. Enjoy immediately or refrigerate.

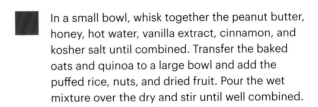

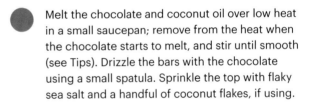

COOK 1

COOK 2

contd.

Of course you can buy power bars just about anywhere. But nothing beats homemade! Each bite tastes beautifully pure and simple. Plus, you know exactly what ingredients are inside.

These bars work as a light way to start the day, or a mid-afternoon snack. Use whatever nuts or dried fruit you have on hand. We like pistachios and dried cranberries, but there are endless combinations: pecan blueberry, oatmeal raisin, almond cherry, and so on. And the chocolate drizzle brings just the right sweet pop.

Tips

You can also microwave the chocolate and coconut oil in a glass bowl or container in 10 second bursts, stirring after each burst. Stop cooking when the chocolate just starts to melt and stir until smooth.

Puffed rice adds light texture and crunch to the bars (they can be overly dense with just oats). It's easy to find at most grocery stores in the cereal section.

To make 16 bars, double the ingredients and use an 8 in [20 cm] or 9 in [23 cm] square pan.

To accommodate nut allergies, you can substitute other types of nut butter or seed butter.

Cooking Together

Have one person toast the oats and quinoa while the other whisks up the other ingredients. Then one of you can shape the bars while the other prepares the chocolate drizzle.

For Vegan

Use agave or brown rice syrup.

Storage

The bars will keep, refrigerated, for up to 3 weeks.

Diet
Vegetarian,
gluten-free,
vegan option

Coffee Shop Banana Bread Crunch Muffins

MAKES 9 MUFFINS

1½ cups [210 g] all-purpose flour

2 tsp cinnamon

¼ tsp nutmeg

1 Tbsp baking powder

1 tsp baking soda

½ tsp kosher salt

1½ cups [320 g] mashed very ripe bananas (about 3 large or 4 medium)

1 egg

¾ cup [150 g] granulated sugar

½ cup [120 ml] neutral oil

2 tsp vanilla extract

Cornflake Streusel

4 Tbsp [55 g] unsalted butter, at room temperature

1 cup [30 g] unsweetened corn flakes (see Tips)

¼ tsp cinnamon

2 Tbsp turbinado sugar, plus more for sprinkling

Preheat the oven to 425°F [220°C]. Line 9 cups of a 12-cup muffin pan with paper liners (see Tips).

In a medium bowl, whisk together the flour, cinnamon, nutmeg, baking powder, baking soda, and kosher salt. In another medium bowl, whisk the bananas, egg, granulated sugar, oil, and vanilla extract.

Mix the wet ingredients into the dry ingredients using a spatula, stirring until a smooth batter forms. Avoid the urge to overmix. Let the batter rest for a few minutes while you make the streusel topping.

To make the cornflake streusel, in a small bowl, mash the butter with a wooden spoon. Add the corn flakes, cinnamon, and turbinado sugar and stir until the butter is fully integrated, crushing the corn flakes until they become broken down and crumbly.

Divide the batter evenly into the muffin cups (the cups will be very full). Sprinkle the tops with cornflake topping, then sprinkle with additional turbinado sugar.

Bake the muffins for 8 minutes, then lower the oven heat to 350°F [180°C] without opening the door. Bake until the tops are browned and a toothpick comes out clean, another 14 to 16 minutes. Cool for 10 minutes in the pan, then gently remove from the pan (wiggling the tops if they stick) and transfer to a rack to cool fully, about 1 hour.

COOK 1

COOK 2

contd.

These muffins are just what you need when you've got a few black bananas, transforming overripe fruit into muffins with massive tops of glittering cornflake streusel. They're less of an everyday bake and more like a treat you'd snag from a bakery display case, making them a fun project for impressing guests or your partner.

We first discovered the magic of cornflake streusel on a blueberry muffin at a local coffee shop, though the concept originated at the Ovenly bakery in New York City. We adapted Ovenly's original topping here, pairing it with an oversized muffin great for savoring with coffee on weekend mornings.

Tips

Don't have corn flakes? Use any unsweetened breakfast cereal. Or simply sprinkle the tops of the muffins with chopped walnuts and turbinado or granulated sugar.

This recipe uses two tricks for big muffin tops: baking at a high temperature for a few minutes to help the muffins rise, and using a large amount of batter in each muffin cup.

This recipe also works to make 12 standard-size muffins: Fill 12 muffin cups and bake for 15 minutes at 400°F [200°C].

Cooking Together

One of you can combine and divide the batter into muffin cups while the other makes the streusel.

For Dairy-Free

Substitute vegan butter.

Storage

To keep the tops crunchy, place the muffins in a storage container with a layer of paper towels on the bottom and on top. They will keep at room temperature for up to 3 days.

Diet
Vegetarian,
dairy-free option

Mini Cardamom Cinnamon Rolls

MAKES 16 SMALL ROLLS

Dough

3 cups [420 g] bread flour

¼ cup [50 g] granulated sugar

2¼ tsp (1 packet) [21 g] instant yeast (see Tips)

1 tsp kosher salt

4 Tbsp [55 g] unsalted butter

1 cup [240 ml] milk

1 egg, beaten

Filling

½ cup [100 g] packed light brown sugar

1 Tbsp cinnamon

1 tsp ground cardamom

1 tsp lightly packed orange zest

1½ Tbsp unsalted butter, melted

Frosting

½ cup [60 g] powdered sugar

1 Tbsp milk

⅛ tsp vanilla extract

To make the dough, in the bowl of a stand mixer, stir together the flour, granulated sugar, yeast, and kosher salt. In a small saucepan, melt the butter over low heat. Add the milk and heat until lukewarm (warm to the touch, but not hot, or between 105° and 115°F [40° and 45°C]).

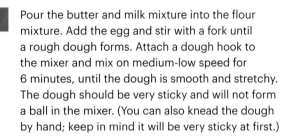

Pour the butter and milk mixture into the flour mixture. Add the egg and stir with a fork until a rough dough forms. Attach a dough hook to the mixer and mix on medium-low speed for 6 minutes, until the dough is smooth and stretchy. The dough should be very sticky and will not form a ball in the mixer. (You can also knead the dough by hand; keep in mind it will be very sticky at first.)

Flour a work surface, scrape the dough onto it, and knead it a few times, then shape it into a rough ball. Place the dough ball in a large clean bowl. Cover the bowl with a damp towel and let it rise in a warm location until doubled in size, 1 to 1½ hours.

To make the filling, stir together the brown sugar, cinnamon, cardamom, and orange zest. Grease a metal 9 x 9 in [23 x 23 cm] baking dish.

Lightly flour a work surface and scoop the dough onto it. Gently roll out the dough into a 12 x 12 in [30 x 30 cm] square. Tug the corners a bit to make them as square as possible. Brush the dough with the melted butter, leaving a ½ in [13 mm] border unbrushed at the left and right edges.

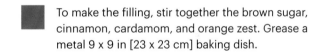

contd.

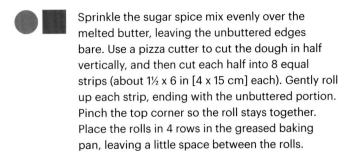 Sprinkle the sugar spice mix evenly over the melted butter, leaving the unbuttered edges bare. Use a pizza cutter to cut the dough in half vertically, and then cut each half into 8 equal strips (about 1½ x 6 in [4 x 15 cm] each). Gently roll up each strip, ending with the unbuttered portion. Pinch the top corner so the roll stays together. Place the rolls in 4 rows in the greased baking pan, leaving a little space between the rolls.

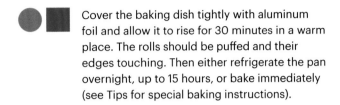 Cover the baking dish tightly with aluminum foil and allow it to rise for 30 minutes in a warm place. The rolls should be puffed and their edges touching. Then either refrigerate the pan overnight, up to 15 hours, or bake immediately (see Tips for special baking instructions).

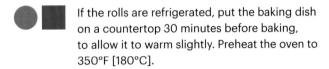 If the rolls are refrigerated, put the baking dish on a countertop 30 minutes before baking, to allow it to warm slightly. Preheat the oven to 350°F [180°C].

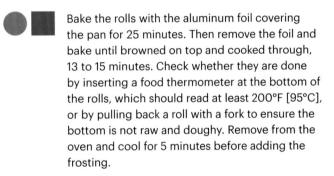 Bake the rolls with the aluminum foil covering the pan for 25 minutes. Then remove the foil and bake until browned on top and cooked through, 13 to 15 minutes. Check whether they are done by inserting a food thermometer at the bottom of the rolls, which should read at least 200°F [95°C], or by pulling back a roll with a fork to ensure the bottom is not raw and doughy. Remove from the oven and cool for 5 minutes before adding the frosting.

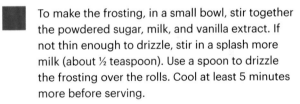 To make the frosting, in a small bowl, stir together the powdered sugar, milk, and vanilla extract. If not thin enough to drizzle, stir in a splash more milk (about ½ teaspoon). Use a spoon to drizzle the frosting over the rolls. Cool at least 5 minutes more before serving.

COOK 1 ———— • ■ ———— COOK 2

contd.

What's a better weekend baking project than ooey, gooey cinnamon rolls? The star here is the cardamom-orange filling, inspired by a cardamom bun we had on a Sunday morning bakery run in Chicago. (We couldn't pass up a visit to Lost Larson bakery, since it's the name of our son, which he found wildly amusing.)

This makes a 9 x 9 pan of mini rolls, so you can eat more than one and have enough to go around! Baking is a two-day process (since who wants to wake up 3 hours beforehand?). Start the rolls the night before and refrigerate overnight, then bake them in the a.m. and enjoy the cinnamon-spiced scent wafting through your kitchen.

Tips

Instant yeast (rather than active dry yeast) is required for this recipe, which allows quick rise times. If using active dry yeast, the rise times will be about double.

To bake the cinnamon rolls the day of, proceed immediately to baking. Bake 20 minutes covered with foil, then uncovered about 10 minutes, checking whether they are cooked through using a food thermometer.

Cooking Together

This is a baking project that's much easier with a partner! It's often helpful to have one person read the recipe out loud while the other gets their hands into the dough. Trade off on tasks and enjoy the process.

Storage

The cinnamon rolls will keep at room temperature, covered with aluminum foil, for up to 2 days. Reheat, covered, at 350°F [180°C] until warmed through, 10 to 12 minutes.

Diet
Vegetarian

Three Smoothies:
Hippie, Sunrise & Blush

MAKES 2 CUPS [480 ML]

Hippie Smoothie

1 large apple, roughly chopped

1 ripe banana, broken into pieces

2 medium ribs celery, roughly chopped

3 cups [60 g] baby spinach leaves, or chopped spinach

½ tsp peeled and grated fresh ginger

¼ cup raw cashews

½ cup water

1 Tbsp fresh lemon juice

1 Tbsp honey

12 ice cubes

Sunrise Smoothie

1 large orange, peeled

½ Tbsp orange zest

1 ripe banana, broken into pieces

1½ cups [210 g] frozen mango

¼ cup [60 ml] milk of choice or orange juice

½ cup [120 g] Greek yogurt (see Tips)

1 Tbsp honey

1½ tsp vanilla extract

8 ice cubes

Blush Smoothie

1 ripe banana, broken into pieces

1 cup [140 g] halved fresh strawberries (10 medium berries) (see Tips)

1 cup [140 g] frozen mango cubes

¼ cup [60 ml] orange juice

½ cup [120 ml] milk of choice

1 Tbsp maple syrup or agave syrup

⅛ tsp cinnamon

8 ice cubes

COOK 1 — ● ■ — COOK 2

 For each smoothie, put all the ingredients in a blender and blend until smooth, stopping and scraping as necessary and adding a splash more liquid if it's too thick (see Tips). For easiest blending, pour the liquids in first, followed by softer ingredients like the banana and other fruits toward the bottom of the blender. Taste and adjust flavors as desired. Drink immediately or refrigerate for up to 1 day.

contd.

Whizzing up brightly colored purées is a fun way to infuse fruit and vegetables into your mornings and snacks. But we've found one thing in our smoothie experiments: Tossing together random items from your vegetable drawer can often make a drink that's bland, bitter, or a lovely shade of brown.

Here are three smoothie recipes guaranteed to work every time. Hippie is a green smoothie, vegan and tinged with celery and ginger like a concoction from a juice bar. Sunrise is bright and citrusy with vanilla notes, reminiscent of a Creamsicle. Blush is sweet and pale pink, inspired by our go-to smoothie at our local climbing gym.

Tips

Make sure to use ripe bananas for sweet, great-tasting smoothies (underripe bananas can make for a bitter aftertaste). The sweetness of the smoothie can also vary based on the brand of frozen fruit. Adjust the amount of sweetener to your liking.

Fresh strawberries are key for the sweetness and color of the Blush Smoothie. You can substitute frozen, but you may need to add additional sweetener to taste. To add protein, the smoothie also works with an additional ¼ cup [60 g] Greek yogurt and ½ tablespoon pure maple syrup to balance the tang.

A high-speed blender is best for smoothies. Depending on your equipment, you may need to stop and scrape several times and add extra liquid. Try not to add too much liquid, or it will dilute the flavors.

Want to pack in more protein? Each of these smoothies tastes great with the addition of a scoop of vanilla protein powder.

For Vegan

For Sunrise, start with ⅓ cup [80 ml] orange juice and omit the Greek yogurt, adding more liquid as needed to blend.

Storage

Drink immediately or refrigerate in a sealed container for up to 1 day. The smoothie may naturally separate; shake it before serving.

Diet
Vegetarian, vegan, gluten-free

Chapter 5

SIDES

Sides aren't just an afterthought—they're the secret weapon that takes a meal from good to magnificent. Dive into this chapter to discover a range of ideas that bring vibrant flavor and color to the plate, such as crisp salads, hearty grains, and crispy roasted vegetables.

Don't be afraid to mix and match! There's no one-size-fits-all rule for side dishes. Each recipe includes variations for different ingredients and seasons: Feel free to make them your own.

SOME HIGHLIGHTS IN THIS CHAPTER:

Make the endlessly versatile, go-to Everyday Arugula Salad (page 187).

Create edible art with the Sunshine Citrus Salad with Orange & Fennel (page 197).

Mix up a fresh and funky Corn & Feta Salad (page 199) or Tomato Artichoke Penne Salad (page 205).

Complement the main dish with Lemon Asparagus with Crispy Prosciutto (page 211).

Mix up Herby Quinoa or Rice to go with any meal (page 226).

Everyday Arugula Salad

SERVES 4

8 cups (5 oz [140 g]) baby arugula (see Tips)

2 Tbsp olive oil

Zest of ½ lemon, plus more for garnishing (optional) (see Tips)

2 Tbsp fresh lemon juice

½ tsp kosher salt

1 crisp, tart apple (like Pink Lady or Honeycrisp), thinly sliced

1 small shallot, thinly sliced into rings

½ cup [35 g] Parmesan cheese shavings (see Tips)

 In a large salad bowl, toss the arugula with the olive oil, lemon zest, lemon juice, and kosher salt. Add the sliced apple, shallot, and Parmesan cheese and toss until combined. Arrange on a platter or individual plates. If desired, garnish with more lemon zest and serve immediately.

COOK 1

COOK 2

contd.

Go ahead and bend down the top corner of this page because you'll be coming back to this recipe again and again. This side salad is beyond simple; there's minimal chopping, and no need to whisk up a dressing! Drizzle olive oil and lemon juice over delicate baby arugula and crisp apple slices—it works like a charm. This is a back-pocket recipe we whip out all the time, both for dinner guests or on busy weeknights.

Tips

Look for baby arugula, sold in bags or boxes in the grocery or farmers' market. Avoid mature arugula, which is sold in bunches, as its flavor is much too spicy. If desired, substitute other delicate or baby greens like watercress, baby kale, or mixed baby greens.

If you can't find pre-shaved Parmesan, shave the Parmesan cheese off a block with a vegetable peeler. Look for a Parmesan that's aged 12 to 16 months for a consistency that's easy to shave.

Make sure to zest the lemon before juicing it! A microplane grater is our tool of choice.

For a seasonal variation, substitute sliced pears for the apple and add a generous handful of chopped walnuts.

For Vegan

Omit the Parmesan cheese and add roasted, salted cashew halves.

Storage

Salad is best served fresh. Leftovers will keep, refrigerated, for up to 1 day.

Diet
Vegetarian, gluten-free, vegan option

Kale Salad *with* Creamy Parmesan Dressing

SERVES 4

2 bunches Tuscan kale, about 1 lb [455 g]

Olive oil

¼ tsp kosher salt

½ cup [70 g] Pickled Red Onions (page 128) or red onion slices, rinsed and dried

½ cup [80 g] cherry tomatoes, sliced, or chopped tomatoes

¼ cup [15 g] seasoned Italian panko

Creamy Parmesan Dressing

¼ cup [60 g] mayonnaise

½ cup [120 g] Greek yogurt

¼ cup [8 g] finely grated Parmesan cheese

1 Tbsp red or white wine vinegar

½ Tbsp Dijon mustard

¼ tsp garlic powder

¼ tsp dry mustard powder (optional)

½ tsp kosher salt

Freshly ground black pepper

 Strip out the kale stems and chop the leaves into bite-size pieces. Put in a large salad bowl and sprinkle with a small drizzle of olive oil and the kosher salt. Massage the leaves with your fingers until the pieces are softened and tender, 2 to 3 minutes.

 To make the dressing, in a medium bowl, whisk together the mayonnaise, Greek yogurt, Parmesan cheese, red wine vinegar, Dijon mustard, garlic powder, mustard powder, kosher salt, and black pepper until a creamy dressing forms. If necessary, stir in 1 tablespoon of water to bring the dressing to a pourable consistency (this varies based on the yogurt brand).

 To serve, put the kale, pickled red onions, and tomatoes in a bowl and toss with ½ cup [120 g] of the dressing. Just before serving, toss with the panko (or use as a garnish for each serving).

COOK 1

COOK 2

Lemon Tahini Sauce (vegan alternative)

½ cup [110 g] tahini

½ cup [120 ml] fresh lemon juice

1 Tbsp olive oil

1 tsp maple syrup or honey

½ tsp kosher salt

2 Tbsp water

In a medium bowl, mix all the sauce ingredients. Leftover dressing will keep, refrigerated, for up to 2 weeks.

contd.

Kale salads have become almost a cliché of the health food world, but don't let that stop you from diving into this one. Massaging Tuscan kale makes its bitter leaves tender and almost sweet, and combined with tangy pickled onions and creamy dressing, it's an explosion of satisfying flavors.

The creamy Parmesan dressing is a go-to twist on a Caesar dressing that is easy to put together and as versatile as the classic! Use leftover dressing on just about anything, from crunchy romaine to fish or chicken, or dip your french fries. For a vegan option, use the Lemon Tahini Sauce recipe instead.

Tips

Seasoned Italian panko contains herbs and salt; it adds a fun crunch to the salad instead of croutons. (If you prefer, substitute homemade or store-bought croutons.)

Convert this recipe to an elegant plated side salad by using butter lettuce instead of kale. Drizzle each serving with the dressing before serving.

The pickled red onions take this salad over the top! A jar will keep, refrigerated, for up to 1 month.

Cooking Together

One of you can prepare the pickled red onions and mix up the dressing, while the other prepares the fresh ingredients and brings the salad together.

For Vegan

Use Lemon Tahini Sauce.

For Gluten-Free

Omit the panko or use gluten-free panko.

Storage

Reserve the remainder of the dressing; it will keep, refrigerated, for up to 2 weeks. Leftover salad without the panko will keep, refrigerated, for up to 3 days; bring to room temperature before serving (about 5 minutes).

Diet
Vegetarian,
vegan option,
gluten-free option

Big Chopped Salad
Three Ways

SERVES 8

Classic Chopped Salad

1 recipe Dijon vinaigrette (recipe follows)

1 romaine heart and ½ head leafy lettuce, chopped (8 cups [440 g] chopped greens)

1 large shallot, thinly sliced

2 cups [240 g] chopped English cucumber (about 1 cucumber)

1 cup [160 g] cherry tomatoes, halved

½ cup [65 g] Castelvetrano olives, halved

½ cup [65 g] jarred sliced pepperoncini

¼ cup [18 g] Parmesan cheese shavings

Cilantro Lime Chopped Salad

½ recipe Cilantro Lime Dressing (recipe follows)

1 romaine heart and ½ head leafy lettuce, chopped (8 cups [440 g] chopped greens)

1 large shallot, thinly sliced

2 cups [120 g] shredded red cabbage (about ¼ head)

1 cup [160 g] cherry tomatoes, sliced

4 radishes, thinly sliced and quartered

¼ cup [35 g] roasted salted pepitas

¾ cup [120 g] canned corn, drained

4 handfuls crushed tortilla chips (optional)

Ginger Miso Chopped Salad

1 recipe Ginger Miso Dressing (recipe follows)

1 romaine heart and ½ head leafy lettuce, chopped (8 cups [440 g] chopped greens)

1 large shallot, thinly sliced

1 cup [120 g] chopped English cucumber (about ½ cucumber)

1 cup [160 g] cherry tomatoes, sliced

1 cup [110 g] shredded carrots

2 tablespoons sesame seeds, toasted in a dry skillet over medium heat until golden brown (3 to 5 minutes)

¼ cup [5 g] roughly chopped cilantro

COOK 1 —————— ● ■ —————— COOK 2

 Make the dressing.

 Prepare the salad ingredients. Immediately before serving, toss all ingredients and dressing together in a large bowl.

contd.

Dijon Vinaigrette

**MAKES A GENEROUS ½ CUP
[120 ML]**

2 Tbsp white wine vinegar

1 Tbsp Dijon mustard

1 Tbsp honey or maple syrup

1 small garlic clove, grated

½ Tbsp Italian seasoning

¼ tsp kosher salt

6 Tbsp olive oil

Freshly ground black pepper

In a medium bowl, whisk together all the ingredients except for the oil and black pepper. Gradually whisk in the olive oil until a creamy dressing forms. Season with black pepper. Dress the salad and serve immediately. Leftover dressing will keep, refrigerated, for up to 2 weeks (it solidifies when cold, so bring to room temperature about 5 minutes prior to serving).

Cilantro Lime Dressing

MAKES 1 CUP [240 ML]

1 small garlic clove, minced

1½ cups [18 g] loosely packed cilantro leaves and tender stems

½ cup [120 g] Greek yogurt

½ cup [120 g] mayonnaise

2 Tbsp fresh lime juice

½ tsp sugar

¼ tsp onion powder

½ tsp kosher salt

Put the garlic and cilantro in a food processor, small blender, or the cup of an immersion blender. Blend to combine, then add the remaining ingredients and blend until smooth. Refrigerate for 15 minutes or until serving. Leftover dressing will keep, refrigerated, for up to 1 week.

Ginger Miso Dressing

MAKES ½ CUP [120 ML]

1 Tbsp peeled and grated fresh ginger (see Tips)

3 Tbsp [40 g] light miso (white or yellow) (see Tips)

2 Tbsp unseasoned rice vinegar

1 Tbsp maple syrup or honey

1 Tbsp olive oil

1 Tbsp toasted sesame oil

¼ tsp garlic powder

Whisk together all the ingredients, or, for a smooth dressing, use a small blender or immersion blender to blend until creamy. (Or make a double recipe in a standard blender.)

If the texture is very thick, stir in water, 1 teaspoon at a time, until it reaches the desired consistency. Dress the salad and serve immediately or refrigerate the dressing for up to 10 days. Before serving, let come to room temperature for about 5 minutes, and stir in a bit of water to loosen if necessary (it can become very thick during storage).

COOK 2

COOK 1

We're always on the lookout for a versatile side dish, and this three-in-one concept is one we eat on repeat. The Classic Chopped Salad is based on the fan-favorite recipe from our website: an Italian-American mix of crunchy veggies, tangy pepperoncini, and a zingy Dijon vinaigrette. It's fantastic with lasagna (page 130), pizza (page 88), and pasta (page 93).

The same base ingredients make two different spins, with new mix-ins and dressings. Cilantro Lime Chopped Salad has a creamy dressing, sweet corn, and crushed tortilla chips, and pairs well with chili (page 123), Sweet Potato Enchiladas (page 31), or tacos (page 62). Ginger Miso Chopped Salad is refreshingly crunchy and works with anything from Sticky Orange Tofu & Broccoli (page 47) to Lentil Soup with Tarragon (page 36).

Tips

A simple way to peel ginger is to scrape it with the side of a spoon—it runs along the uneven surface much better than a vegetable peeler.

Look for packages marked light miso (yellow or white), which are fermented for a shorter time and taste milder. Avoid red or dark miso, which is stronger and saltier.

Cooking Together

Assign a dressing master to mix the dressing while the other person preps the fresh ingredients.

For Vegan

Omit the Parmesan cheese from the Classic and use maple syrup in the dressing, or make the Ginger Miso Chopped Salad.

Storage

If you're planning to keep the salad as leftovers or make it in advance, refrigerate the chopped vegetables separate from the dressing. Keep out any crunchy items (tortilla chips, pepitas), as they'll become soggy during storage.

Diet

Vegetarian, gluten-free, vegan option

Sunshine Citrus Salad
with Orange & Fennel

SERVES 4

2 Tbsp sliced almonds

5 small oranges, plus zest of ½ orange (a mix of navel and blood oranges, if desired) (see Tips)

1½ Tbsp white wine vinegar

½ Tbsp Dijon mustard

½ Tbsp honey or maple syrup

⅛ tsp garlic powder

⅛ tsp kosher salt

¼ cup [60 ml] olive oil

Freshly ground black pepper

1 head frisée, or the crunchy interior leaves of 1 head green leafy lettuce, torn into pieces (about 1 cup [40 g])

½ fennel bulb, thinly sliced into half-moons, plus fronds for garnishing

1 small shallot, thinly sliced into rings

1 oz [30 g] soft goat cheese, crumbled (optional)

In a small dry skillet over medium heat, toast the almonds, stirring often, until they are fragrant and golden brown, 3 to 5 minutes. Remove immediately from the heat and transfer to a bowl.

To create orange rounds, use a large chef's knife to cut off both ends of each orange, then cut around the fruit to remove the peel and the pith. Slice the peeled oranges widthwise into rounds.

In a medium bowl, whisk together the white wine vinegar, Dijon mustard, honey, garlic powder, and kosher salt. Gradually mix in the olive oil until a creamy emulsion forms. Season with black pepper.

Place the greens on a platter or four separate salad plates. On top, artfully arrange the orange rounds. Top with the sliced fennel, fennel fronds, shallot, toasted almonds, goat cheese, if using, and orange zest. Drizzle with half of the dressing; reserve remainder for serving or future use.

COOK 1

COOK 2

contd.

This "Fancy Pants Salad" (as we like to call it) is simple but looks like a piece of art. And what a delight it is to eat, with a juicy burst from the orange, frilly lettuce, nutty toasted almonds, creamy goat cheese, and bright zingy dressing. Fresh fennel brings subtle licorice notes and a refreshing crunch.

Using a mix of oranges is lovely here. If they're in season, use sweet blood oranges. You can also use different types of greens, like green leafy lettuce, frisée, or Belgian endive. This recipe makes a platter for four, but it's easy to double the quantities for a party size.

Tips

Get creative with your plating! Arrange the ingredients as you like, and keep in mind that the amounts listed are only suggestions.

Make sure to zest an orange before slicing into rounds: removed orange peels are virtually impossible to zest.

If using Belgian endive in place of the other greens, cut off the bottom ½ in [13 mm] of the endive, then cut the leaves in half lengthwise, leaving most of the smaller leaves whole (or thinly slice the endive leaves). Rinse the leaves, then blot them dry with a towel or use a salad spinner.

Wine Pairing

Complement the juicy burst of orange and the fennel's licorice notes with a bottle of effervescent prosecco. Its lively bubbles and bright profile make it a festive choice, especially if you're sharing it at a holiday gathering.

For Vegan

Omit the goat cheese, use maple syrup in the dressing, and garnish with flaky sea salt.

Storage

This salad tastes best the day it is made.

Diet

Vegetarian, gluten-free, vegan option

Corn & Feta Salad

SERVES 6

Two 15 oz [480 g] cans corn, drained (about 3 cups kernels) or 4 ears corn

1 cup [160 g] cherry tomatoes, quartered

½ cup [70 g] minced red onion

¼ cup [10 g] roughly chopped fresh cilantro (see Tip)

½ tsp smoked paprika

½ tsp chili powder

½ tsp garlic powder

½ tsp kosher salt

1 cup [120 g] feta cheese crumbles

2 Tbsp olive oil

2 Tbsp mayonnaise

1½ Tbsp red wine vinegar

Freshly ground black pepper

If using ears of corn, boil the corn on the cobs in a large pot of water until bright yellow, about 4 minutes. Drain and rinse under cold water, then slice the kernels from the cob.

Toss the corn kernels with all of the remaining ingredients and stir to combine. Serve immediately or refrigerate to allow the flavors to meld; bring to room temperature (about 5 minutes) before serving.

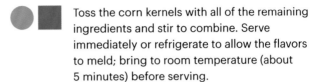

COOK 1

COOK 2

contd.

Here's a summer salad for lazy patio meals and picnics on blankets. But it tastes just as great with canned corn, making it work in any season!

Use it as a side dish for a cookout or barbecue, or serve it up with Crispy Black Bean Tacos with Spicy Ranch (page 29), Sweet Potato–Enchiladas (page 31), or Blackened Shrimp Tacos with Avocado Lime Sauce (page 62). It also works great as a chip dip: Finely dice the tomatoes and serve with crunchy tortilla chips.

Tip

Don't love cilantro? Use fresh basil or parsley instead. (Note: Basil browns after refrigeration, but parsley stays bright green.)

Storage

Leftovers will keep, refrigerated, for up to 3 days.

Diet
Vegetarian,
gluten-free

Brussels Sprouts & Apple Slaw

COOK 2 —————— ■ ● —————— COOK 1

SERVES 6 TO 8

½ cup [120 g] mayonnaise

2 Tbsp apple cider vinegar

1½ Tbsp honey

¼ tsp dried dill

1 pinch cayenne (see Tips)

Freshly ground black pepper

1 lb [455 g] Brussels sprouts
(off the stalk)

3 medium carrots, peeled

1 large crisp, tart apple (like Pink
Lady or Granny Smith)

1 medium shallot, thinly sliced

¾ tsp kosher salt, plus more
to taste

In a medium bowl, whisk together the mayonnaise, apple cider vinegar, honey, dill, cayenne, and a few grinds of black pepper.

Use the slicing blade attachment on a food processor to shred the whole Brussels sprouts (no need to discard the root ends). Or to shred them by hand, first remove any tough outer leaves with your fingers. With a large chef's knife, slice a sprout in half lengthwise. Place the cut side down and thinly slice crosswise to create shreds. Separate the shreds with your fingers and discard the root end. Repeat for all the Brussels sprouts.

Grate or shred the carrots and apple into 2 in [5 cm] pieces using a food processor with a large grater blade or a handheld grater.

Put the shredded vegetables, apples, and shallot in a large bowl and toss with the kosher salt. Add half the dressing and stir until coated, then add the remaining dressing and stir again. Let stand for 10 minutes before serving, or refrigerate until serving. Taste and add additional salt as necessary until the flavor pops.

This slaw is the epitome of fresh and light! Shaved raw Brussels sprouts add a feathery texture that balances the sweet crunch of carrots and apples. The dressing is an ode to the classic picnic coleslaw, made with just enough mayo to give it a satisfying richness while still tasting refreshing.

This one is a favorite on our table: We love serving it as a weeknight side dish with chicken or fish. It's great for picnics, pitch-ins, or as a make-ahead salad for lunches throughout the week.

Tips

Cayenne adds just the right complexity to this slaw; omit it only for the most heat-sensitive eaters.

A crisp, tart apple is key. Pink Lady is our favorite variety, which has a lovely rosy pink color and intense sweet-tart flavor.

Customize your slaw by adding sunflower seeds, sliced almonds, raisins, dried cranberries, Parmesan cheese shreds, and more.

For Vegan

Use vegan mayonnaise and maple syrup.

Storage

Leftovers will keep, refrigerated, for up to 3 days.

Diet
Vegetarian, gluten-free, vegan option

Tomato Artichoke
Penne Salad

SERVES 5 TO 6

8 oz [230 g] penne (see Tips)

2 cups [80 g] baby spinach
or roughly chopped spinach

1 handful fresh mint or basil
leaves, loosely torn

One 14 oz [400 g] can artichoke
hearts, chopped (8½ oz [240 g]
drained weight)

2 cups [320 g] cherry tomatoes,
halved

¼ cup [60 g] sun-dried tomatoes
(packed in oil), roughly chopped

¼ cup [8 g] shredded Parmesan
cheese

2 Tbsp pine nuts

2 Tbsp white wine vinegar

2 Tbsp olive oil

2 Tbsp neutral oil (like
organic vegetable, canola,
or grapeseed) (see Tips)

½ Tbsp granulated sugar

½ Tbsp Dijon mustard

1 tsp dried oregano

½ tsp garlic powder

½ tsp kosher salt, plus more for
the pasta water

Freshly ground black pepper

Bring a large saucepan of water to boil with ½ tablespoon kosher salt. Boil the pasta until it is al dente. Drain the pasta and return it to the pot (stir in a drizzle of olive oil to keep the pasta from sticking if the remaining components are not yet done).

Combine the spinach, mint, artichoke hearts, cherry tomatoes, sun-dried tomatoes, and Parmesan cheese in a large bowl.

Add the pine nuts to a small dry skillet. Toast over medium heat, stirring often, until golden, about 3 minutes. Immediately add to the bowl with the vegetables.

In a small bowl, whisk together the white wine vinegar, olive oil, neutral oil, sugar, Dijon mustard, oregano, garlic powder, kosher salt, and black pepper. When the pasta is cooked, add it to the bowl with the vegetables. Toss with the dressing until fully coated. Serve immediately.

COOK 1

COOK 2

contd.

Every cook needs a good pasta salad, and this one gets rave reviews every time we serve it. The secret to its success lies in the combination of flavors and textures. Savory sun-dried tomatoes, rich buttery pine nuts, tangy dressing, and the bright burst of fresh herbs are just the right accessories for chewy penne.

Even better, it holds up in the refrigerator for days, which is no mean feat for a pasta salad. This makes it incredibly versatile—use it for a summer picnic or barbecue, as a simple side dish, or even as a make-ahead lunch.

Tips

You can use any short pasta shape for this salad, including fusilli (spirals), shells, rigatoni, orecchiette, and more. We like using penne ritorte, an oversized version of penne with ridges.

Using a mix of neutral oil and olive oil makes this pasta salad hold up well in the refrigerator (dressings using only olive oil tend to solidify when cold).

Cooking Together

While one of you boils the pasta, toasts the pine nuts, and mixes the dressing, the other can chop and prepare the fresh ingredients.

For Vegan

Omit the Parmesan cheese or use plant-based cheese.

Storage

Leftovers will keep, refrigerated, for up to 5 days.

Diet
Vegetarian,
vegan option

French Carrot Salad

SERVES 4

1 lb [455 g] carrots (about 8 medium), peeled and grated on the large holes of a box grater (see Tip)

¼ cup [10 g] finely chopped parsley

1 Tbsp finely chopped chives

½ Tbsp fresh tarragon, or ½ tsp dried tarragon

2 Tbsp fresh lemon juice

½ Tbsp Dijon mustard

1 tsp granulated sugar

½ tsp kosher salt

3 Tbsp olive oil

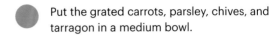 Put the grated carrots, parsley, chives, and tarragon in a medium bowl.

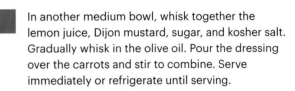 In another medium bowl, whisk together the lemon juice, Dijon mustard, sugar, and kosher salt. Gradually whisk in the olive oil. Pour the dressing over the carrots and stir to combine. Serve immediately or refrigerate until serving.

COOK 1

COOK 2

This bright salad tastes like sunbeams. Called *salade de carottes rapées* in France, it's a national specialty served at cafes and bistros, and you can buy it by the pound at supermarkets. One taste and you'll see why: It's addictingly good (kind of like American coleslaw, but better). If you have tarragon on hand, the hint of anise takes it to the next level. Enjoy it for picnics and lunches, or as a side for chicken or fish.

Tip

Want to speed up the grating? Grate the carrots in a food processor using the grater disk.

Storage

Leftovers will keep, refrigerated, for up to 3 days.

Diet
Vegetarian, vegan, gluten-free

Crunchy Green Panzanella

COOK 2

COOK 1

SERVES 6

2 garlic cloves

2 Tbsp fresh lemon juice, plus zest from 1 lemon

1 Tbsp white wine vinegar

7 Tbsp [105 ml] olive oil

¼ cup [25 g] thinly sliced red onion

4 cups [200 g] crusty artisan bread, torn into 1 to 2 in [2.5 to 5 cm] pieces (see Tips)

¾ teaspoon kosher salt

3 cups [375 g] English cucumber (1 large or 2 small), halved lengthwise and sliced ⅜ in [9.5 mm] thick

2 green onions, sliced diagonally

1 cup [80 g] celery heart ribs and leaves, sliced diagonally

2 cups [160 g] snap peas, sliced in half widthwise

¼ cup [1 g] roughly chopped fresh dill

⅔ cup (3 oz [80 g]) feta cheese crumbles

Freshly ground black pepper

Grate one garlic clove. Whisk it with the lemon juice and zest, white wine vinegar, and 4 tablespoons [60 ml] of the olive oil. Add the red onion to the bowl with the dressing to marinate and set aside.

Smash the other garlic clove. In a large skillet over medium heat, heat the remaining 3 tablespoons of olive oil and the smashed garlic clove. Add the bread pieces and stir with tongs until coated with oil. Sprinkle with ¼ teaspoon of the kosher salt. Cook, stirring occasionally, until browned and crispy, 5 to 6 minutes. Discard the garlic. Let it cool while making the remainder of the salad.

Combine the cucumber, green onions, celery, snap peas, dill, and feta cheese crumbles in a bowl. Add the bread cubes and dressing. Add the remaining ½ teaspoon of kosher salt and black pepper, and toss to combine. Serve within 30 minutes (see Tips).

contd.

A COUPLE COOKS

This classic Italian bread salad is traditionally made with juicy summer tomatoes, but this spin with green veggies is an excuse to eat it any time of the year. The crunchy, garlicky bites of pan-fried bread are worth their weight in gold, and they might not even make it into the salad if you sneak bites like we do. Toss them with fresh dill, feta, and a tangy vinaigrette to dress them up into a next-level side dish.

This recipe is loosely inspired by a Spring Panzanella created by author Molly Baz for *Bon Appétit*. We made it for a spring dinner with family, and everyone's still talking about it.

Tips

This is a great way to use up leftover Crusty Rosemary Artisan Bread (page 245), but any store-bought artisan loaf will do.

For meal prep up to 24 hours in advance, refrigerate the fresh ingredients and dressing in separate containers, and store the bread in a sealed container at room temperature. Stir together immediately before serving.

Cooking Together

Have one person manage the dressing and chopping the vegetables while the other pan-fries the bread.

For Vegan

Omit the feta cheese (or use dairy-free cheese).

Storage

The salad is best enjoyed the day it is made (see Tips).

Diet
Vegetarian, vegan option

Lemon Asparagus
with Crispy Prosciutto

SERVES 4

1 lb [455 g] thin asparagus spears, tough bottom ends removed

1½ Tbsp olive oil

½ tsp kosher salt

Freshly ground black pepper

1 medium lemon, cut in half

2 slices prosciutto (1 oz [30 g]), chopped into very small pieces

Grated Parmesan cheese, for serving

Preheat the broiler to high. Line a baking sheet with aluminum foil and lay the asparagus on the foil. Drizzle with 1 tablespoon of the olive oil and add the kosher salt and a few grinds of black pepper. Toss until well combined. Slice one half of the lemon into 4 wheels, then slice them in half to make half-moon shapes and place them on top of the asparagus.

Broil for 3 minutes. Remove the pan from the oven and stir, then broil until the spears are tender when pierced by a fork at the thickest part, 2 to 3 minutes more. (If not tender, continue cooking until tender.)

Meanwhile, heat the remaining ½ tablespoon of olive oil in a large nonstick skillet over medium heat. Sauté the chopped prosciutto until browned and crisp, 2 to 3 minutes. Transfer to a plate.

When the asparagus is cooked, remove from the oven. Zest and juice the remaining half of the lemon over the asparagus and toss to combine. Transfer to a serving platter and top with the crispy prosciutto and a sprinkle of Parmesan cheese. Serve immediately.

COOK 1 ——————•——— COOK 2

contd.

Just a hint of prosciutto, crisped up in a hot skillet, turns into salty confetti that makes any vegetable taste like candy. Here it dresses up asparagus as a side that will wow everyone. Broiling makes the green stalks tender with lightly charred edges, and you don't even have to wait for the oven to preheat. Cook the spears with lemon slices, then add lemon juice and zest before serving to give it a citrus punch.

Tip

Thin asparagus spears have a nice tender texture and sweet flavor. If all you can find is thicker asparagus, you can use it too. Simply broil for a few minutes longer until tender when pierced with a fork.

Storage

Leftovers will keep, refrigerated, for up to 2 days.

Diet
Gluten-free

Heart-Melting
Garlicky Greens

COOK 2 ——— ■ ● ——— COOK 1

SERVES 4

1 Tbsp salted butter

1 Tbsp olive oil

4 garlic cloves, peeled and smashed

1 lb [455 g] Tuscan kale or Swiss chard, or a mix of both, stemmed and chopped (about 2 bunches) (see Tips)

1 Tbsp fresh lemon juice

¼ heaping tsp kosher salt

2 Tbsp shredded Parmesan cheese (optional)

 In a large skillet, heat the butter and olive oil over medium-high heat.

 Add the garlic cloves and cook until fragrant and lightly browned, about 1½ minutes. Add the kale, which will be mounded in the pan at first, and stir until all the leaves are coated with oil. Cook until the leaves are fully wilted but still bright green, 3 to 4 minutes. Remove from the heat and discard the garlic cloves. Stir in the lemon juice and kosher salt. Taste and add more salt if desired. Top with Parmesan cheese, if desired, and serve.

A COUPLE COOKS

Three minutes is all it takes to "melt" a massive mound of chopped kale into a mouthwatering side dish. The bright, lemony zing complements chicken, fish, or pasta, and you can dress it up with toasted pine nuts. If you're cooking for two, it's easy to make a half recipe for quick weeknight meals.

Tips

Step it up for a fancy dinner party or a Thanksgiving side by topping with lemon zest and toasted pine nuts. To toast the nuts, put a handful in a dry skillet and heat over medium heat, shaking the pan and stirring often with a wooden spoon, until the nuts are fragrant and golden brown, about 3 minutes. Remove from the heat immediately and transfer to a plate to stop the browning.

Look for Tuscan kale when shopping, also known as Lacinato or dinosaur kale. Its mild flavor is preferable to spicier curly kale, though either work. Or use a mix of greens by adding in some Swiss or rainbow chard.

For Vegan

Substitute olive oil for the butter and omit the Parmesan cheese.

Storage

Leftovers will keep, refrigerated, for up to 4 days.

Diet
Vegetarian,
gluten-free,
vegan option

Blistered Green Beans Almondine

SERVES 4

1 lb [455 g] green beans, trimmed

1 Tbsp olive oil

½ tsp kosher salt

¼ cup [25 g] sliced almonds

1 Tbsp salted butter

2 medium garlic cloves, minced

Freshly grated whole nutmeg, or 1 pinch ground nutmeg (see Tips)

Heat the broiler to high heat. Line a baking sheet with aluminum foil. Add the green beans, olive oil, and kosher salt and toss with your hands until evenly coated. Spread the beans into a single layer.

Broil, removing the pan from the oven and stirring every few minutes, until all the beans are tender and charred, 7 to 12 minutes. Check often, since each broiler is different (see Tips).

In a large dry skillet over medium heat, toast the almonds until they start to brown, 2 to 4 minutes. Transfer to a bowl and turn off the heat. In the same skillet with no heat, melt the butter, then add the garlic and stir until fragrant, about 1 minute (the residual heat from the pan cooks the garlic).

Return the toasted almonds to the skillet with the garlic butter, add the broiled green beans, and toss to combine. Finish with a few grates of nutmeg from a whole nutmeg. Taste and add more salt if desired. Serve immediately.

COOK 1

COOK 2

contd.

Our secret to green beans: blister them in the broiler instead of the stovetop or the oven. It's fast and easy and adds a charred finish to the tender beans. Even better, they maintain their brilliant bright green color.

Combine the tender, charred beans with nutty toasted almonds, butter, and garlic, and it's enough to make this side dish take over as star of the plate. Nutmeg adds a floral complexity as a finishing touch—don't leave it out!

Tips

All broilers work differently; some may cook much faster than others. The first time you make this recipe, check early and often.

Use a microplane grater to add a hint of fresh grated nutmeg to add a unique, heightened element. Otherwise, ground nutmeg works as a substitute.

Haricots verts or French green beans also work here. Since they are thinner, cut the cooking time by half and cook until browned.

For Vegan

Substitute olive oil for the butter.

Storage

Leftovers will keep, refrigerated, for up to 2 days; reheat in a skillet before serving.

Diet
Vegetarian, gluten-free, vegan option

Lemon Pepper
Broccolini

SERVES 4

2 Tbsp olive oil

2 bunches (14 oz [400 g])
broccolini, tough lower stems
removed and large pieces sliced
in half lengthwise (see Tips)

½ tsp garlic powder

½ tsp kosher salt

1 Tbsp fresh lemon juice
(see Tips)

Freshly ground black pepper

1 Tbsp grated Parmesan cheese

Zest of ½ lemon (see Tips)

In a medium skillet, heat the olive oil over
medium-high heat. Add the broccolini and
cook for 3 to 5 minutes, stirring often, until the
florets are bright green and starting to brown
at the edges.

Stir in the garlic powder and kosher salt. Add
¼ cup [60 ml] of water to the pan and continue
to cook until the stems are just tender, 2 to
3 minutes. Remove the pan from the heat and
toss the broccolini with the lemon juice.

Place the broccolini in a serving bowl or on a
platter and garnish with the Parmesan cheese
and lemon zest. Serve immediately.

COOK 1 — ● — ■ — COOK 2

contd.

Broccolini makes a lightning-fast side dish that feels fancier than it is. This sophisticated cousin of broccoli is a cross between Chinese broccoli and the standard variety, giving it long, elegant stems and a sweet, mild flavor. It's versatile, pairing with a variety of mains from risotto (page 95) to fish (page 53) to meatballs (page 79). With a cooking time of just 6 minutes, you can throw it on at the last minute to round out any meal.

Tips

Make sure to zest the lemon before juicing it! A microplane grater is quicker and easier than a zester.

Can't find broccolini? This method works with broccoli florets just as well.

For Vegan

Omit the Parmesan cheese and garnish with flaky sea salt.

Storage

Leftovers will keep, refrigerated, for up to 3 days.

Diet
Vegetarian,
gluten-free,
vegan option

Crispy Potato Wedges

SERVES 4

1½ lb [680 g] 3 in [7.5 cm] long yellow or red potatoes (about 5 medium potatoes)

2 Tbsp salted butter, melted, or olive oil

1 tsp garlic powder

½ tsp onion powder

½ tsp dry mustard powder

¼ tsp ground black pepper

½ tsp fine sea salt, plus more for seasoning

⅓ cup [10 g] grated Parmesan cheese (optional, see Tips)

 Preheat the oven to 425°F [220°C].

 To cut the potatoes into wedges, slice them in half lengthwise, then place the cut side of the potato down onto the cutting board and cut it in half again. Place each potato quarter cut side up, then slice down the center to create 2 wedges.

 Add the potatoes to a large bowl with the melted butter, garlic powder, onion powder, mustard powder, black pepper, and fine sea salt, and mix until fully coated. Mix in the Parmesan cheese, if using.

 Line two baking sheets with parchment paper. Lay the wedges on the sheet in a single layer, with as much space between the wedges as possible. Bake for 20 minutes, then remove the sheets from the oven and flip the potatoes. Reverse the sheets and bake until browned, with a crisp exterior, another 10 to 12 minutes. Let them cool for a few minutes, then taste a wedge. Toss with a few more pinches of fine sea salt, if desired, and serve warm.

COOK 1 ———— ● ■ ———— COOK 2

Parmesan Aioli

¼ cup [60 g] high-quality mayonnaise

½ garlic clove, grated

1 Tbsp grated Parmesan cheese

Curried Ketchup

¼ cup [65 g] high-quality ketchup

½ tsp curry powder

Special Fry Sauce

2 Tbsp high-quality ketchup

2 Tbsp mayonnaise

1 Tbsp Dijon mustard

 To make each dip, in a small bowl, mix all the ingredients. Refrigerate until ready to serve.

contd.

Who needs fries when you've got potato wedges? They're simpler than homemade fries, and they come out crispy and irresistibly seasoned. Serve them up as a fun appetizer or side for Chicken Cutlets with Honey Mustard Pan Sauce (page 68) or Seared Tuna Steaks with Chimichurri (page 50).

Our favorite part? The dips! These quick sauces are inspired by the long list of french fry dips we love to order at our local brewpub. Each one takes just a few minutes to whip up.

Tips

The grated Parmesan is optional but recommended; it adds a crispy coating to the wedges.

Repurpose the Parmesan Aioli or Special Fry Sauce as a sandwich spread.

Cooking Together

One person can mix up the sauces while the other bakes the potatoes.

For Vegan

Use olive oil instead of butter and omit the Parmesan cheese or use a dairy-free substitute. Use vegan mayonnaise in the dips.

Storage

Wedges are best served immediately but can be refrigerated for up to 2 days; reheat in the oven until crispy. The sauces will keep, refrigerated, for up to 2 weeks.

Diet
Vegetarian, gluten-free, vegan option

Roasted Butternut Squash & Onions *with Garlic Butter*

SERVES 4

One butternut squash (about 2 lb [910 g]), peeled, or 1½ lb [680 g] sweet potatoes (about 3 medium), unpeeled, cut into ¾ in [2 cm] dice, about 6 cups (see Tip)

1 small red onion, cut into ¾ in [2 cm] slices

1½ Tbsp olive oil

1 tsp garlic powder

1 tsp kosher salt

Freshly ground black pepper

1½ Tbsp salted butter

1 small garlic clove, finely minced

1 Tbsp finely chopped fresh parsley

⅓ cup [40 g] feta cheese crumbles, for garnishing

COOK 2

COOK 1

Preheat the oven to 425°F [220°C] and line two baking sheets with parchment paper.

In a large bowl, stir together the squash and red onion with the olive oil, garlic powder, and kosher salt. Add a few grinds of black pepper. Arrange in a single layer on the prepared baking sheets, spaced apart as far as possible.

Roast for 20 minutes, stir, then roast until tender, another 10 to 15 minutes.

Meanwhile, melt the butter with the garlic and parsley in a small saucepan over low heat, then set aside. When the squash is roasted, toss with the garlic butter and feta cheese crumbles. Serve immediately.

Make almost any veggie taste amazing with this trick: Roast it until browned and caramelized in a hot oven, then toss with garlic butter and feta cheese! Butternut squash is notoriously time-intensive to peel and dice, so if you prefer, use sweet potato instead. The recipe is a versatile platform for whatever orange vegetable you have on hand. Pair with Salmon Piccata (page 60) or Creamy Mediterranean Chicken Skillet (page 70).

Tip

To peel and chop butternut squash:

Use a large chef's knife to cut off the stem of the butternut squash. Then cut off the neck where it meets the round base.

Use a serrated vegetable peeler to peel the neck and the base. A serrated peeler is much easier than a standard peeler, which tends to slip on the tough skin.

Cut the base in half and use a spoon to scoop out the seeds.

Cut a slice off of one side of the neck and lay it cut side down. Cut the neck into ¾ in [2 cm] slices, then cut the slices into strips and chop crosswise to dice.

Slice off the end of the base, and set it cut side down. Cut it into ¾ in [2 cm] slices, then chop crosswise to dice.

Cooking Together

For quick prep, have one person peel and chop the butternut squash while the other preps the remaining ingredients.

For Vegan

Use vegan butter, omit the feta, and add extra kosher salt to taste.

Storage

Leftovers will keep, refrigerated, for up to 3 days.

Diet
Vegetarian, gluten-free, vegan option

Herby Quinoa or Rice

COOK 2 ——— COOK 1

SERVES 4

1 cup [180 g] dry quinoa or 1 cup [200 g] white rice, or 3 cups cooked whole grain

½ tsp kosher salt

1 Tbsp salted butter or olive oil

1 small garlic clove, finely minced, or ¼ tsp garlic powder

2 Tbsp chopped fresh herbs, like thyme, oregano, Italian parsley, or chives, or 1 tsp dried oregano (see Tips)

For quinoa: Rinse the quinoa in cold water using a fine-mesh strainer, then drain and shake it dry. Put the quinoa in a saucepan with 1¾ cups [415 ml] of water and ¼ teaspoon kosher salt. Bring it to a boil, then turn down the heat to low. Cover the pot and simmer until the water is completely absorbed, 15 to 18 minutes (test by pulling back the quinoa with a fork). Remove from the heat. Cover and let rest for 5 minutes.

For rice: Rinse the rice in cold water using a fine-mesh strainer, then drain and shake it dry. Put the rice in a saucepan with 1½ cups [360 ml] of water and ¼ teaspoon of the kosher salt. Bring it to a boil, then turn down the heat to low. Cover the pot and simmer until the water is completely absorbed, 12 to 15 minutes (test by pulling back the rice with a fork). Remove from the heat. Cover and let rest for 10 minutes.

Fluff the quinoa or rice with a fork. Stir in the butter, garlic, herbs, and the remaining ¼ teaspoon of kosher salt. Taste and add additional salt if necessary.

When we first started cooking together, fresh herbs transformed our approach to simple, nutritious meals. We started growing fresh herbs in pots on our small patio and fell in love with the way a small handful of chives or basil could transform a dish.

Here are some basic instructions for turning bland quinoa or rice into a side dish you'll be snacking on straight from the pot. It's best with fresh herbs, ideal for the growing season when they are abundant. But in winter, store-bought fresh herbs or even a few shakes of dried herbs do the trick. Try a combination of herbs for the most impact (like thyme and chives), and remember, you can always add more to taste.

Tips

Experiment with different dried herbs or spice blends from your spice rack. With dried herbs, we like a combination of dried oregano and dill. If you use dried thyme, sage, or rosemary, use ¼ to ½ teaspoon, since these herbs have a very strong flavor.

Dress this up by stirring in a spritz of lemon juice or a sprinkle of feta cheese.

Storage

Leftovers will keep, refrigerated, for up to 4 days.

Diet
Vegetarian, vegan, gluten-free

Growing Fresh Herbs

Fresh herbs are the rock stars of the kitchen. There's nothing quite like the peppery scent of summer basil or the grassy burst of delicate fresh dill. We have two large planters on our deck dedicated to herbs, and from spring to fall we're regularly running outside to snip a handful for our meals.

Growing your own herbs is much more effective than buying them at the store. It's more economical, they taste better, and they're always on hand. Plus, there's no garden space required; all you need are a handful of pots and a sunny step or ledge.

Here are our top herbs to grow at home, grouped by how to care for them. Keep in mind the categories vary based on your climate (we're in the American Midwest):

- **Thyme, oregano, tarragon, and rosemary (annual or perennial, depending on your zone):** Plant these herbs from starter plants in the early summer. They'll last until the early fall or even through winter if cared for properly.

- **Mint, sage, and chives (perennials):** These herbs are very hardy, even in cooler climates. Plant them from starter plants and let them go wild. (Keep in mind that mint spreads like wildfire, so contain it in a planter or pot.)

- **Dill, parsley, and cilantro:** These herbs are fun to grow from seeds. Because they're more delicate, they tend to not last all summer and will go to seed when the weather gets too hot. (We often buy parsley and cilantro from the store because a big bunch is inexpensive and available in all seasons.)

- **Basil (annuals):** Plant basil from starter plants in the early summer. It will last until the early fall if cared for properly.

Not sure where to start? Get one pot and grow basil, thyme, and rosemary in the pot. This combination makes for a big impact, both visually and in recipes.

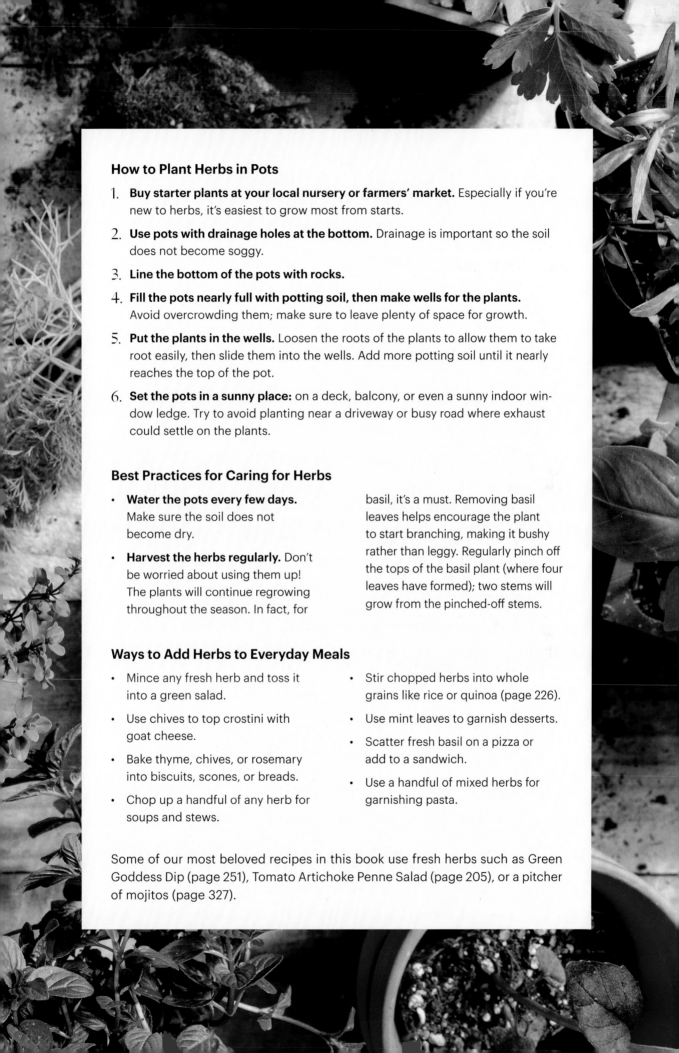

How to Plant Herbs in Pots

1. **Buy starter plants at your local nursery or farmers' market.** Especially if you're new to herbs, it's easiest to grow most from starts.

2. **Use pots with drainage holes at the bottom.** Drainage is important so the soil does not become soggy.

3. **Line the bottom of the pots with rocks.**

4. **Fill the pots nearly full with potting soil, then make wells for the plants.** Avoid overcrowding them; make sure to leave plenty of space for growth.

5. **Put the plants in the wells.** Loosen the roots of the plants to allow them to take root easily, then slide them into the wells. Add more potting soil until it nearly reaches the top of the pot.

6. **Set the pots in a sunny place:** on a deck, balcony, or even a sunny indoor window ledge. Try to avoid planting near a driveway or busy road where exhaust could settle on the plants.

Best Practices for Caring for Herbs

- **Water the pots every few days.** Make sure the soil does not become dry.

- **Harvest the herbs regularly.** Don't be worried about using them up! The plants will continue regrowing throughout the season. In fact, for basil, it's a must. Removing basil leaves helps encourage the plant to start branching, making it bushy rather than leggy. Regularly pinch off the tops of the basil plant (where four leaves have formed); two stems will grow from the pinched-off stems.

Ways to Add Herbs to Everyday Meals

- Mince any fresh herb and toss it into a green salad.

- Use chives to top crostini with goat cheese.

- Bake thyme, chives, or rosemary into biscuits, scones, or breads.

- Chop up a handful of any herb for soups and stews.

- Stir chopped herbs into whole grains like rice or quinoa (page 226).

- Use mint leaves to garnish desserts.

- Scatter fresh basil on a pizza or add to a sandwich.

- Use a handful of mixed herbs for garnishing pasta.

Some of our most beloved recipes in this book use fresh herbs such as Green Goddess Dip (page 251), Tomato Artichoke Penne Salad (page 205), or a pitcher of mojitos (page 327).

Chapter 6

BAKES

There's something about making time and space to bake with someone you love. Sure, the kitchen might be a wreck, and you might end up wearing more flour than goes into the recipe. But when that stunning crusty artisan loaf or those pillowy garlic knots come out of the oven, you'll be left with a whole new set of memories made together (not to mention a delicious baked treat).

Got a bit of extra time to spend baking together? Try the baking projects in this chapter.

Garlic *Herb* Knots

MAKES 12 KNOTS

2 cups [280 g] bread flour

½ Tbsp active dry yeast
(not instant)

1 tsp kosher salt

½ tsp garlic powder

½ tsp onion powder

½ tsp dried oregano

2 Tbsp minced fresh basil

¾ cup [177 ml] lukewarm water
(see Tips)

½ Tbsp olive oil

2 Tbsp salted butter, melted

1 garlic clove, grated

Flaky sea salt, for sprinkling

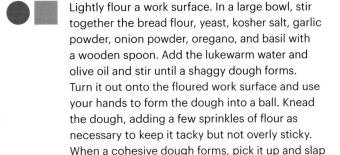 Lightly flour a work surface. In a large bowl, stir together the bread flour, yeast, kosher salt, garlic powder, onion powder, oregano, and basil with a wooden spoon. Add the lukewarm water and olive oil and stir until a shaggy dough forms. Turn it out onto the floured work surface and use your hands to form the dough into a ball. Knead the dough, adding a few sprinkles of flour as necessary to keep it tacky but not overly sticky. When a cohesive dough forms, pick it up and slap it against the counter 5 or 6 times to work up the gluten, then continue kneading with your hands until the dough is very smooth, pillowy, and a bit tacky, 7 to 8 minutes.

Form the dough into a ball by wrapping it under itself until the top is taut and smooth. Put the ball in a large bowl and rub the top with a drizzle of olive oil. Cover the bowl with a clean damp towel. Let rest until doubled in size, 45 minutes to 1 hour.

Line a baking sheet with parchment paper.

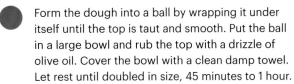 After the rise, remove the dough from the bowl and divide it into 12 equal pieces (about ⅓ cup [40 g] each). Roll each piece into an 8 in [20 cm] long rope, then tie it in a knot and set on the parchment paper. Cover the knots with a damp towel and let rise until puffy, an additional 45 minutes.

Meanwhile, preheat the oven to 425°F [220°C].

After the rise, remove the towel and bake the knots for 12 minutes. Meanwhile, in a small saucepan, melt the butter and stir in the garlic.

Remove the pan from the oven, leaving the heat on. Brush the knots with the garlic butter, making sure the garlic that's settled to the bottom of the bowl is evenly distributed, and sprinkle them with flaky sea salt. Return to the oven and bake until fragrant and golden brown, 2 to 3 more minutes. Cool for 5 minutes before serving.

COOK 1 —— ●—■—— COOK 2

contd.

Some of our early forays into the kitchen as a couple were baking breads together. The magic of flour, salt, and yeast never ceases to delight us. Here, we've jazzed up our basic pizza dough (page 88) with a shower of fresh basil and garlic butter. It's a fun baking project, and the resulting soft, chewy knots pair nicely with just about any meal. Leftover knots reheat well, so you can enjoy them all through the week (or freeze them and enjoy for months).

Tips

For baking, lukewarm water should be warm on your finger, but not hot. A thermometer should register 105° to 115°F [40° to 45°C].

Make-ahead instructions: Bake as instructed but leave out the garlic butter, baking the knots 14 to 15 minutes total. Allow the knots to cool fully, wrap in foil, and store at room temperature. When ready to serve, preheat the oven to 375°F [190°C]. Make the garlic butter and brush it onto the knots. Bake until warmed through, about 5 minutes. If reheating frozen knots, bake for 5 minutes at 375°F [190°C], then add the garlic butter and bake for another 5 minutes.

For Vegan

Use vegan butter.

Storage

Allow the knots to cool fully. Store wrapped in foil or in a sealed container or plastic bag at room temperature for up to 4 days. Or freeze leftover knots for up to 3 months. Reheat in a 375°F [190°C] oven for 5 minutes (from room temperature) or 10 minutes (from frozen).

Diet
Vegetarian,
vegan option

Sour Cream & Onion Savory Scones

MAKES 8 SCONES

½ cup [120 g] sour cream

2 large eggs

2 Tbsp milk of choice, plus more if needed

2 cups [280 g] all-purpose flour

½ Tbsp granulated sugar

1 Tbsp baking powder

½ Tbsp onion powder

½ tsp kosher salt

3 green onions (white and light and dark green parts), finely minced

½ cup [113 g] unsalted butter, frozen for at least 30 minutes or overnight

Flaky sea salt, for topping

Preheat the oven to 400°F [200°C]. Line a baking sheet with parchment paper and lightly flour a work surface.

In a medium bowl, whisk together the sour cream, 1 of the eggs, and the milk.

In a large bowl, whisk together the flour, sugar, baking powder, onion powder, kosher salt, and green onions (reserve ½ tablespoon of the green onions for topping). Using a box grater, grate the frozen butter into the flour mixture, then toss it with a spatula until the butter is coated.

Pour the wet mixture into the center of the dry ingredients and stir with a spatula until the dough just comes together. If it is very crumbly, stir in more milk, ½ tablespoon at a time, until the dough just comes together.

Turn the crumbly dough out onto the floured surface. Use your hands to gently pat it into a large rectangle. Fold the rectangle in half, placing any floury crumbles in the middle of the fold, then continue patting the dough into another rectangle. Fold one more time in the same manner, then pat it into an 8 in [20 cm] circle. Sprinkle with the reserved green onions and pat them into the top.

Use a large knife to slice the dough into 8 wedges and carefully transfer the wedges to the prepared baking sheet.

In a small bowl, whisk the remaining egg. Lightly brush the top of the scones with the beaten egg and sprinkle the tops with flaky sea salt.

Bake until puffed and golden, 17 to 19 minutes. Transfer to a cooling rack to cool for a few minutes, then serve.

COOK 1 ———— ● ■ ———— COOK 2

contd.

These scones are flaky, salty, and everything you want in a good pastry! This savory spin on the classic works equally as a dinner biscuit or for brunch with scrambled eggs, warm from the oven. These get two thumbs up all around in our house.

For brunch, they go with a Sheet-Pan Egg Bake (page 161) or a Spinach & Sun-Dried Tomato Crustless Quiche (page 166). Or for dinner, pair them with One-Pan Roast Chicken & Herby Veggies (page 142), Hearty Black Bean Chili ("The Chili") (page 123), or Lentil Soup with Tarragon (page 36).

Tip

Leftover scones reheat well. Pop them into a 300°F [150°C] oven until warmed through, about 10 minutes.

Storage

Scones are best the day of baking. They keep at room temperature in a sealed container for 2 days or in the refrigerator for 5 days. Before serving, reheat at 300°F [150°C] for 10 minutes.

To freeze, cool to room temperature, then place the scones in a freezer-safe bag or container and freeze for up to 2 months. To thaw, set them out at room temperature for a few hours or in the refrigerator overnight.

Diet
Vegetarian

Gouda Cheddar Ranch Pull-Apart Bread

MAKES 1 LOAF (6 TO 8 SERVINGS)

1 medium round sourdough loaf (1 lb [455 g])

6 Tbsp [85 g] salted butter, melted

2 tsp dried parsley

1 tsp dried dill

1 tsp garlic powder

1 tsp onion powder

1 tsp dried onion flakes

⅛ tsp kosher salt

Freshly ground black pepper

1 cup (3 oz [85 g]) shredded Gouda cheese

1 cup (3 oz [85 g]) shredded mild Cheddar cheese (see Tips)

1 Tbsp chopped chives, or a finely minced green onion top

Preheat the oven to 375°F [190°C].

Using a large serrated knife, cut through the bread diagonally about 1 in apart, leaving about ¾ in [2 cm] attached at the bottom of the bread. Then turn the bread and carefully slice the loaf in the other direction to make 1 in [2.5 cm] diamond shapes.

Stir together the melted butter with the parsley, dill, garlic powder, onion powder, onion flakes, kosher salt, and a few grinds of black pepper.

Line a baking sheet with a large sheet of aluminum foil and set the bread in the center. Gently lift the bottom of the bread to open space between the diamonds. Brush the seasoned butter all over the inside surfaces (this is easiest with two people, having one hold the bread and the other brush). Brush the remaining butter over the top of the bread.

Using your fingers, evenly stuff the shredded cheese between the bread chunks on all sides, making sure that you are pushing the cheese evenly to the bottom. Sprinkle the top with the chopped chives.

Wrap the bread in the foil and place it back on the baking sheet. Bake for 15 minutes. Uncover the bread and bake until the cheese is melted, another 10 to 12 minutes. Serve immediately.

COOK 1 ——— COOK 2

contd.

Pull-apart bread is an interactive side dish that we find is universally loved (really, who can turn this down?). Scoring the bread lets you pull off individual portions with a satisfying cheesy pull.

The top comes out crispy, the middle is cheesy, and the bottom is gooey from the ranch butter. It's all we can do not to eat the whole loaf ourselves! Serve it with Hearty Black Bean Chili ("The Chili") (page 123) or Tortellini Vegetable Soup (page 39), or as part of an appetizer spread.

Tips

Be sure to use mild Cheddar; sharp Cheddar doesn't melt as well.

An electric carving knife (like the one you get out at Thanksgiving) is a great tool for slicing bread. It works especially well for this recipe.

Cooking Together

Have one person slice the bread while the other makes the seasoned butter. Then get all four hands dirty and stuff the bread together!

Storage

Leftovers will keep, wrapped in aluminum foil and refrigerated, for up to 2 days. Reheat from refrigerated in a 375°F [190°C] oven until the cheese melts, about 20 minutes.

Diet
Vegetarian

Maple-Glazed Buttermilk Cornbread

COOK 2 ——————— COOK 1

**MAKES 12 MEDIUM OR
16 SMALL PIECES**

1½ cups [210 g] yellow cornmeal
(medium grind or stone ground)

1 cup [140 g] all-purpose flour

¼ cup [50 g] packed light brown
sugar

1½ tsp baking powder

½ tsp baking soda

1 tsp kosher salt

2 eggs

7 Tbsp [100 g] unsalted butter,
melted

1½ cups [360 ml] buttermilk

Maple Glaze

1 Tbsp unsalted butter

¼ cup [60 ml] maple syrup

¼ tsp cinnamon

Preheat the oven to 375°F [190°C]. Grease a
9 x 9 in [23 x 23 cm] baking dish.

In a medium bowl, stir together the cornmeal,
flour, brown sugar, baking powder, baking soda,
and kosher salt.

In a separate bowl, whisk together the eggs,
melted butter, and buttermilk. Add the wet
ingredients to the dry ingredients and stir with a
spatula until just combined.

Pour the batter into the prepared pan and smooth
the top evenly with a spatula. Bake until the
cornbread is puffed and golden and a toothpick
comes out clean, 24 to 26 minutes. Remove from
the oven.

To make the maple glaze, in a small saucepan,
melt the butter with the maple syrup and
cinnamon. Pour the glaze over the top of the
bread and brush it to evenly cover. Let it cool for
at least 15 minutes, then cut into pieces and serve.

Every home cook's got to have a go-to cornbread, and this one's ours. Each square is thick and ultra-moist (because dry cornbread is a true kitchen crime). The trick? Buttermilk adds moisture and brings a robust, developed flavor.

Take it over the top with the cinnamon maple glaze, a handy trick so there's no need to serve it with honey (though don't let us hold you back!). This one pairs well with big bowls of Hearty Black Bean Chili ("The Chili") (page 123) or a plate of Barbecue Beans & Greens (page 26).

Tips

The maple glaze seeps deeper into the cornbread the longer it sits, enhancing the flavor. It works well to make in advance and bring as a side dish to a dinner or potluck. Refrigerated leftovers also work well reheated.

Use medium grind cornmeal if possible; it lends a robust flavor and texture that's preferable to fine ground.

Storage

Cover with foil and store for 1 day at room temperature; thereafter it will keep, refrigerated, for up to 5 days, or freeze for up to 3 months. Reheat leftovers in a 350°F [180°C] oven until warmed through, 10 to 15 minutes.

Diet
Vegetarian

Spiced *Latte* Loaf

**MAKES ONE 9 X 5 IN
[23 X 13 CM] LOAF**

1½ Tbsp ground cinnamon

2 tsp ground ginger

1 tsp ground cardamom

¼ tsp ground cloves

¼ cup [52 g] packed light brown
sugar

2¼ cups [315 g] all-purpose
flour

2 Tbsp unsalted butter, melted

1 cup [200 g] granulated sugar

1 Tbsp baking powder

½ tsp kosher salt

1 egg

1 cup [240 ml] milk of choice

¼ cup [60 ml] neutral oil

¼ cup [60 ml] unsweetened
applesauce

2 tsp vanilla extract

● Preheat the oven to 350°F [180°C]. Butter a
9 x 5 in [23 x 13 cm] metal loaf pan.

● In a small bowl, stir together the spice mix:
cinnamon, ginger, cardamom, and cloves.

■ In a medium bowl, make the streusel topping:
Add the brown sugar, ¼ cup [35 g] of the flour,
and 1 teaspoon of the spice mix to the bowl and
mix lightly with a fork. Continue mixing while
pouring in the melted butter until a crumbly
mixture forms. Set aside.

● In a separate medium bowl, whisk together
the remaining 2 cups [280 g] of flour and the
granulated sugar, baking powder, and kosher salt.

■ In a large bowl, whisk together the egg, milk, oil,
applesauce, and vanilla extract until completely
smooth. Gradually add the flour mixture to the wet
ingredients, stirring with a spatula until a smooth
batter forms. Pour ¾ cup [180 g] of the batter into
a liquid measuring cup and stir the remaining
spice mix into the measuring cup to create a
darker spiced batter.

● ■ Pour about half the vanilla batter into the prepared
loaf pan and smooth it into an even layer with a
spatula. Pour the spiced batter on top and smooth
it, then pour on the remaining vanilla batter and
smooth it. To swirl the batters together, insert a
butter knife in the top corner of the pan so it just
touches the bottom. Draw about 3 large S shapes
through the entire pan, then repeat in a slightly
different position. Rotate the pan 90 degrees
and make 2 large S shapes in the other direction.
Sprinkle the top of the batter with the streusel.

● ■ Bake the loaf for 50 to 55 minutes, until the top
springs back when touched and a toothpick
inserted in the center comes out clean. Cool
the bread in the pan for 30 minutes. Run a
knife around the edge and invert the loaf onto a
cooling rack. Let cool fully to room temperature
(30 minutes to 1 hour) before cutting into slices.

COOK 1 ——— ● ■ ——— COOK 2

contd.

The moist slices of this fun and funky quick bread are reminiscent of a chai latte, with notes of milky vanilla, cinnamon, cardamom, and ginger. The best part is when you cut the first slice to show the beautiful spiced swirl decoration inside.

There are a few components to assemble, so it's nice to have a partner to help with this baking project. One day we had the crazy idea of slicing up leftovers into strips and baking it to make biscotti, and it's surprisingly effective. The crunchy strips pair well with morning coffee or an afternoon snack.

Tip

Turn leftovers into biscotti! Cut ¾ in [2 cm] thick slices into 1 in [2.5 cm] wide strips, then bake at 300°F [149°C] for 45 to 55 minutes, until golden brown and mostly crisp (they will firm up as they cool). Let cool for 30 minutes. Store in a sealed container with a paper towel. Serve with coffee or tea.

Cooking Together

Have one person start with the streusel topping while the other makes the batter. Then assemble the loaf together.

Storage

The loaf will keep, wrapped in aluminum foil, at room temperature for 4 days, or refrigerated for 10 days (bring to room temperature before enjoying). To store frozen for up to 3 months, slice the loaf, wrap it in plastic wrap, and place in a freezer-safe container.

Diet
Vegetarian

Crusty Rosemary Artisan Bread

MAKES 1 LOAF

Bread

1½ cups [210 g] all-purpose flour

1½ cups [210 g] bread flour (see Tips)

½ Tbsp kosher salt

½ Tbsp active dry yeast

2 Tbsp roughly chopped fresh rosemary

½ tsp freshly ground black pepper

1¼ cups [295 g] lukewarm water (see Tips)

Olive oil, for rising

Brine

½ Tbsp olive oil

½ tsp kosher salt

To make the bread, in the bowl of a stand mixer, use a wooden spoon to combine the all-purpose flour, bread flour, kosher salt, yeast, rosemary, and black pepper. Stir in the lukewarm water. Attach the dough hook to the mixer and knead on low speed for 7 minutes (see Tips). Meanwhile, lightly flour a work surface and lightly oil a large bowl.

Turn out the dough onto the floured counter and flour your hands. Gently shape the dough into a boule by stretching it out and folding it under itself several times until the top is taut and smooth like a ball. Pinch the bottom of the boule and put it in the oiled bowl. Rub the top lightly with olive oil. Cover the bowl with a damp towel and allow it to rise at room temperature for 1½ hours.

After the rise, lay a piece of parchment paper on the work surface. With wet hands, punch down the dough in the bowl. Still in the bowl, lift one side of the dough straight up so it stretches, then fold it across the center. Turn the bowl a quarter turn and repeat 4 times. Then pick up the dough and gently shape it into a boule again as before. Set the boule on the parchment paper and rub the top lightly with olive oil. Cover with an inverted bowl and allow it to rest for 30 minutes.

Set a Dutch oven in the oven and preheat to 450°F [230°C].

After the rest, make the brine. In a small bowl, stir together the olive oil, ½ tablespoon of water, and the kosher salt. Brush the brine evenly over the boule. Using a sharp knife, cut an X shape in the top about ½ in [13 mm] deep.

Using a hot pad, carefully remove the hot Dutch oven lid. Set the parchment paper with the bread inside and cover with the lid. Bake for 15 minutes, then lower the oven temperature to 400°F [200°C] and remove the lid. Bake the bread until it is golden brown on top (the internal temperature should be 205°F [96°C]), about 20 minutes more. Let cool on a rack for at least 1 hour before slicing.

contd.

No matter your skill level, you can bake up a boule at home that's worthy of a French boulangerie! It takes a little time and practice, but it's especially satisfying to pull your own glorious golden loaf out of the oven.

After years of practice, here's our masterpiece: one outstanding crusty, rustic loaf that's doable as a home baking project. Baking in a Dutch oven holds in the steam released from the bread, making a light, airy crumb and a crispy crust. Fresh rosemary and a salty brine subtly hint at the flavors of focaccia bread, making for one irresistible loaf.

Tips

Bread flour has a higher protein content than all-purpose flour. Using it in this recipe helps the bread to hold its shape while baking.

For baking, lukewarm should feel warm on your finger, but not hot. A thermometer should register 105° to 115°F [40° to 45°C].

You can knead this bread by hand, but due to the high water content in the recipe, it's much easier to let a mixer do the work! If you do try hand kneading, resist the urge to add too much flour as you knead. You can add a bit of flour to make it workable, but it should remain rather sticky.

Making a boule is easier than it sounds. If bread making is new to you, a simple internet search on "how to shape a boule" shows a visual of this technique.

If you know you're not going to eat the entire loaf in a few days, freeze half of it (see the following instructions). Or use up crusty leftovers in Crunchy Green Panzanella (page 208), Sheet-Pan Egg Bake (page 161), Gambas al Ajillo with Crusty Bread (page 101), or Pressed Manchego & Prosciutto Sandwiches (page 67).

Storage

This loaf tastes best on the day of baking. To preserve it, consider freezing half when it's fresh. Let cool to room temperature, then slice the bread, wrap in plastic wrap, and put in a sealable plastic bag. Suck out as much air as possible with a straw, then seal it tightly. It will keep, frozen, for up to 6 months. At room temperature, it will keep in a sealed plastic bag, as airtight as possible, for up to 3 days.

Diet
Vegetarian, vegan

Chapter 7

APPETIZERS
& Snacks

Whip up these small bites for noshing on while you cook together, or serve them to get a party started. You can even combine a few of them to make a "happy hour dinner" for two: Grab one or two appetizer recipes, a cheese board, and a bottle of wine, and you've got a meal. They also work for picnic lunches, cookouts, or your contribution to a big table of party snacks.

SOME HIGHLIGHTS IN THIS CHAPTER:

Go fresh and creamy with Green Goddess Dip (page 251).

Assemble a big festive Charred Corn Guacamole & Black Bean Hummus Snacking Platter (page 258).

Make simple baked Warm Goat Cheese with Jam for any season (page 263).

Bake up juicy Spanakopita-Stuffed Mushrooms (page 265).

Style a colorful pile of Whipped Ricotta Crostini with Hot Honey (page 269).

Green *Goddess* Dip

**MAKES 2 CUPS [480 G]
(8 SERVINGS)**

1½ cups [12 g] loosely packed
Italian parsley, leaves and
tender stems

2 Tbsp chopped chives

1½ cups [360 g] 2 percent or
whole-milk Greek yogurt

½ cup [120 g] mayonnaise

2 tsp dried dill

1 tsp onion powder

1 tsp garlic powder

1 tsp dried tarragon

½ tsp kosher salt

Freshly ground black pepper

Assorted vegetables, for
serving

Place all the ingredients except the assorted
vegetables in a food processor or small blender
and process until combined. Taste and add more
salt as necessary. Serve immediately with crunchy
colorful veggies, or refrigerate until serving.

COOK 1 ———— ● ■ ———— COOK 2

contd.

We're always looking for more ways to enjoy creamy, herbaceous Green Goddess salad dressing, so here we've morphed it into a party dip! It's lightened up with a bit of Greek yogurt and loaded with those signature herbs.

This one is simply begging to be brought to a party, surrounded with colorful crudités. Or use it as part of a snack to munch on while you're cooking together.

Storage

The dip will keep, refrigerated, for up to 5 days.

Diet
Vegetarian, gluten-free

Burst Garlicky Tomato Dip

**MAKES 2 CUPS [480 G]
(8 SERVINGS)**

2 Tbsp olive oil

2 pints (20 oz [570 g]) grape tomatoes or cherry tomatoes

4 garlic cloves, minced

1 tsp smoked paprika

½ tsp dried oregano

½ tsp kosher salt

2 Tbsp finely chopped fresh basil, or ½ Tbsp dried Italian seasoning

1 tsp balsamic vinegar

Freshly ground black pepper

Crostini or crackers, for serving (see Tips)

In a large skillet, heat 1 tablespoon of the olive oil over medium-high heat. Add the tomatoes and cook, stirring occasionally, until lightly browned on both sides, about 4 minutes. Add the garlic and cook, stirring often, until fragrant, 1 to 2 minutes.

Lower the heat and carefully mash the tomatoes with a potato masher (taking care to avoid spitting hot juices), until most of the liquid is released but the texture is slightly chunky. Add the smoked paprika, oregano, and kosher salt. Return to medium heat and cook until thickened to the desired consistency, 2 to 3 minutes.

Remove from the heat and stir in the basil, balsamic vinegar, and the remaining 1 tablespoon of olive oil. Pour into a serving dish and let cool for at least 10 minutes to serve warm, or 30 minutes for room temperature (the flavor intensifies as it cools). Serve with crostini or crackers.

COOK 1

COOK 2

contd.

Here's one for a lazy Sunday night with friends, crisp rosé, and twinkling patio lights. Throw tomatoes into a sizzling hot pan until they burst forth their juices, then add garlic, oregano, and fresh basil. Serve the dip warm with crackers or crusty bread, and your friends won't be able to tear themselves away. Grape tomatoes work surprisingly well here: Their sturdier flesh makes a thicker, juicier sauce than cherry tomatoes.

Tips

Sprinkling with crumbled feta or goat cheese takes this dip over the top.

To make homemade crostini for serving, preheat the oven to 425°F [220°C]. Slice a baguette into thin slices on the bias (diagonally) and arrange on a baking sheet in a single layer. Bake until lightly browned and very crisp, 7 to 10 minutes. Cool to room temperature.

For Gluten-Free

Serve with gluten-free crackers or crostini.

Storage

The dip will keep, refrigerated, for up to 1 week.

Diet
Vegetarian, vegan, gluten-free option

Charred Corn Guacamole & Black Bean Hummus Snacking Platter

SERVES 8

Black Bean Hummus

MAKES 1½ CUPS [360 G]

1 small garlic clove, peeled

One 15 oz [430 g] can black beans, drained and rinsed, or 1½ cups [240 g] cooked beans

2 Tbsp fresh lime juice

¼ cup [55 g] tahini

1 Tbsp olive oil

¾ tsp smoked paprika

½ tsp kosher salt

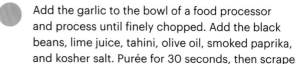 Add the garlic to the bowl of a food processor and process until finely chopped. Add the black beans, lime juice, tahini, olive oil, smoked paprika, and kosher salt. Purée for 30 seconds, then scrape down the bowl. Purée until creamy, about 1 more minute.

Charred Corn Guacamole

MAKES ABOUT 2 CUPS [480 G]

1 cup [160 g] frozen corn or fresh corn cut off the cob

3 ripe avocados, pitted

1 small Roma tomato, seeds removed, finely chopped

¼ cup [70 g] minced white onion

¼ cup [10 g] finely chopped cilantro

2 Tbsp fresh lime juice

¾ tsp kosher salt

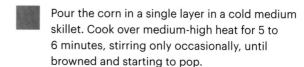 Pour the corn in a single layer in a cold medium skillet. Cook over medium-high heat for 5 to 6 minutes, stirring only occasionally, until browned and starting to pop.

Scoop the flesh from the avocados into a medium bowl or molcajete. Mash it with a large fork or pestle until mostly creamy. Stir in the charred corn, tomato, onion, cilantro, lime juice, and kosher salt. Taste and add more salt if desired.

For the platter

Salsa or pico de gallo

Tortilla or plantain chips

Pita wedges

Carrots

Celery

Radishes or jicama strips

Small sweet peppers

Cherry tomatoes

A big platter of dips always makes a splash at parties! The star of this one is black bean hummus, a smooth purée that's smoky, savory, and creamy. Pair it with this simple guacamole, embellished with bits of charred corn to add a sweet pop to each bite. The rest is up to you, and more of a concept than a recipe. Surround the bowls with salsa, veggies, and chips for a colorful platter with something for everyone.

Tip

Place the bowls of dips on a large platter and surround them with vegetables and various types of chips. Vary the colors and textures for the best presentation. Different colors and types of chips look nice (vegetable or plantain chips are a great option). Garnish with extra cilantro.

Cooking Together

Have each partner mix up one of the dips, then artfully arrange the platter together.

Storage

Hummus will keep, refrigerated, for up to 5 days. Guacamole will keep, refrigerated, for up to 3 days in a sealed container with plastic wrap pressed onto the surface to prevent oxidizing (if necessary, add a few pinches of kosher salt after storage).

Diet
Vegetarian, vegan, gluten-free

Roasted Red Pepper
Tapenade

**MAKES ABOUT 1 CUP
[240 G] (ENOUGH FOR
20 TO 24 CROSTINI)**

1 garlic clove, peeled

1¼ cups [175 g] pitted kalamata
or niçoise olives, drained (one
10 oz [290 g] net weight jar,
5.6 oz [160 g] drained)

⅓ cup [90 g] jarred roasted red
pepper, sliced into strips (about
1 medium pepper)

2 Tbsp drained capers

1 small handful fresh parsley

¼ cup [60 ml] olive oil

Freshly ground black pepper

Crackers, bread, or crostini
(page 254)

In the bowl of a food processor, process the garlic
until finely chopped. Add the olives, roasted
red pepper, capers, and parsley and pulse until
roughly chopped. Scrape down the bowl. Add
the olive oil and pepper and pulse until a chunky
paste forms. Serve immediately as a dip with
crackers or bread, or spread onto crostini as an
appetizer.

As two olive lovers, we couldn't help but include a recipe for tapenade, that popular French olive spread. Eating it makes us feel like we're picnicking in the olive groves of Provence. The burst of savory, briny umami works on small toasts as an appetizer or spread on sandwiches.

Tapenade is traditionally made with olives, capers, and anchovies, but we prefer to swap in roasted red pepper for the anchovy, which mellows out the salty kalamata olives.

Tip

Tapenade is very versatile. Stir it into white beans or chickpeas for a quick lunch, use as a sandwich spread, slather over fish or chicken, or add to dips, soups, or stews.

Storage

Leftovers will keep, refrigerated, for up to 2 weeks; bring to room temperature before serving (about 5 minutes).

Diet
Vegetarian, vegan, gluten-free

Warm Goat Cheese
with Jam

SERVES 6 TO 8

One 10 oz [280 g] goat
cheese log

½ cup [150 g] jam or marmalade
of any flavor (see Tips)

2 Tbsp chopped pecans
or pistachios

1 tsp fresh thyme leaves

2 pinches flaky sea salt
or kosher salt

Crackers, bread, or crostini

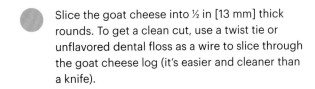

Preheat the oven to 350°F [180°C].

Slice the goat cheese into ½ in [13 mm] thick
rounds. To get a clean cut, use a twist tie or
unflavored dental floss as a wire to slice through
the goat cheese log (it's easier and cleaner than
a knife).

Put a spoonful of jam in the bottom of a small
baking dish (approximately 6 x 9 in [15 x 23 cm]),
spreading it to cover with the back of a spoon.
Arrange the goat cheese rounds on top. Dollop
the remaining jam on top. Top with chopped nuts,
thyme, and flaky sea salt.

Bake until the goat cheese is soft, 10 to
12 minutes. Serve with crackers, bread,
or crostini (see page 269).

COOK 1 ———— COOK 2

contd.

Here's one to pull out when company is coming—the perfect marriage of a few simple ingredients. Creamy goat cheese paired with fruity jam and a sprinkle of fresh thyme makes a dip that has everyone scraping the dish clean. We love its versatility: Make it with fig jam in the winter, apricot orange marmalade in the fall, and blueberry jam in the summer.

Tips

Vary the nuts based on the season. Pecans and walnuts are great for fall and winter, and pistachios and almonds work well in summer.

Shop your local gourmet jam and marmalade section for seasonal ideas like these:

- **Spring:** Strawberry Rhubarb with Mint
- **Summer:** Blueberry Jam with Thyme
- **Fall:** Caramelized Onion Jam with Sage
- **Winter:** Citrus Marmalade with Rosemary

For Gluten-Free

Serve with gluten-free crackers or bread.

Storage

Leftovers will keep, refrigerated, for up to 1 week; reheat in a 350°F [180°C] oven.

Diet
Vegetarian,
gluten-free option

Spanakopita-Stuffed Mushrooms

MAKES 18 TO 20 MUSHROOMS

1 lb [455 g] cremini (a.k.a. baby bella) mushrooms, about 18 to 20 mushrooms

1 Tbsp olive oil, plus more for drizzling

¾ tsp kosher salt

Freshly ground black pepper

¾ cup (4½ oz [130 g]) ricotta cheese

¼ cup (1 oz [30 g]) feta cheese crumbles, crumbled very small

¼ cup (1 oz [30 g] thawed) frozen spinach, thawed, squeezed completely dry, and chopped

1 green onion, finely minced

½ tsp lemon zest

½ tsp garlic powder

¾ tsp dried dill

½ tsp dried oregano

2 Tbsp panko or bread crumbs, for topping

Snipped chives, for garnish

Preheat the oven to 400°F [200°C] and line a baking sheet with parchment paper.

Gently remove the stems of the mushrooms and discard them (if the stem doesn't immediately pop out, use a butter knife to help remove it). Clean any dirt off the mushrooms by wiping the outside with a paper towel. Use a melon baller or a small measuring spoon to slightly hollow out the flesh beneath where the stem was attached to make extra room for the filling.

In a large bowl, gently mix the mushrooms with the olive oil, ½ teaspoon of the kosher salt, and black pepper. Arrange the mushrooms on the prepared pan in a single layer.

In a medium bowl, mix the ricotta cheese, feta cheese crumbles, spinach, green onion, lemon zest, garlic powder, dill, oregano, and the remaining ¼ teaspoon of kosher salt. Spoon the filling into the mushrooms. Top with the panko. Lightly drizzle the tops with olive oil.

Bake until the mushrooms are cooked and lightly brown on top, about 20 minutes (they will release moisture onto the parchment paper as they cook). Transfer the mushrooms to a platter and allow them to cool for at least 5 minutes. Garnish with chives and serve warm.

COOK 1

COOK 2

contd.

These stuffed mushrooms are so tasty that you might want to keep the entire sheet pan to yourself!

The filling is inspired by the classic Greek spinach pie, made with filo dough, spinach, and cheese. Each bite has a savory pop of feta, lemon, and herbs, with a sprinkle of crunchy bread crumbs for texture. They're ideal for parties, and they disappear in minutes (consider a double batch).

Tips

The filling freezes well. If desired, you can make a half batch of stuffed mushrooms and freeze the remaining filling for enjoying another batch later.

It's easy to double this recipe for a large party. Keep in mind that two pans of mushrooms may need a few extra minutes in the oven.

Cooking Together

Have one person prepare the mushroom caps while the other mixes up the filling.

For Gluten-Free

Omit the panko or use gluten-free bread crumbs.

Storage

Leftovers will keep, refrigerated, for up to 2 days; reheat in a 350°F [180°C] oven until warmed through.

Diet
Vegetarian, gluten-free option

Whipped Ricotta Crostini
with Hot Honey

MAKES 20 CROSTINI

1 baguette, cut into twenty ½ in [13 mm] slices

1 cup [240 g] ricotta cheese

½ Tbsp olive oil

1 Tbsp milk of choice

¼ tsp kosher salt

½ tsp lemon zest (optional)

¼ cup [85 g] honey

2 tsp jarred chopped Calabrian chile peppers, or 2 tsp hot sauce

1 apple, pear, or ripe peach, thinly sliced (see Tips)

¼ cup [30 g] finely chopped pistachios

Preheat the oven to 425°F [220°C]. Arrange the baguette slices on a baking sheet. Bake until lightly browned and very crisp, 7 to 10 minutes. Cool to room temperature.

In a food processor, process the ricotta cheese, olive oil, milk, kosher salt, and lemon zest until light and creamy, about 1 minute (see Tips).

In a small bowl, stir together the honey and the Calabrian chile peppers.

To serve, spread the crostini with the whipped ricotta, then top with the fruit slices, hot honey, and chopped pistachios.

COOK 1 ———— COOK 2

contd.

We love trying to make a "perfect bite" of food, and this appetizer comes pretty close, pairing creamy, rich ricotta with sweet fruit, spicy honey, and crusty bread. Every time we set these out at a party, they disappear immediately.

If you can find them, Calabrian chiles take the spicy honey to the next level. They're a type of Italian chile grown in the region of Calabria that infuses a dish with both heat and smoky, fruity flavor notes. If you can't find them, your favorite hot sauce makes a great substitute.

Tips

Don't have a food processor? Whip the ricotta with the other ingredients using a whisk or mixer. The texture won't be as smooth, but it's just as tasty.

Customize the fruit based on the season. Apples work for much of the year, but it's fantastic with peaches in the summer. Try peaches, blackberries, plums, or apricots when they are in season.

Calabrian chiles are sold in jars in the grocery or online (either chopped or whole), packed in oil. You can use up the rest of the jar as a pizza topping for Date-Night Pizza (page 88), or add a tablespoon or two chopped peppers to make a spicy pasta sauce for Smoky Spinach & Artichoke Lasagna (page 130), Meatballs with Fire-Roasted Marinara (page 79), or Rigatoni with Fennel & Pancetta (page 136).

For Gluten-Free

Use gluten-free bread for the crostini.

Storage

Crostini are best served immediately after topping. To prep in advance, make all the components ahead and refrigerate the ricotta and fruit slices, tossed with a bit of lemon juice to prevent browning. Assemble just before serving.

Diet
Vegetarian,
gluten-free option

Smoked Salmon Bites

**MAKES 24 SMALL OR
12 LARGE BITES**

1 baguette, cut into 12 thin
slices, then cut in half

8 oz [230 g] cream cheese,
softened

½ Tbsp milk of choice

2 Tbsp chopped chives, plus
more for garnishing

2 tsp everything bagel
seasoning, plus more for
sprinkling

¼ tsp garlic powder

¼ tsp kosher salt

4 oz [113 g] cold smoked salmon

● Preheat the oven to 425°F [220°C]. Place the
baguette slices on a baking sheet. Bake until
lightly browned and very crisp, 7 to 10 minutes.
Cool to room temperature.

■ In a food processor or a stand mixer, process or
mix the cream cheese and milk on high until fluffy,
stopping and scraping the bowl as necessary,
about 1 minute. Add the chives, everything bagel
seasoning, garlic powder, and kosher salt and mix
again for a few seconds to combine.

● ■ Place a dollop of cream cheese on each crostini,
then add a small piece of smoked salmon. Top
with a sprinkle of chives and everything bagel
seasoning.

COOK 1 ●──── ■ COOK 2

contd.

Ever get a feeling of dread when you're invited to a party but chips and salsa has already been claimed at the snack table? These smoked salmon bites are nearly as easy to throw together and way more likely to elicit an "oh yum!" from your friends. Each umami-packed bite combines buttery smoked salmon and everything bagel–spiced chive cream cheese.

Tips

Leave the cream cheese at room temperature for 1 hour to soften. Or to soften cream cheese quickly, set the block of cheese on a plate and microwave for 5 seconds. Flip over the block and microwave for another 5 seconds.

Don't have time for crostini? Use thin, round store-bought crackers instead.

You'll have some leftover chive cream cheese; use it as a spread for bagels, sandwiches, and wraps.

For Gluten-Free

Use gluten-free crackers or English cucumber slices in place of crostini.

For Dairy-Free

Use dairy-free cream cheese.

Storage

Crostini are best served immediately after topping, but you can make the bites up to 2 hours in advance and refrigerate. You can also make the cream cheese up to 1 week in advance and refrigerate until time to assemble.

Diet
Pescatarian,
gluten-free option,
dairy-free option

Table Setting & Styling

Eating is as much about the ambience as it is about the food. Of course, there's no need to have white linen tablecloths and fresh bouquet centerpieces on a regular basis! But for special occasions, we see it as an act of love to set a beautiful tablescape for enjoying food together.

Our philosophy? Invest in a quality neutral set of everyday tableware that you can mix and match with some fun pieces for entertaining.

Here are the pieces we recommend as essential everyday tableware:

- A quality set of salad-sized plates for everyday eating (8 to 12)
- Large, wide, shallow bowls for bowl meals and soups (4 to 8)
- Small cereal bowls (4 to 8)
- A set of high-quality silverware (we received a set of high-quality minimalist stainless steel as a wedding gift that we still use today)
- Large and small drinking glasses (8 to 12); we use a combination of Ball jars and French cafe glasses
- A large supply of cloth napkins (these are both stylish and eco-friendly; toss them in the washer whenever you're doing laundry)
- Stainless steel plates, bowls, and cups for kids; they're durable and have a minimalist look that goes with anything

Make sure your dishes are high-quality and dishwasher safe. Don't make the mistake we did with our first set of everyday dishes—we opted for lower quality and ended up replacing them within a few years.

For entertaining and dinner parties, adding these items is key:

- A set of place mats (4 to 8), made with natural fibers or felt, or a tablecloth.
- One set of wine glasses (8). We like stemless wine glasses that easily go in the dishwasher and are less prone to tipping over or crowding the table.
- One set of larger dinner plates (8). We use an assortment of large dinner plates we've collected over the years rather than one big set.
- A selection of large platters for serving. It's fun to mix new and antique pieces for an interesting look.
- One large wooden cutting board, to use as a cheese board or for serving appetizers.

When it's time to party, here are a few tips for setting the stage:

- **Infuse character and uniqueness by using a few antique or funky pieces, mixed in with the more neutral tableware.** For example, use an old wooden cutting board and a few pieces of Grandma's china with neutral earthenware.

- **Use a bouquet of flowers or greenery to set the mood.** However, be mindful of blocking the view with a big bouquet or tall candles; a low arrangement or single blooms in short vases ensure an open view of fellow diners to encourage conversation.

- **Add lighting!** Candles and twinkle lights are a simple way to create ambience. Avoid harsh overhead lighting, if possible.

Chapter 8

SWEETS

A good meal has a sweet ending, in our opinion. On a date night out, we always take a peek at the dessert menu (even if we're stuffed). It's even more fun to make that sweet treat at home with your special someone, sharing the kitchen while simmering a homemade caramel sauce or stirring up a chocolate ganache.

Brown Butter–Miso Chocolate Chip Cookie Bars

MAKES 16 BARS

½ cup [113 g] unsalted butter

¾ cup [105 g] all-purpose flour

1¼ cups [125 g] old-fashioned rolled oats

½ cup [100 g] packed light brown sugar

½ cup [100 g] granulated sugar

1 teaspoon baking powder

3 Tbsp light miso (white or yellow) (see Tips)

1 tsp vanilla extract

1 large egg

1 cup [180 g] bittersweet chocolate chips

Flaky sea salt, for sprinkling (optional)

Preheat the oven to 375°F [190°C]. Grease a 9 x 9 in [23 x 23 cm] baking dish. Line the pan with a piece of parchment paper, cut so that it extends on two sides to easily remove the bars from the pan.

Heat the butter in a small skillet over medium heat. When it starts to bubble, cook, stirring occasionally, until it just starts to turn brown and becomes fragrant, 3 to 5 minutes. Immediately remove from the heat and pour the butter into a large bowl.

In a separate medium bowl, mix the flour, oats, brown sugar, granulated sugar, and baking powder and set aside.

In the bowl with the butter, whisk in the miso and vanilla extract, then whisk in the egg. Pour the dry ingredients into the wet mixture and mix with a spoon until a thick dough comes together. Stir in ¾ cup [135 g] of the chocolate chips.

Pour the dough into the prepared pan and gently spread it to the edges with your fingers, until it is evenly distributed (the dough spreads as you work). Leave the top rough rather than flattening it out. Add the remaining ¼ cup [45 g] of chocolate chips and lightly press them into the top.

Bake until the bars start to brown at the edges, 20 to 22 minutes. Transfer the pan to a cooling rack. If desired, sprinkle a few pinches of flaky sea salt over the bars. Let cool completely (at least 1 hour) before cutting. Run a knife around the edges, then lift the bars out of the pan with the parchment paper. Cut into 16 pieces and serve or store.

COOK 1 ———————— COOK 2

contd.

On weekends we love to wander the farmers' market or explore a new bakery and split an indulgent treat. These bars are just that sort of delight: chewy, rich, and salty-sweet—with a generous helping of chocolate, of course.

These cookie bars get their magic from an unexpected ingredient: miso. Using this Japanese fermented soybean paste in a cookie is a baking trend that's here to stay, we think. The flavor is heightened even more by browning the butter before stirring it into the batter, which infuses a nutty caramel essence.

Tips

Make it an over-the-top dessert by serving the bars warm, topped with ice cream!

Look for miso packages marked light miso (yellow or white), which are fermented less time and have a mild flavor. Avoid red or dark miso in this recipe.

Cooking Together

Have one person brown the butter and prep the wet ingredients while the other prepares the pan and dry ingredients.

Storage

Place layers of parchment paper in between the bars and store in a sealed container. The bars will keep, at room temperature, for 5 days; refrigerated, for 2 weeks; or frozen, for up to 3 months.

Diet
Vegetarian

Chocolate Ganache Tart
for Two

MAKES ONE 4 IN [10 CM] TART (2 SERVINGS)

2 graham cracker sheets (1 oz [30 g])

1 tsp cocoa powder

1 tsp granulated sugar

¼ tsp ground cinnamon

¼ tsp ground cardamom

1½ Tbsp salted butter, melted, plus more for greasing

3 Tbsp best-quality semisweet or dark chocolate chips

2 Tbsp heavy cream

½ tsp vanilla extract

Fresh raspberries and edible gold dust or powdered sugar (optional), for garnishing

Butter a 4 in [10 cm] fluted tart pan, making sure to fully coat all of the fluted surfaces.

Place each graham cracker on a cutting board and slowly roll over them with a rolling pin until finely ground. Transfer the crumbs to a small bowl and stir in the cocoa powder, sugar, cinnamon, and cardamom. Add the melted butter and stir with a fork until combined. Firmly press the crust into the tart pan with your fingers, leaving a ¼ in [6 mm] rim all the way around. Chill the crust in the freezer while you make the ganache.

In a small saucepan over low heat, combine the chocolate chips, heavy cream, and vanilla extract, stirring very slowly and gently with a spatula, until the chocolate is fully melted and the ganache is glossy, about 1 minute. Let it rest at room temperature for 1 minute, then pour it into the prepared tart crust.

Transfer the tart to the freezer and freeze for 20 minutes. Transfer to the refrigerator until serving.

When ready to serve, allow the tart to sit at room temperature for 5 minutes, then remove the tart pan ring (if it sticks, use a thin knife to slide between the bottom and the ring). Garnish with fresh raspberries and edible gold dust or powdered sugar, if desired, then serve.

COOK 1

COOK 2

contd.

This mini sweet treat is inspired by the glass case at our local pastry shop, where we pick up tiny gold-dusted tarts and colorful macarons for after-dinner treats. Chocolate ganache may sound fancy, but it's easy to make—just melt chocolate chips with cream for a luscious, glossy filling.

Whip up this no-bake dessert before you start the main dish, then let it chill until you're ready to eat. Edible gold dust is optional, but it sure takes it over the top! The two-serving tart is perfect for date nights, or make the eight-serving version for parties (see Tips).

Tips

Keep the chocolate on low heat and stir very slowly: This makes a smooth ganache with no air bubbles. Be careful not to overheat the ganache, which can cause it to seize and separate.

Look for a 4 in [10 cm] mini tart pan with fluted edges and removable bottom. You can also make eight servings in an 8 in [20 cm] tart pan. Both sizes are easy to find online.

Ground cardamom adds subtle floral notes to the crust. Don't neglect this lovely spice. Use it in Mini Cardamom Cinnamon Rolls (page 175).

Want to make this for a party? Multiply the ingredients by 4 and make it in an 8 in [20 cm] tart pan (the crust will come about halfway up the sides). Ingredients are as follows:

- 8 graham cracker sheets
- 1½ Tbsp cocoa powder
- 1½ Tbsp granulated sugar
- 1 tsp cinnamon
- 1 tsp cardamom
- 6 Tbsp [85 g] salted butter
- ¾ cup [135 g] chocolate chips
- ½ cup [120 ml] heavy cream
- 2 tsp vanilla extract

Wine Pairing

Elevate this treat with a pour of a tawny port. Its rich, nutty undertones highlight the luscious chocolate ganache.

For Vegan

Use vegan butter and substitute full-fat coconut milk for the heavy cream. Use dark chocolate chips marked "dairy free."

Storage

The tart will keep, refrigerated, for up to 3 days.

Diet
Vegetarian,
vegan option

Lemon Poppy Seed Cake
with Raspberry Jam & Cream Cheese Frosting

SERVES 10 TO 12

Lemon Poppy Seed Cake

2½ cups [300 g] cake flour
(see Tips)

1 tsp baking powder

½ tsp baking soda

½ tsp kosher salt

2 Tbsp poppy seeds

1⅔ cups [333 g] granulated
sugar

Zest from two lemons

10 Tbsp [140 g] unsalted butter,
at room temperature

3 large eggs, at room
temperature

¼ cup [60 ml] neutral oil

1 tsp vanilla extract

1 tsp lemon extract (see Tips)

1 cup [240 ml] buttermilk, at
room temperature

contd.

To make the cake, preheat the oven to 350°F [180°C]. Grease three 6 in [15 cm] cake pans and line the bottoms with parchment paper.

In a medium bowl, whisk together the cake flour, baking powder, baking soda, kosher salt, and poppy seeds.

In the bowl of stand mixer, beat the granulated sugar and lemon zest on medium-low speed for 1 minute. Add the butter and beat on medium speed until fluffy, 3 to 4 minutes, scraping once.

Turn the mixer speed to medium-low and add the eggs, 1 at a time, beating each until incorporated. Then add the oil, vanilla extract, and lemon extract and beat until combined.

Turn the mixer speed to low and alternate adding increments of the buttermilk and the flour mixture, mixing until just combined each time, until all of the ingredients are added. Scrape once to ensure the batter is fully integrated.

Divide the cake batter evenly among the three prepared pans. Use a spatula to smooth the tops. Tap the pans several times on the counter to release any air bubbles. Bake, rotating the pans after 28 minutes, until a toothpick comes out clean and the center of the cake is springy when tapped, 33 to 38 minutes (the cakes may be done at slightly different times, depending on your oven). Cool the pans on a rack for 30 minutes. Remove the cakes from the pans and let cool completely, about 2 hours.

contd.

Cream Cheese Frosting

½ cup [113 g] unsalted butter, softened for 30 minutes

8 oz [230 g] cream cheese, softened for 15 minutes

2½ cups [250 g] powdered sugar, sifted

¼ tsp vanilla extract

¼ tsp lemon extract (see Tips)

Filling and Decoration

½ cup [150 g] raspberry jam, or other berry jam like strawberry, blueberry, or blackberry

Poppy seeds

Lemon slices or lemon twist (page 325)

Raspberries

Fresh flowers, like baby's breath (optional) (see Tips)

To make the frosting, add the butter to the bowl of a stand mixer and beat on medium speed until fluffy, about 1 minute, scraping once. Add the cream cheese and beat on medium speed until fluffy and smooth, 1 to 2 minutes. Stop mixing as soon as it is smooth.

Turn the mixer speed to low and incorporate about half of the powdered sugar. Add the vanilla extract and lemon extract and beat until incorporated. Add the remaining powdered sugar and mix on medium until all of the sugar is incorporated, scraping once or twice.

To fill and decorate the cake, use a serrated knife to carefully slice the top dome off of each cake so that it is level across the top. Add a small dollop of frosting to the center of the cake stand (to keep the bottom layer from shifting) and set one cake on top. Using a piping bag with no tip or a large round tip, pipe a ¾ in [2 cm] bead around the edge of the cake. Spread ¼ cup [75 g] of raspberry jam inside the bead of frosting. Set the second cake on top and repeat the bead of frosting and the jam. Set the third cake on top and use an offset spatula to carefully spread a thin layer of frosting across the top (to capture any crumbs), followed by a thicker ¼ in [6 mm] layer on top. Spread frosting very thinly on the sides of the cake, using the edge of the offset spatula to scrape off and discard any excess to achieve the naked cake look.

Decorate the top of the cake with poppy seeds, lemon slices, raspberries, and baby's breath or other edible flowers, if using (see Tips).

Refrigerate the cake for 30 minutes to set the frosting. Then carefully wrap the cake in plastic, inserting toothpicks at intervals to dome the wrap over the decorations on top. Remove from the refrigerator 1 hour before serving.

COOK 2

COOK 1

Here's the treat to make everyone swoon at birthdays, anniversaries, showers, or outdoor parties. The moist citrus cake is light and fluffy, layered with pops of tart berry jam, and it's covered in tangy cream cheese frosting, a delicious alternative to the common buttercream. We've had multiple people who claim to "not like cake" polish off a slice and wander back for another taste.

It takes a bit of effort to assemble, but the process is pretty simple, even for the novice baker. Do your best baking show impression and decorate with lemon slices and wheels, berries, and fresh flowers.

Tips

Using cake flour is important for achieving a fluffy texture in the cake layers.

Lemon extract is key for infusing intense citrusy essence. It's easily found in the baking aisle at most grocery stores.

A lazy Susan or cake decorating turntable is helpful for decorating. Place the cake stand in the center and spin while scraping the sides of the cake.

If the cake seems a bit wobbly after initially setting the layers, refrigerate for 30 minutes before the final frosting and decorating.

If you choose to use baby's breath for decoration, try to avoid its touching the frosting, since the buds are an allergen (do not ingest). Look for edible flowers at your local grocery (or in your garden).

Cooking Together

While making the batter, have one person read the recipe out loud while the other does the tasks to make sure everything is accurate. Then bake and decorate the cake together.

Storage

Leftover cake will keep, refrigerated, for up to 3 days.

Diet
Vegetarian

Molten Brownie Batter Pudding

SERVES 8 TO 10

¾ cup (6 oz [165 g]) salted butter

2 tsp instant espresso (see Tips)

1 tsp vanilla extract

3 large eggs

1½ cups [250 g] granulated sugar

⅔ cup [70 g] cocoa powder

½ cup [70 g] all-purpose flour

⅛ tsp ground nutmeg

1 oz [30 g] dark chocolate, chopped, or ¼ cup chocolate chips

For serving

Vanilla ice cream

Chopped hazelnuts or sprinkles (optional)

Preheat the oven to 325°F [165°C].

Lightly butter a 9 in [23 cm] pie plate (standard or deep dish). In a small saucepan, melt the butter. Whisk in the espresso and vanilla extract, then set aside to cool.

Fit an electric mixer with the paddle attachment. Add the eggs and sugar to the bowl and beat on medium-high speed until thick and fluffy, about 7 minutes.

Meanwhile, in a medium bowl whisk together the cocoa powder, flour, and nutmeg.

Add the flour mixture to the egg and sugar mixture and mix on low speed until just combined. Leaving the mixer running, slowly pour in the melted butter mixture and mix until just combined, scraping down the bowl once with a spatula and mixing again. Add the chocolate and mix for a few seconds until combined.

Pour the mixture into the prepared dish and smooth it into an even layer. The dish can rest at this stage for up to 1 hour at room temperature (see Tips), or you can proceed directly to baking.

Bake until the pudding is puffed and the top is shiny, with the outer 1 in [2.5 cm] baked but the interior still liquid, 27 to 30 minutes. Test by inserting a toothpick about 1 in [2.5 cm] from the edge; it should be coated with molten "pudding" underneath. (The batter cooks to over 160°F [71°C], which removes any risk of salmonella.)

Remove from the oven and let rest for 10 minutes. Scoop into small bowls and serve warm, with vanilla ice cream and chopped hazelnuts or sprinkles, if desired. (Note: The molten part of the brownie pudding solidifies as the dessert sits at room temperature. To warm it back up, reheat for a few minutes in a 300°F [150°C] oven. It's still delicious solidified, though the texture is more gooey than molten.)

contd.

COOK 1 ——————— COOK 2

A COUPLE COOKS

To us, making dessert is all about sneaking bites of the batter or dough! Here's a decadent way to eat the batter for dessert instead. The outside rim of this "pudding" is set like a brownie, but the interior is pure warm molten chocolate goo. It's a spin on a popular recipe by Ina Garten, but done up our way with notes of espresso, nutmeg, and dark chocolate.

Scoop it into small bowls and top with a touch of melty ice cream: The contrast of cold vanilla against warm chocolate is pretty darn heavenly.

Tips

Don't skip the instant espresso! Often used in chocolate desserts like brownies and cake, it brings a deeper chocolate flavor to the dish. It's often available in a small jar in the baking aisle in grocery stores; if not, check the coffee aisle.

This recipe is flexible: You can mix up the batter before eating your main dish, then pop it into the oven 45 minutes before you'd like your dessert.

For Gluten-Free

Use almond flour or gluten-free flour.

Storage

This is best served immediately after baking. Leftovers will keep, refrigerated, for up to 5 days but will become solidified in the refrigerator. It tastes good cold or reheated.

Diet
Vegetarian,
gluten-free option

Glazed Applesauce Spice Cake

MAKES 16 SERVINGS

Applesauce Cake

1½ cups [210 g] all-purpose flour

¾ cup [150 g] packed light brown sugar

1½ tsp ground cinnamon

½ tsp ground ginger

½ tsp allspice

½ tsp cloves

¾ tsp baking powder

¾ tsp baking soda

¼ tsp kosher salt

1 egg

1 tsp vanilla extract

½ cup [120 ml] neutral oil

½ cup [120 g] plain Greek yogurt

¾ cup [185 g] unsweetened applesauce

Cinnamon stick, or more ground cinnamon, for garnishing (optional) (see Tips)

Sour Cream Icing

¾ cup [90 g] unsifted powdered sugar (see Tips)

2 Tbsp sour cream

½ tsp vanilla extract

To make the cake, preheat the oven to 350°F [180°C]. Grease a metal 9 x 9 in [23 x 23 cm] baking dish. Line the pan with a piece of parchment paper, cut so that it extends on two sides to easily remove the cake from the pan.

In a medium bowl, whisk together the flour, brown sugar, cinnamon, ginger, allspice, cloves, baking powder, baking soda, and kosher salt.

In another medium bowl, whisk together the egg, then add the vanilla extract, oil, Greek yogurt, and applesauce and whisk until smooth. Pour the dry ingredients into the wet mixture and stir gently with a spoon or spatula until a thick batter forms and no dry streaks remain. Pour the batter into the prepared pan.

Bake until the cake is fairly firm when you press lightly on the center, 28 to 32 minutes. Remove from the oven and let cool completely on a baking rack, for at least 1 hour. Use the parchment to remove the cake from the pan, then remove the paper and transfer the cake to a cutting board.

To make the icing, in a small bowl, use a spoon to stir together the powdered sugar, sour cream, and vanilla extract; it will seem dry and thick at first, but keep stirring until it comes together as a smooth icing (if it still seems very dry, add ½ teaspoon of milk of choice; if it is too thin, add a bit more powdered sugar). Pour the icing over the cake and smooth it over the top with a spatula. If desired, top with a few grates of a cinnamon stick or a pinch or two of ground cinnamon. Before the icing sets, cut into 16 pieces. Enjoy immediately or allow the icing to set for about 30 minutes.

COOK 1

COOK 2

contd.

This sweetly spiced cake gets five-star reviews from all our friends and family, including a raving "1,560 thumbs up" from our son. Make it, and the loved ones in your life will thank you! It's tender, moist, and fluffy thanks to applesauce and Greek yogurt, and seasoned with warming spices.

Cover it all in a simple icing glaze—just three ingredients make a creamy, lightly tangy drizzle. Make it into a decadent winter dessert with vanilla ice cream and Bourbon Salted Caramel (page 297), or serve it in summer with sliced peaches and homemade Whipped Cream (page 303).

Tips

Finely grating a cinnamon stick makes for a polished garnish for the top of the applesauce cake; ground cinnamon is so fine that it can look messy. But you can use it if it's all you have. Use a small pinch and sprinkle it from several feet above the cake to ensure an even coating.

If you have a food scale, weigh the powdered sugar for the icing. It's the easiest way for an accurate measurement.

Storage

Leftovers will keep, refrigerated, for up to 1 week. Freeze the uniced cake wrapped in plastic and sealed in a plastic bag for up to 3 months, then bring to room temperature and add icing.

Diet
Vegetarian

Apple Galette *with* Bourbon Salted Caramel

COOK 2 ———— ■ ● ———— COOK 1

SERVES 8

Galette Dough

1½ cups [210 g] all-purpose flour

1 Tbsp granulated sugar

¾ tsp kosher salt

¼ tsp baking powder

10 Tbsp [150 g] cold unsalted butter or vegan butter

5 to 6 Tbsp [80 to 90 ml] cold water

1 egg, for the egg wash

1 Tbsp Demerara or turbinado sugar, for sprinkling

Filling

1 lb [455 g] crisp, tart apples like Granny Smith, Pink Lady, or Honeycrisp (about 2 large), unpeeled, thinly cut into ⅛ in [3 mm] slices (3½ cups sliced)

2 Tbsp light brown sugar

2 Tbsp granulated sugar

1½ tsp cinnamon

½ tsp allspice

⅛ tsp nutmeg

½ tsp cornstarch

1 Tbsp unsalted butter, cut into very small pieces

Bourbon Salted Caramel (recipe follows)

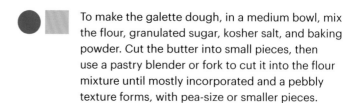 To make the galette dough, in a medium bowl, mix the flour, granulated sugar, kosher salt, and baking powder. Cut the butter into small pieces, then use a pastry blender or fork to cut it into the flour mixture until mostly incorporated and a pebbly texture forms, with pea-size or smaller pieces.

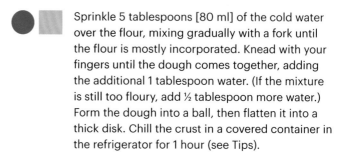 Sprinkle 5 tablespoons [80 ml] of the cold water over the flour, mixing gradually with a fork until the flour is mostly incorporated. Knead with your fingers until the dough comes together, adding the additional 1 tablespoon water. (If the mixture is still too floury, add ½ tablespoon more water.) Form the dough into a ball, then flatten it into a thick disk. Chill the crust in a covered container in the refrigerator for 1 hour (see Tips).

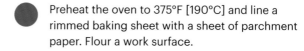 Preheat the oven to 375°F [190°C] and line a rimmed baking sheet with a sheet of parchment paper. Flour a work surface.

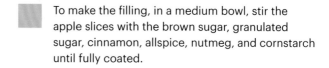 To make the filling, in a medium bowl, stir the apple slices with the brown sugar, granulated sugar, cinnamon, allspice, nutmeg, and cornstarch until fully coated.

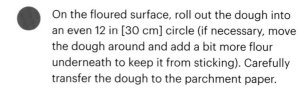 On the floured surface, roll out the dough into an even 12 in [30 cm] circle (if necessary, move the dough around and add a bit more flour underneath to keep it from sticking). Carefully transfer the dough to the parchment paper.

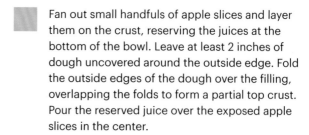 Fan out small handfuls of apple slices and layer them on the crust, reserving the juices at the bottom of the bowl. Leave at least 2 inches of dough uncovered around the outside edge. Fold the outside edges of the dough over the filling, overlapping the folds to form a partial top crust. Pour the reserved juice over the exposed apple slices in the center.

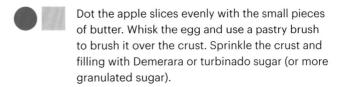

Dot the apple slices evenly with the small pieces of butter. Whisk the egg and use a pastry brush to brush it over the crust. Sprinkle the crust and filling with Demerara or turbinado sugar (or more granulated sugar).

Bake until the crust is golden brown, 38 to 40 minutes. Transfer the galette on the parchment paper to a baking rack and let cool to room temperature (about 30 minutes) before cutting into pieces and serving. Drizzle with Bourbon Salted Caramel (recipe follows) before serving, or top with ice cream.

COOK 1 — COOK 2

Bourbon Salted Caramel

MAKES ⅔ CUP [160 ML]

½ cup [100 g] granulated sugar

¼ cup [60 ml] water

½ tsp kosher salt

⅓ cup [80 ml] heavy cream

½ Tbsp bourbon (see Tips)

¼ tsp vanilla extract

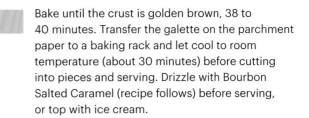

In a medium saucepan over medium heat, stir together the sugar, water, and kosher salt. Cook, stirring constantly with a spatula, until the sugar and salt are dissolved and it starts to boil, about 2 minutes.

Reduce the heat slightly to a simmer and cook, constantly bubbling, until the sugar turns deep amber, 8 to 11 minutes. Occasionally give a gentle stir with a spatula to ensure even cooking. Watch closely toward the end of the cooking time, as the color darkens quickly.

Once the sugar turns deep amber, immediately reduce the heat to low. Add the cream, which will cause the mixture to bubble vigorously; stir constantly with a spatula, until it is a rich caramel color, about 90 seconds. Stir in the bourbon and vanilla extract and cook for 20 seconds more.

Transfer the caramel to a small bowl to cool, leaving any hardened bits of sugar in the pan. Let cool and thicken for 10 minutes before serving. It will keep thickening the longer it sits; if it becomes too thick, reheat gently before serving (see Tips).

contd.

This rustic French tart lets you skip fiddling with pie dough to make free-form folded layers of golden pastry. Piling the crust full of cinnamon-spiced apples is a fun fall treat, but of course you can indulge any time of the year. There are endless variations on this type of fruit tart.

Serve with melty vanilla ice cream, or even better, drizzle with gooey Bourbon Salted Caramel. The mad scientist in you will love how easy it is to make a caramel sauce out of a few basic ingredients. Pour leftover caramel over ice cream or French Toast Waffles (page 158).

Tips

Galettes are endlessly customizable! For the filling, use 3 cups of any seasonal fruit, ⅓ to ½ cup [65 to 100 g] of granulated sugar, 1 tablespoon of cornstarch, and ½ teaspoon of cinnamon. Taste and adjust the filling as desired based on the sweetness of the fruit. Try peaches, pears, plums, blueberries, and more.

Make the crust in advance for easy prep. The dough will keep, refrigerated, for up to 3 days. Before rolling, allow the dough to sit at room temperature for 30 minutes. Or wrap it in plastic wrap or aluminum foil and freeze for up to 3 months, then defrost overnight in the refrigerator and let stand for 30 minutes at room temperature before rolling.

You can also make the caramel sauce in advance. Refrigerate the sauce, then reheat it on the stovetop or in the microwave before serving.

Omit the bourbon in the caramel sauce if desired. It's just as tasty!

Liqueur Pairing

After the galette, enjoy a small glass of Amaro Nonino Quintessentia or Amaro Averna. These caramel-colored liqueurs have a bittersweet, smooth finish and an herbal complexity that complements the apples' natural tartness. (For more on amari, see page 325.)

Cooking Together

After the dough is chilled, have one person roll out the dough while the other person makes the filling. Then whip up the caramel sauce together while the galette bakes.

For Vegan

Use vegan butter and, instead of using the egg wash, brush the crust with nondairy milk. Omit the salted caramel.

Storage

Leftovers will keep, refrigerated, for up to 4 days; bring to room temperature before serving.

Diet
Vegetarian, vegan option

Nectarine & Blueberry Crumble

SERVES 8

3 cups sliced (¼ in [6 mm]) ripe nectarines (about 1 lb [455 g]), 2 to 3 nectarines, or ripe peaches

2 cups [280 g] fresh blueberries

1 cup [200 g] granulated sugar

2 Tbsp cornstarch

½ Tbsp vanilla extract

1 Tbsp fresh lemon juice

1 tsp cinnamon

¾ cup [105 g] all-purpose flour

½ tsp ground ginger

¼ tsp baking powder

¼ tsp kosher salt

6 Tbsp [85 g] unsalted butter, melted

Vanilla ice cream, for serving (optional)

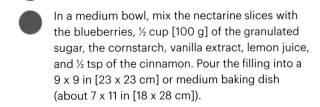

Preheat the oven to 375°F [190°C].

In a medium bowl, mix the nectarine slices with the blueberries, ½ cup [100 g] of the granulated sugar, the cornstarch, vanilla extract, lemon juice, and ½ tsp of the cinnamon. Pour the filling into a 9 x 9 in [23 x 23 cm] or medium baking dish (about 7 x 11 in [18 x 28 cm]).

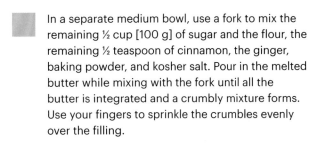

In a separate medium bowl, use a fork to mix the remaining ½ cup [100 g] of sugar and the flour, the remaining ½ teaspoon of cinnamon, the ginger, baking powder, and kosher salt. Pour in the melted butter while mixing with the fork until all the butter is integrated and a crumbly mixture forms. Use your fingers to sprinkle the crumbles evenly over the filling.

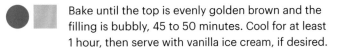

Bake until the top is evenly golden brown and the filling is bubbly, 45 to 50 minutes. Cool for at least 1 hour, then serve with vanilla ice cream, if desired.

COOK 1 ——— ● ——— COOK 2

contd.

No summer is complete for us without a trip to Michigan to go blueberry picking. There's something about wandering the rows of tall berry bushes that's almost spiritual, picking plump berries and sneaking the occasional one into your mouth for a taste of sweet-tart. Each year we come home with a mountain of berries for just a few dollars, and we bake them into a stream of bars, cobblers, and crumbles.

This nostalgic crumble is just right for all of that summer fruit, baked until syrupy and topped with chewy cinnamon crumbles.

Often bypassed for peaches or plums, nectarines are a natural pairing with berries and can sometimes be easier to find ripe at the grocery store (though ripe summer peaches work, too). Feel free to substitute 5 cups of your favorite fruit and make it all year long.

Tips

Substitute frozen peaches and blueberries, and it's just as tasty (no need to defrost). Or use any combination of stone fruits and berries, like peaches, plums, strawberries, raspberries, or blackberries.

Turn it into a winter crisp by substituting peeled apples and pears and a hint of ginger or cardamom in the filling.

For Vegan

Use vegan butter.

For Gluten-Free

Use almond flour or gluten-free flour.

Storage

The crumble will keep, covered, at room temperature for up to 1 day. After 1 day, refrigerate any leftovers for up to 5 days. Freeze in a sealed container for up to 3 months; reheat it in a 375°F [190°C] oven until bubbly.

Diet
Vegetarian, vegan option, gluten-free option

Ricotta Shortcakes *with* Lemon Curd & Berries

SERVES 8

Ricotta Shortcakes

⅔ cup [160 ml] cold buttermilk, plus more for brushing (see Tips)

½ tsp vanilla extract

½ cup [120 g] cold whole-milk ricotta cheese

2 cups [280 g] all-purpose flour

¼ cup [50 g] granulated sugar

2 tsp baking powder

½ tsp baking soda

¾ tsp kosher salt

4 Tbsp [55 g] cold unsalted butter

Turbinado sugar

For serving

Lemon Curd (recipe follows)

Whipped Cream (recipe follows)

Raspberries, blueberries, or blackberries

Preheat the oven to 425°F [220°C]. Line a baking sheet with parchment paper.

To make the ricotta shortcakes, in a medium bowl, whisk together the buttermilk, vanilla extract, and ricotta.

In a large bowl, whisk together the flour, granulated sugar, baking powder, baking soda, and kosher salt. Using the large holes of a grater (see Tips), grate the cold butter into the flour and mix with a fork until the butter is coated with the flour mixture.

Pour the wet mixture into the flour mixture and stir with a spatula until it comes together into a shaggy dough. Knead once or twice in the bowl with your hands to ensure that the flour is fully incorporated. Form the dough into 8 equal-size pieces and set them on the prepared pan (you can roll them into balls with your fingers or keep them in a rough organic shape).

Brush the shortcake tops lightly with buttermilk and sprinkle with turbinado sugar (or more granulated sugar). Bake until golden brown on top, 12 to 15 minutes. Let cool before serving. To serve, slice the shortcakes in half horizontally. On the bottom half, spread a generous layer of lemon curd, then add a small dollop of whipped cream and a handful of berries. Add the shortcake top and another small dollop of whipped cream.

COOK 2

COOK 1

contd.

A COUPLE COOKS

Whipped Cream

MAKES 1 CUP [120 G]

½ cup [120 ml] heavy cream

1 Tbsp powdered sugar

¼ tsp vanilla extract

In the bowl of a stand mixer fitted with the whisk attachment, mix the cream, powdered sugar, and vanilla extract on medium speed until soft or stiff peaks form. Or put the ingredients in a medium bowl. With a large whisk, whip the cream by moving the whisk back and forth quickly in a line instead of a circular motion. Whip until the cream thickens and the desired consistency is reached, 2 to 3 minutes.

Lemon Curd

MAKES 1½ CUPS [360 G]

3 eggs

½ cup [100 g] granulated sugar

6 Tbsp [90 ml] fresh lemon juice

2 tsp lemon zest

6 Tbsp [85 g] unsalted butter, cut into ½ in [13 mm] pieces

To make the lemon curd, in a medium saucepan, whisk the eggs until smooth. Whisk in the granulated sugar, lemon juice, and lemon zest. Cook over medium heat, stirring slowly and constantly with a spatula, until the mixture is steaming and starts to thicken to a yogurt-like consistency, 2 to 3 minutes. This happens at a temperature of 160°F to 170°F [70°C to 76°C] when measured with a food thermometer. Avoid simmering or overcooking, which makes the curd lumpy. Immediately remove from the heat and whisk in the pieces of butter until they are melted. Scrape the lemon curd into a container and press plastic wrap onto the surface to prevent a skin from forming. Refrigerate for at least 2 hours before using.

Memorize this lemon curd recipe in case you ever find yourself on the *Great British Bake Off*. It's intensely citrusy and absolutely brilliant. Pair it with a moist, tender shortcake made with ricotta cheese along with seasonal fruit, and it's a lovely summer dessert for outdoor meals and celebrations. It's easy to prepare in advance: Make both the curd and shortcakes ahead of time for an easy-to-assemble treat.

Tips

For best results, use full-fat or whole buttermilk.

If you don't have a box grater, cut the butter for the shortcakes into ⅛ in [3 mm] cubes.

The lemon curd makes 1½ cups [360 g], more than you'll need for the recipe. Use leftovers as a topping for waffles or pancakes, or with biscuits, scones, English muffins, or crumpets.

For Gluten-Free

Omit the shortcakes and serve the lemon curd topped with berries and whipped cream in small bowls.

Storage

Leftover lemon curd will keep, refrigerated, for up to 1 week. Leftover shortcakes will keep at room temperature for up to 3 days between layers of paper towel (to reduce moisture) in a storage container.

Diet
Vegetarian, gluten-free option

Strawberry *Limeade* Sorbet

**MAKES 1 QUART [945 G]
(8 SERVINGS)**

2 lb [910 g] fresh strawberries,
hulled

1 cup [200 g] granulated sugar

1 Tbsp lime zest

6 Tbsp [90 ml] fresh lime juice
(from 2 large or 3 medium
limes)

1 pinch kosher salt

½ cup [90 g] ice

 Freeze the base of the ice cream maker overnight.

 In a high-speed blender or food processor, blend
the strawberries until fully puréed. Add the sugar,
lime zest, lime juice, kosher salt, and ice and blend
again until smooth.

 Pour the mixture into the ice cream maker
and churn until thickened and smooth, 20 to
25 minutes. Transfer to a loaf pan and freeze for
at least 2 hours to ripen to a scoopable texture.

COOK 1

COOK 2

This extra zingy, fruity homemade sorbet is simple and made for
highlighting ripe berries. Investing in an ice cream maker is worth it
for the silky, luxurious texture that can come only from churning. You
can make a half recipe if you like, but we like to have leftovers so we
can sneak late-night spoonfuls from the freezer!

Tips

Don't have an ice cream maker? Use this
no-churn method for a less smooth but
just as delicious version. Pour the sorbet
mixture into a loaf pan and freeze for
3 hours. Stir to fully incorporate any icy
bits, then smooth out the top. Freeze for
at least 1 hour, until mostly solid, then
serve. This variation tastes best the day
of making, as the texture becomes icier
the longer it is stored.

**Make other sorbet flavors using
this ratio:** 2 pounds [910 g] of fruit,
1 cup [200 g] of sugar, and at least
2 tablespoons of lemon or lime juice.
Try it with blueberries, raspberries,
pineapple, fresh peaches, or mangoes.

Storage

Sorbet will keep, frozen, for 1 week in a
loaf pan with parchment paper pressed
onto the top or in a sealed freezer-proof
container. After freezing overnight,
thaw at room temperature for about
20 minutes.

Diet
Vegetarian, vegan,
gluten-free

Tiramisu Sundaes

SERVES 4

1 cup [240 ml] heavy cream

¼ cup [30 g] powdered sugar

2 Tbsp amaretto liqueur
(see Tips)

8 ladyfinger cookies, 6 roughly
crumbled and 2 cut in half

One 1½ oz [45 g] piece of dark
chocolate, cut into shavings
with a knife

8 small scoops vanilla ice cream

½ cup [120 ml] cold espresso
or very strong coffee, regular
or decaf

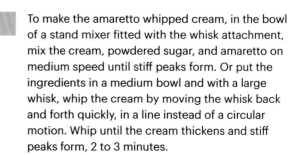 To make the amaretto whipped cream, in the bowl of a stand mixer fitted with the whisk attachment, mix the cream, powdered sugar, and amaretto on medium speed until stiff peaks form. Or put the ingredients in a medium bowl and with a large whisk, whip the cream by moving the whisk back and forth quickly, in a line instead of a circular motion. Whip until the cream thickens and stiff peaks form, 2 to 3 minutes.

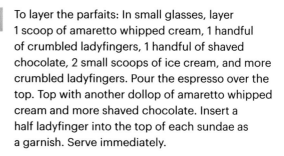 To layer the parfaits: In small glasses, layer 1 scoop of amaretto whipped cream, 1 handful of crumbled ladyfingers, 1 handful of shaved chocolate, 2 small scoops of ice cream, and more crumbled ladyfingers. Pour the espresso over the top. Top with another dollop of amaretto whipped cream and more shaved chocolate. Insert a half ladyfinger into the top of each sundae as a garnish. Serve immediately.

contd.

Enjoy all the fun of classic Italian tiramisu with none of the effort or wait time. It's fun and easy to make and great as a date-night treat or a no-cook dessert at parties.

Layer a homemade amaretto whipped cream with vanilla ice cream, crushed ladyfinger cookies, and shaved dark chocolate. Just before serving, pour on a shot of espresso like an Italian *affogato*, which makes rich coffee-soaked bites of cookies and cream. Tiramisu, without the fuss! For a sweet ending to a date night, cut the recipe in half and serve it as a double-sized sundae with two spoons.

Tips

You can assemble the sundaes in advance if you like. Layer them without the coffee and the final whipped cream and chocolate. Freeze until ready to serve. Pour over the coffee, then top with 1 dollop of whipped cream and the reserved chocolate.

You can make the whipped cream up to 6 hours in advance; transfer to a sealed container and refrigerate until serving time.

If you like a stronger amaretto flavor, increase the amaretto by up to 1 table-spoon. Some brands are stronger than others; high-quality brands tend to be more balanced. Our favorite, Lazzaroni, tastes great at 3 tablespoons total. If using a different brand, start with 2 tablespoons and adjust to taste.

Looking to use up your amaretto bottle? Try the Amaretto Whiskey Sour (page 333).

Storage

This dessert is best enjoyed immediately.

Diet
Vegetarian

Chapter 9

DRINKS

Aperol spritz slushies turn an evening on the patio into a date, and a big pitcher of mojitos or sangria makes a get-together of friends into a party. And what's better than a good "happy hour" night, pairing a signature drink with loads of small bites?

In this chapter, we're diving into the world of cocktails for every occasion: signature cocktails for two, pitcher cocktails for a crowd, simple drinks to build in a glass, and warming winter cocktails to savor by the fire. Plus, several mocktail variations provide alcohol-free alternatives.

SOME HIGHLIGHTS IN THIS CHAPTER:

Mix up cocktails for two, like Perfect Margaritas for Two (page 313) or Amaretto Whiskey Sours (page 333).

Pour up a laid-back Lillet Spritzer—no real measuring required (page 316).

Set up the patio with a pitcher of Red Wine Sangria, with Sangria Mocktails (made with kombucha) for the kids (page 319).

Poolside, sip a citrusy-sweet Aperol Spritz Slushie (page 330).

Perfect Margaritas *for Two*

MAKES 2 DRINKS

6 oz [180 ml] tequila reposado

4 oz [120 ml] Cointreau

3 oz [90 ml] fresh lime juice

For serving

2 Tbsp flaky sea salt, like Maldon

Lime wedge

Lime wheels

2 clear ice cubes (page 326)

● To prepare the glasses for serving: Spread the flaky sea salt on a plate in an even layer. Cut a notch in a lime wedge, then run it around the rim of two lowball glasses. Dip the rim of each glass into the salt and rotate to coat the rim.

■ Add the tequila reposado, Cointreau, and lime juice to a cocktail shaker. Fill it with 8 ice cubes. Shake vigorously until cold.

■ Add a clear ice cube to each glass. Strain the drink into the two glasses and garnish each with a lime wheel.

This classic recipe from the 1930s is a three-ingredient sour, made with tequila, orange liqueur, and lime juice. We've tried all sorts of margarita variations (from grapefruit to prickly pear cactus!), but we always come back to the original. It's simply perfect.

Like any great drink, the best margarita requires quality ingredients. We prefer tequila reposado, which is aged for 2 to 12 months in oak barrels, infusing hints of oak, vanilla, and caramel. Cointreau orange liqueur adds a warm depth versus the traditional triple sec. The resulting cocktail for two is our pick for an evening in—just add chips and guac.

Jalapeño Margarita: Add 6 thin jalapeño pepper slices to the cocktail shaker before shaking the drink (for a more subtle heat, remove the seeds).

Mezcal Margarita: Replace half the tequila with mezcal for a smoky margarita.

Pitcher Margarita (8 servings): In a large pitcher, stir together 3 cups (24 oz [710 ml]) tequila, 2 cups (16 oz [475 ml]) Cointreau, and 1½ cups (12 oz [360 ml]) lime juice with 3 large handfuls of ice cubes.

Elderflower Gin & Tonic

MAKES 1 DRINK

Clear ice (optional; page 326)

1½ oz [45 ml] gin

1 oz [30 ml] St-Germain or other elderflower liqueur

3 lemon wedges

Fresh rosemary, dill, or mint leaves

4 oz [120 ml] tonic water

 Fill a large, stemmed cocktail glass or wine glass with clear ice or ice and swirl until the glass is chilled. Stir in the gin and St-Germain. Squeeze in the lemon wedges and add them to the glass, along with lots of fresh dill and mint.

 Pour the tonic water over the back of a bar spoon into the glass (this maximizes the effervescent bubbles). Stir once and serve immediately.

Riffing on gin and tonics is endless fun at parties. We love to make a big tray of garnishes: lemon and lime wedges, fresh mint, dill, rosemary, cucumber slices, citrus peels, and juniper berries. Once the deck lights are glowing and the music is on, it's easy to refill the drinks with endless flavor combinations.

This G&T spin adds St-Germain liqueur to the classic ingredients. Its floral, fragrant notes make a drink that's bright, lightly sweet, and funky. Make sure to load up on the garnishes, which give an herbaceous aroma to each sip.

Mocktail: Use 2 ounces [60 ml] of elderflower lemonade in place of the gin and St-Germain. Garnish generously with fresh dill.

Classic G&T: Use 2 ounces [60 ml] of gin and omit the St-Germain.

Tips

The gin and tonic is a classic cocktail that's dependent on great ingredients: The brand of tonic water, freshness of garnishes, and type of gin all matter. Try our favorite gin, Malfy Gin Originale, or find a local distiller you love.

Serve the gin and tonic in a large, round, stemmed glass to allow plenty of room for ice and garnishes.

The pretty bottle looks historic, but St-Germain was invented in 2007. It's quite versatile; pair it with champagne in a French 77 (page 317), or substitute it for Lillet blanc to make an Elderflower Spritzer (page 316).

COOK 2

COOK 1

A COUPLE COOKS

Lillet Spritzer

MAKES 1 SPRITZER

3 oz [90 ml] Lillet blanc, chilled

3 oz [90 ml] soda water, chilled
(or club soda)

Fresh thyme sprig and a lemon
wheel, for garnishing

 Pour the Lillet blanc and soda water into a
stemmed wine glass and gently stir. Add the
thyme and lemon wheel and serve immediately.

Here's a simple drink that's hardly a cocktail at all: the wine spritzer!
The spritzer concept originated in Austria, and we became smitten
with it while visiting dear friends in Vienna. It's made by diluting
wine with soda water, resulting in a refreshing, low-alcohol aperitif
that's made for sipping on a warm day.

This one stars Lillet blanc, a French aromatized wine that's
infused with fruits, herbs, and other botanicals to give it subtly
floral notes. Spritzers are typically watered down 50 percent or
more, but there's really no need to measure. It's a fun and carefree
drink that's meant for laid-back summer afternoons.

Red wine spritzer: Replace the Lillet
blanc with red wine and garnish with an
orange wheel.

Rosé or white wine spritzer: Replace the
Lillet blanc with rosé or white wine.

Tips

Feel free to play around with the dilution
level here to fit your own tastes.

Lillet is a family of French aromatized
wines that includes Lillet blanc, Lillet
rosé, and Lillet rouge. Feel free to use
any of them in this drink.

Amari—bittersweet Italian herbal
liqueurs—work great as spritzers as well.
Adding soda water to Campari (with a
splash of sweet vermouth) makes the
refreshing Americano cocktail, an Italian
classic from the 1860s. Experiment with
any other type of amaro to create a light
yet complex drink.

French 75 & 77

French 75

2 DRINKS

2 oz [60 ml] gin

1½ oz [45 ml] fresh lemon juice

1 oz [30 ml] simple syrup

1 mini bottle (187 ml [6 oz]) dry champagne
or prosecco

Lemon twist

For 2 servings: Add the gin, lemon juice, and simple syrup to a cocktail mixing glass. Add a handful of ice and stir until cold. Strain 2 ounces [60 ml] of the mixture into each champagne flute. Top each glass with 3 ounces [90 ml] of the champagne or prosecco. Garnish with a lemon twist (page 325).

8 DRINKS

8 oz [240 ml] gin

6 oz [180 ml] fresh lemon juice

4 oz [120 ml] simple syrup

1 bottle (750 ml [24 oz]) dry champagne
or prosecco

Lemon twist

For 8 servings: Add the gin, lemon juice, and simple syrup to a pitcher. Add two handfuls of ice and stir until cold. Remove the ice and pour 2 ounces [60 ml] of the mixture into each champagne flute. Top each glass with 3 ounces [90 ml] of the champagne or prosecco. Garnish with a lemon twist (page 325).

French 77

2 DRINKS

1½ oz [45 ml] St-Germain elderflower liqueur

1 oz [30 ml] fresh lemon juice

1 mini bottle (187 ml [6 oz]) dry champagne
or prosecco

Lemon twist

For 2 servings: Add the St-Germain and lemon juice to a cocktail mixing glass. Add a handful of ice and stir until cold. Strain 2 ounces [60 ml] of the mixture into each champagne flute. Top each glass with 3 ounces [90 ml] of the champagne or prosecco. Garnish with a lemon twist (page 325).

8 DRINKS

6 oz [180 ml] St-Germain elderflower liqueur

4 oz [120 ml] fresh lemon juice

1 bottle (750 ml [24 oz]) dry champagne
or prosecco

Lemon twist

For 8 servings: Add the St-Germain and lemon juice to a pitcher. Add two handfuls of ice and stir until cold. Remove the ice and pour 2 ounces [60 ml] of the mixture into each champagne flute. Top each glass with 3 ounces [90 ml] of the champagne or prosecco. Garnish with a lemon twist (page 325).

COOK 1

COOK 2

contd.

The French 75 has always held an allure for us, possibly because of its mysterious name. The drink combines bubbly champagne, floral gin, and zingy lemon and is just the thing for celebrations where you want to pop open a bottle, be it New Year's Eve, an anniversary, or a birthday.

This classic cocktail was likely invented around 1915 in Paris, named after the 75mm French field gun. We like it even better as the French 77, a variation that uses St-Germain elderflower liqueur in place of the gin.

Tips

Any dry sparkling wine works here. While champagne is classic for this drink, prosecco is more economical and tastes just as good.

Any large glass or the bottom half of your cocktail shaker will work for a mixing glass.

Red Wine Sangria

MAKES 6 DRINKS

Juice of 1 orange

1 green apple, chopped into bite-size pieces

1 ripe stone fruit (peach or plum), sliced

1 lemon, sliced

1 lime, sliced

1 cinnamon stick

750 ml bottle fruity, full-bodied red wine (we prefer a Crianza from the Rioja region of Spain)

⅓ cup [80 ml] Cointreau

⅓ cup [80 ml] simple syrup (page 325), plus more to taste

 Combine all ingredients in a pitcher and stir. Taste and add additional simple syrup if you prefer a sweeter sangria. Refrigerate for 1 to 4 hours.

 To serve, pour the sangria into ice-filled glasses and garnish with some of the soaked fruit (served on a skewer if desired).

COOK 1 —————— • ■ —————— COOK 2

contd.

In the States we often get sangria wrong, making it overly sweet, like fruit punch. This red wine sangria is closer to the Spanish method: dry but fruity, with a subtle citrus lift to the finish. (Of course, if you prefer a sweeter sangria, feel free to add more simple syrup.) Mix it up for a dinner al fresco, or make a half batch for a date night with Gambas al Ajillo with Crusty Bread (page 101).

White Sangria: Replace the red wine with 1 bottle dry white wine, like Albariño or pinot grigio. Remove the cinnamon stick and use more peaches.

Fall Sangria: Use pear instead of stone fruit. Substitute ½ teaspoon of ground cinnamon for the cinnamon stick. When serving, fill half the glass with sparkling apple cider and half with the red wine mixture.

Sangria Mocktail: Replace the wine and Cointreau with one 16 oz [475 ml] bottle kombucha and one 16 oz [475 ml] bottle cranberry juice blend. Replace the orange juice with the juice of 1 lemon and 1 lime.

Bar Cart

We started to dabble in cocktails early in our marriage, but it wasn't until a few years in that we really started to appreciate the art of the homemade cocktail. We learned about egg-white drinks and dry shakes, Prohibition-style sours and modern classics, amari and bitters, clear ice techniques, and herb-infused simple syrups. After making over three hundred different cocktail recipes and documenting them all on our *A Couple Cooks* website, we became, more or less, amateur bartenders. The best part of it all was doing it together as a couple: mixing, garnishing, taste testing, and of course . . . enjoying the drinks!

Cocktails are all about the finer details: The ice, garnishes, and glassware are as much a part of the experience as the alcohol. Becoming well-acquainted with citrus twists and lime wheels, cocktail picks, and how to make clear ice is just as important as a well-stocked bar. Here's what you need to start mixing up great drinks at home.

Bar Cart Gear

- **Bartender measuring glass or jigger:** This is essential for measuring up cocktails, which are specified in ounces.

- **Cocktail shaker and strainer:** This tool quickly mixes, chills, and slightly dilutes cocktails when shaking them with the ice.

- **Cocktail mixing glass:** A cocktail shaker can double as a mixing glass, but true mixologists use a mixing glass for stirred cocktails (like a Manhattan and Martini) to chill the drink without watering it down.

- **Bar spoon:** This tall spoon is used for stirring in a mixing glass.

- **Muddler:** The flat end of a wooden muddler is used to smash fruits and herbs in a cocktail shaker, releasing their flavor into the drink.

- **Press citrus juicer:** Fresh citrus juice is a common ingredient in cocktails; avoid substituting bottled juice at all costs! A citrus press juicer is easiest to use.

Glassware

- **Stemmed cocktail glass:** A stemmed cocktail glass is customary for shaken and stirred cocktails, from Prohibition-era drinks to modern classics.

- **Lowball:** A lowball glass works for everything from the Perfect Margaritas for Two (page 313) to an Old Fashioned.

- **Highball:** Highball glasses are customarily used for drinks that are diluted, like an Elderflower Gin & Tonic (page 314), Party Mojitos (page 327), Tom Collins, and more.

- **Wine glass:** Use these to serve wine-based cocktails, like sangria or a Lillet Spritzer (page 316). They also work well for a Gin & Tonic (page 314).

- **Champagne flute:** Champagne-based drinks are often served in a flute, like a good French 75 (page 317).

Essential Ingredients

- **Soda water (a.k.a. seltzer or sparkling water):** Carbonated water with no additives. Club soda, carbonated water infused with added minerals, can be used interchangeably with soda water.

- **Tonic water:** Carbonated water with added quinine and sugar. It tastes both sweet and bitter, and is used in cocktails like the classic gin and tonic or vodka tonic.

- **Simple syrup:** A liquid sweetener made with sugar and water, commonly used in cocktails and coffee drinks. It's easy to make your own; see the following recipe.

- **Bitters:** Small bottles of spirits infused with botanicals (herbs and spices) that are used to add nuance to cocktails. The most popular is Angostura bitters, but there are lots of unique types to try, like celery, chocolate, lemon, cherry, and more.

Liquors

As a home mixologist, you don't have to try to stock every liquor! Buy a bottle for a cocktail, then try using it up in different drinks before buying something new. If you need inspiration for using up a bottle, we have hundreds of cocktail ideas on our website www.acouplecooks.com.

Primary liquors

The most common hard liquors to use in American cocktails are

- Gin
- Whiskey (bourbon and rye)
- Tequila

- Vodka
- Rum (white and aged)
- Brandy

Secondary liquors

These are the supporting actors, liquors used in cocktails in smaller amounts to add nuance in flavor. They can also be used on their own in drinks like a spritzer (page 316). Here are some of our favorite secondary liquors to stock:

- Italian amari Aperol, Campari, and/ or a caramelly bittersweet amaro (Amaro Nonino Quintessentia, Meletti, Averna, or Cynar)
- Vermouth (sweet and dry)
- Lillet blanc

- Cointreau, triple sec, or other orange liqueur
- Maraschino liqueur
- Amaretto
- Elderflower liqueur, such as St-Germain

How to make a lemon twist

Cut a circular lemon slice ¼ in [6 mm] thick. Run a paring knife around the edge of the circle to remove the peel from the pith and flesh. Make a small cut to open the circle of peel into a long strip and twist into a spiral, holding it for several seconds until the shape is kept.

How to make simple syrup

MAKES ¾ CUP [180 ML]

½ cup [100 g] sugar

½ cup [120 ml] water

Heat the sugar and water in a saucepan over medium heat. Stir until the sugar is dissolved, 1 to 2 minutes. Cool to room temperature before using. It will keep, refrigerated in a sealed container, for up to 1 month.

Variations: If desired, you can use brown sugar or Demerara sugar to add nuttier caramel notes. **Or make an herb-based syrup:** Throw in handfuls of an herb like mint or thyme and allow to steep for 30 minutes, then strain (see the Party Mojitos, page 327).

How to make clear ice

Taking the time to make clear ice turns your homemade drinks into craft cocktails. These crystal clear cubes are frozen directionally to avoid the air bubbles that make standard ice cubes cloudy. Large cubes also melt more slowly than regular ice, cooling the drink without watering it down. These days there are clear ice makers on the market, but you can also make your own at home with a small cooler that fits in your freezer.

Here's the basic science: Normal ice cubes are frozen from all sides at the same time, which traps all air and particles in the center of the cube. For clear ice, you freeze the water in a cooler instead of an ice tray. This forces the water to freeze directionally from the top down, allowing the ice to form perfectly clear crystals. All of the dissolved air and particles end up in the water beneath the ice block.

Small cooler that fits in your freezer (see Tip)

Warm tap water

Fill the small cooler with 4 to 5 inches of warm tap water. Put the cooler in the freezer with the lid off. Freeze until several inches have frozen, 18 to 24 hours. Some water should be left under the ice, which is important to ensure that the ice stays clear.

To remove the ice, turn the cooler upside down and set in a sink for 5 minutes. Then gently shake the ice block out (it may fall out on its own).

Set the ice block on a cutting board. Hold the ice with a towel or oven mitt and lightly score the top of the ice with a serrated knife until a strip of the ice snaps off. Then cut each strip into cubes that fit inside a glass.

Store the clear ice cubes in a closed container or freezer-safe bag and freeze until needed. Before using, allow the ice cubes to sit at room temperature for 2 minutes to temper them. Tempering prevents cracking and also allows the outer layer and any freezer burn flavor to melt off.

Tip

You can also use a clear ice cube tray to make clear ice for cocktails; several options are available online. Follow the instructions that come with the ice tray.

Party Mojitos

MAKES 8 DRINKS

¾ cup [150 g] sugar

¾ cup [15 g] loosely packed mint leaves, plus 2 more handfuls for the garnish

1 cup [240 ml] fresh lime juice (about 8 limes), plus 2 limes for garnishing

16 oz (2 cups [480 ml]) white rum

16 oz (2 cups [480 ml]) sparkling water

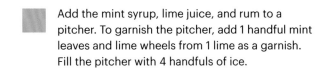 In a small saucepan, heat the sugar, mint, and ¾ cup [180 ml] of water over medium heat. Bring to a simmer and stir until all the sugar is dissolved. Turn off the heat and let stand for at least 30 minutes. Then strain it into a jar (or directly into the pitcher, if making immediately). Makes 1 cup [240 ml]; it will keep, refrigerated, for up to 5 days.

Add the mint syrup, lime juice, and rum to a pitcher. To garnish the pitcher, add 1 handful mint leaves and lime wheels from 1 lime as a garnish. Fill the pitcher with 4 handfuls of ice.

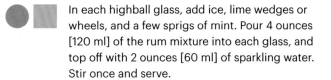 In each highball glass, add ice, lime wedges or wheels, and a few sprigs of mint. Pour 4 ounces [120 ml] of the rum mixture into each glass, and top off with 2 ounces [60 ml] of sparkling water. Stir once and serve.

COOK 1

COOK 2

contd.

This minty, bubbly concoction has been an iconic Cuban cocktail since the 1930s, when writer Ernest Hemingway became its number one fan. Today the mojito has star status all over the world.

Pitchers are perfect for entertaining, so you don't have to muddle and shake each individual drink. Make a mint-infused simple syrup ahead of time and combine it with lime juice and rum. When it's time to serve, simply pour the mixture into glasses, top each with sparkling water, and garnish with plenty of fresh mint. This is the best summer cocktail for when garden-fresh mint is abundant—we even let ours go wild so we can serve mojitos on repeat.

Classic one-serving mojito: Muddle 6 mint leaves in a cocktail shaker, then add 1 ounce [30 ml] of simple syrup, 1 ounce [30 ml] of lime juice, and 2 ounces [60 ml] of rum and shake until cold. Strain the mixture into the prepared glass and top with 2 ounces [60 ml] of sparkling water.

Strawberry mojitos: Hull, halve, and muddle 1 pint [240 g] of strawberries (24 berries). Mix the muddled strawberries into the pitcher with the mint syrup. Add additional sliced strawberries to the pitcher as a garnish.

Tips

If you want a lighter drink, use 3 oz [90 ml] of sparkling water per glass.

To make ahead, mix up the pitcher of mint syrup, lime juice, and rum up to 1 day in advance.

Aperol Spritz Slushies

2 DRINKS

6 oz [180 ml] Aperol

4 oz [120 ml] orange juice

1 mini bottle (187 ml [6 oz]) prosecco, chilled

Orange wedges or wheels

8 DRINKS

One 750 ml bottle (24 oz) Aperol

16 oz [475 ml] orange juice

1 bottle (750 ml [24 oz]) prosecco, chilled

Orange wedges or wheels

 Stir together the Aperol and orange juice in a freezer-proof container. Freeze for at least 6 hours or until solid (it can be made up to 1 week in advance).

To serve, use a fork to scrape the frozen mixture into a fluffy texture. Scoop ½ cup [120 ml] of the frozen mixture into stemmed wine glasses. Top each glass with 3 ounces [90 ml] of prosecco. Garnish with an orange wedge or wheel.

COOK 2

COOK 1

Here's a fun, frozen spin on the Italian classic where effervescent prosecco injects some serious sparkle into a granita-like mixture of bittersweet Aperol and orange juice. It's simple to whip up in advance for a special brunch, lazy day by the pool, or happy hour date with someone special. The recipe can be scaled up or down to serve two or eight by simply adjusting the size of your prosecco bottle.

Tip

Use up extra Aperol by mixing it with bourbon or rye whiskey in the Four of a Kind or Paper Plane (page 334), or make it into a free-form spritzer (page 316).

Amaretto *Whiskey* Sour

MAKES 2 DRINKS

2 clear ice cubes (page 326)

2 oz [60 ml] amaretto

3 oz [90 ml] whiskey

2 oz [60 ml] fresh lemon juice

½ oz [15 ml] maple syrup or simple syrup

1 egg white (optional)

Cocktail cherries, orange wheels, for garnishing

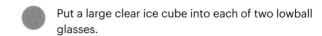 Put a large clear ice cube into each of two lowball glasses.

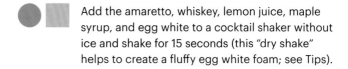 Add the amaretto, whiskey, lemon juice, maple syrup, and egg white to a cocktail shaker without ice and shake for 15 seconds (this "dry shake" helps to create a fluffy egg white foam; see Tips).

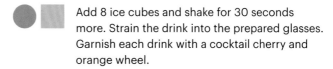 Add 8 ice cubes and shake for 30 seconds more. Strain the drink into the prepared glasses. Garnish each drink with a cocktail cherry and orange wheel.

COOK 1

COOK 2

The whiskey sour is one of the first cocktails we made together, so it holds a special place in our hearts. First recorded in the 1862 manual *The Bartender's Guide* by Jerry Thomas, it mixes liquor, citrus, and sweetener to make a balanced, sweet-tart drink.

Here we've added a few subtle touches to the classic: A hint of amaretto adds nutty notes, and maple syrup adds caramel flavor. The finishing touch is an egg white: a classic bartender trick that adds froth and a creamy mouthfeel to sour cocktails, counteracting the acid to make a pleasantly balanced drink.

Tips

Make sure to use clean, fresh eggs in cocktails. In general, it is safe to consume raw eggs, except for the immuno-compromised and elderly. For a vegan substitute, use 2 tablespoons of aquafaba (the liquid from a can of chickpeas), and shake for double the time.

The frothiest egg white foam is achieved with a dry shake. The first shake without ice lets the protein in the egg begin to form foam before being diluted by the ice. The second shake with ice cools the drink and strengthens the foam.

Whiskey & Amaro
Two Ways

MAKES 2 DRINKS

Four of a Kind

1½ oz [45 ml] rye whiskey

1½ oz [45 ml] Aperol

1½ oz [45 ml] maraschino liqueur (see Tips)

1½ oz [45 ml] fresh lemon juice

Lemon twist (page 325), for garnishing

Paper Plane

1½ oz [45 ml] bourbon whiskey

1½ oz [45 ml] Aperol

1½ oz [45 ml] Amaro Nonino Quintessentia (see Tips)

1½ oz [45 ml] fresh lemon juice

Lemon twist (page 325), for garnishing

 Add the ingredients except the lemon twist to a cocktail shaker and fill it with ice. Shake until cold. Strain the drink into a stemmed cocktail glass and garnish with the lemon twist.

If there's a drink formula we love, it's the "equal parts" cocktail: a drink that uses all ingredients in equal measure, making it simple to shake up. One of the most famous of the equal parts cocktails is the Last Word, a Prohibition-era mix of gin, Chartreuse, maraschino, and lime that makes a balanced green drink.

Here are two whiskey cocktails that riff on the equal parts formula, both using Italian amari. Inspired by the Last Word, the Paper Plane is a modern classic using bourbon that was created by the bartender Sam Ross in 2007. The Four of a Kind is our own invention, an equal-parts cocktail with rye whiskey, Aperol, and maraschino. Both drinks are irresistibly sippable, delightfully balancing sweet and tart with a funky finish.

Tips

Amaro is part of a family of Italian herbal liqueurs that taste bitter (*amaro* means "bitter" in Italian). The category encompasses a wide range of spirits, from the ultra-bitter Campari to sweet Aperol, and many different varieties in between.

Amaro Nonino Quintessentia is the type of amaro originally used for the Paper Plane. It has hints of caramel, vanilla, allspice, and bitter orange. However, it can be hard to find. If you can't find it, substitute any caramelly bittersweet amaro, like Meletti, Averna, or Cynar.

Maraschino liqueur is a clear, cherry-flavored liqueur (not, as you might assume, the liquid from a jar of maraschino cherries). Sweet with notes of sour cherry and almond, it features in several classic 1920s cocktails. It's essential to building the Four of a Kind—no substitutes!

Cranberry Orange Hot Toddy

MAKES 2 DRINKS

2 cinnamon sticks

2 star anise

3 oz [90 ml] aged rum
(a.k.a. añejo rum)

2 oz [60 ml] maple syrup

2 oz [60 ml] fresh orange juice

2 oz [60 ml] 100 percent
cranberry juice

2 orange wheels, for garnishing

Fresh or frozen cranberries,
for garnishing (optional)

 In a small saucepan over medium-low heat, toast the cinnamon sticks and star anise until fragrant, about 3 minutes. Turn down the heat to low. Add 4 ounces [120 ml] of water, the rum, maple syrup, orange juice, and cranberry juice and simmer for 3 more minutes.

 Divide the mixture between two heatproof mugs. Garnish with the cinnamon sticks, star anise, and orange wheels. If desired, add fresh cranberries as an additional garnish.

COOK 2

COOK 1

contd.

This classic British drink has been enjoyed for centuries; it was originally thought to be a cure for the common cold. The long-standing allure of the toddy lies in its simplicity: hot water, liquor, honey, and lemon.

You can build an individual toddy right in the glass, but we prefer to simmer a batch on the stovetop. It makes this two-serving drink easier and simple to scale up for a big crowd. We infuse ours with warm spices like cinnamon and anise, which add a subtle depth to the boozy concoction.

Party variation: In a large pot or Dutch oven, simmer 12 ounces [360 ml] of rum, 8 ounces [240 ml] each of maple syrup, orange juice, and cranberry juice, 16 ounces [475 ml] of water, 8 cinnamon sticks, and 8 star anise.

Bourbon or Scotch Hot Toddy: Swap out the rum for bourbon or a blended Scotch whisky.

Brandy Hot Toddy: Swap out the rum for brandy.

Apple Cider Hot Toddy: Use apple cider in place of the orange juice and cranberry juice. Reduce the maple syrup to ½ ounce [15 ml] and add 6 whole cloves.

Tip

Aged rum, also known as añejo rum, has notes of vanilla, coconut, almond, citrus, or caramel. You can use other types of rum, like white rum, which has a more straightforward flavor, or dark rum, which has notes of caramel, cinnamon, and spices.

Essential Kitchen Gear

What's the most important tool for any home cook? We wouldn't hesitate to answer: a large, sharp chef's knife! It's essential for efficiently chopping, slicing, and preparing a wide variety of foods. Of course, when you cook as frequently as we do, you'll need a bit more gear to fit out the space.

Here's our list of essentials for setting up a kitchen. We try to refrain from purchasing items that are hard to find space for or not often used. Items in the Specialty Gear section are those that you'll use only in special cases, but they're handy for preparing the recipes in this book.

Pots and pans

- 10 in [25 cm] nonstick frying pan
- 10 or 12 in [25 or 30 cm] nonstick skillet
- 12 in [30 cm] cast-iron skillet
- 12 in [30 cm] stainless skillet
- 5 qt [4.7 L] Dutch oven
- 8 qt [7.5 L] stainless pasta pot
- Nonstick griddle (a large double burner is nice to have)

Utensils

- Can opener
- Chef's knife (we like an 8 in [20 cm] santoku)
- Coarse microplane paddle grater (for grating cheese)
- Fine-mesh strainer
- Fine microplane paddle grater
- Fish spatula
- Ladle
- Lemon juicer (we recommend a press juicer)
- Paring knife
- Pastry brush
- Pastry cutter
- Pizza cutter
- Serrated bread knife
- Silicon spatula
- Spatula tongs
- Vegetable peeler and julienne peeler
- Whisk
- Wine bottle opener
- Wooden spoons

Baking

- 2 rimmed baking sheets
- 7 x 11 in [18 x 28 cm] medium baking dish
- 9 in [23 cm] pie plate
- 9 x 5 in [23 x 13 cm] metal loaf pan
- 9 x 9 in [23 x 23 cm] metal baking dish
- 9 x 13 in [23 x 33 cm] baking dish
- 12-cup muffin pan
- 15 x 10 in [38 x 25 cm] jelly roll pan

Bowls and Measuring

- Dry measuring cups (2 sets)
- Liquid measuring cups, 2-cup [475 ml] (2)
- Measuring spoons (2 sets)
- Mixing bowls—small, medium, and large
- Poly cutting boards (2)

Miscellaneous

- Clear plastic ruler
- Food scale
- High-speed blender
- Instant-read food thermometer
- Kitchen twine
- Large food processor
- Salt cellar
- Stand mixer
- Toothpicks

Specialty Gear

- 4 in [10 cm] fluted tart pan
- 6 in [15 cm] cake pans (3)
- Butter warmer
- Cake decorating turntable
- Cake stand
- Ice cream maker
- Melon baller
- Piping bags
- Pizza stone
- Waffle maker

Sample Menus

Fall Chili Night with Friends

Hearty Black Bean Chili ("The Chili") (page 123)

Maple-Glazed Buttermilk Cornbread (page 240)

Kale Salad with Creamy Parmesan Dressing (page 189) or Cilantro Lime Chopped Salad (page 193)

Glazed Applesauce Spice Cake (page 291)

Pizza Friday

Date-Night Pizza (page 88)

Classic Chopped Salad (page 193)

Tiramisu Sundaes (page 306)

Valentine's Day Date

Truffle Pasta with Mixed Mushrooms & Goat Cheese (page 93) or Seared New York Strip Steak with Garlic Mushrooms (page 117)

Lemon Pepper Broccolini (page 219)

Everyday Arugula Salad (page 187)

Chocolate Ganache Tart for Two (page 281)

Spring Brunch

Spinach & Sun-Dried Tomato Crustless Quiche (page 166)

Spiced Latte Loaf (page 243)

Fruit and yogurt

Coffee

Spring Date for Two

Risotto with Asparagus, Peas & Pine Nuts (page 95)

Everyday Arugula Salad (page 187)

Lemon Curd and Berries (without the Ricotta Shortcakes; see page 302)

Birthday Dinner

Creamy Mediterranean Chicken Skillet (page 70)

Crunchy Green Panzanella (page 208)

Herby Quinoa or Rice (page 226)

Molten Brownie Batter Pudding (page 288) or Lemon Poppy Seed Cake with Raspberry Jam & Cream Cheese Frosting (page 284)

Breakfast in Bed

French Toast Waffles (page 158)

Fresh fruit

Sunrise Smoothie (page 181)

Mother's Day Surprise

Mini Cardamom Cinnamon Rolls (page 175)

Sheet-Pan Egg Bake (page 161)

Fresh fruit

Big Family Party

Nacho-Loaded Sweet Potato Bar (page 125)

Corn & Feta Salad (page 199)

Charred Corn Guacamole & Black Bean Hummus Snacking Platter (page 258)

Brown Butter–Miso Chocolate Chip Cookie Bars (page 279)

Summer Barbecue

Curry Salmon Burgers with Cilantro Chutney (page 139)

Corn & Feta Salad (page 199)

Tomato Artichoke Penne Salad (page 205)

Nectarine & Blueberry Crumble (page 299)

Grazing Date Night

Perfect Margaritas for Two (page 313)

Charred Corn Guacamole & Black Bean Hummus Snacking Platter (page 258)

Strawberry Limeade Sorbet (page 305)

Picnic Lunch

Smoked Salmon Bites (page 271)

Green Goddess Dip with crudités (page 251)

Roasted Red Pepper Tapenade with crostini (page 260)

French Carrot Salad (page 207)

Sour Cream & Onion Savory Scones with butter (page 235)

Tomato Artichoke Penne Salad (page 205)

Assorted cheeses

Fresh fruit

Brown Butter–Miso Chocolate Chip Cookie Bars (page 279)

Impress Anyone Dinner

Salmon Piccata (page 60)

Blistered Green Beans Almondine (page 217)

Herby Quinoa or Rice (page 226)

Tiramisu Sundaes (page 306)

Summer Date Night

Aperol Spritz Slushies (page 330)

Whipped Ricotta Crostini with Hot Honey (page 269)

Grilled Eggplant Parmesan with Burrata (page 99)

Tiramisu Sundaes (page 306)

Autumn Feast (Thanksgiving)

One-Pan Roast Chicken & Herby Veggies (page 142) or Cozy Vegetable Pot Pie (page 133)

Roasted Butternut Squash & Onions with Garlic Butter (page 224)

Blistered Green Beans Almondine (page 217)

Everyday Arugula Salad (page 187) with pear and walnuts

Crusty Rosemary Artisan Bread (page 245)

Apple Galette with Bourbon Salted Caramel (page 296)

Holiday Appetizer Spread

Roasted Red Pepper Tapenade with crostini (page 260)

Warm Goat Cheese with Jam (page 263)

Spanakopita-Stuffed Mushrooms (page 265)

Smoked Salmon Bites (page 271)

Garlic Herb Knots (page 233)

Cranberry Orange Hot Toddy (page 336)

Winter Feast

Smoky Spinach & Artichoke Lasagna (page 130)

Lemon Asparagus with Crispy Prosciutto (page 211)

Sunshine Citrus Salad with Orange & Fennel (page 197)

Apple Galette with Bourbon Salted Caramel (page 296)

Soup for a Rainy Evening

Tortellini Vegetable Soup (page 39) or Lentil Soup with Tarragon (page 36)

Gouda Cheddar Ranch Pull-Apart Bread (page 237)

Everyday Arugula Salad (page 187)

Quick Italian Dinner

Pressed Manchego & Prosciutto Sandwiches (page 67)

Classic Chopped Salad (page 193)

Cozy Comfort Food

Barbecue Beans & Greens (page 26)

Maple-Glazed Buttermilk Cornbread (page 240)

Glazed Applesauce Spice Cake (page 291)

Acknowledgments

To our agent, Jane Dystel: Thank you for making our book dream come true! This book is everything it is because of you.

To our photographer, Shelly Westerhausen Worcel: The way you capture food is out of this world. What a thrill to see you bring these pages to life! It's such a gift to finally work together professionally after "growing up" in food blogging together.

To our cookbook consultant, Breana Killeen: You helped shape this vision from day one! Thank for you believing in us and always being available to brainstorm and advise.

To our editor, Sarah Billingsley: Working together has been a true dream. Thank you thank you for your brilliant guidance in catching the vision and making it a reality.

To the Chronicle team: Seeing this book take shape as a beautiful volume is a true pleasure, and it has turned out even more stellar than we could imagine! The design is genius. Thank you to the entire team for every piece and part that came together to bring this book to print. Also thanks to copyeditor Kristi Hein for poring over every word.

To our parents: Thank you beyond measure to our parents for supporting us every step of the way and being our first examples of a loving, supportive partner team. Special thanks to our moms Kristi Kuhnau and Lin Gorman for being constant taste-testers and recipe sounding boards. The way you use food as hospitality is a huge inspiration!

Also big thanks to Kylia Rowe for hair styling, and moms, mother-in-laws, and aunties who watched babies during the shooting of these lifestyle images!

To our loyal readers of *A Couple Cooks*: We are beyond grateful for your support of our website and family throughout the years. Creating recipes that nourish and inspire you is an enormous privilege.

To our friends and family: What can we say? You've been the most incredible support system, cheering us on and being first-line testers for recipes hot off the press. We love you so much and would not be here without you. Special thanks to Kelly Burson, Dan and Megan Pino, Lisa Kuhnau, and Evan Scandling for overall support, and Milena Klimek for our recipe brainstorming sessions.

To our recipe testers: You are the true rock stars! You tested recipes and provided hundreds of pieces of feedback on how they worked in real-life kitchens. And along the way you were funny, fun, and a huge source of encouragement. Hats off to you: This book is better because of each one of you! Thank you to: Carrie Abbott, Lisa Abrahams, Kelly Agee, Corina Allender, Amy Ballard, Caralyn Blouin, Kristy Brooks, Amanda Bureau, Joanne Burke-Vernon, Annika Carnes, Nicole Carpenter, Christine Chapman, Sarah Chivers, Amanda Conforti, Hilary Cunningham, Patty Day, Jill Delaney, Nicole Clark Denny, Roshni Dhoot, Theresa Diulus, Kate Downes, Abbie Downes, Susan Dritt, Sarah Epplin, Elizabeth Evans, Emmy Evans, Sonya Frymoyer, Debbe Geiger, Erin Gladstone, Sharon Halkovics, Karen Harris, Jayme Harvey, Julie Hatlem, Buffy Heldt, Steve and Renata Hepler, Katie Hughes, Andrea and Ryan Hunley, Betsy Hutson, Chelsea James, Jennifer Keller, Jennifer Knickel, Bree Kruse, Kristi Kuhnau, Lisa Kuhnau, Laura Lachowecki, Angela Lengerich, Cami Lica and Charles Masters, Anna Limauro, Elle Mann, Megan McAnally, Lexi Mumma, Julie O'Connell Roberts, Sydney Overcast, Elizabeth and Joe Parker, Kathy Peterson, Daniel and Megan Pino, Jill Delaney Racine, Stephanie Raymond, Colleen Richardson, Mary Rosenberg, Kyley Scofield, Hannah Searcy, Julia Shaheen, Brianna Shamsuddoha, Rachel Short, Suzanne Siegel, Eliza and Lynne Smiley, Kelly Sparrer, Tracie Stamm, Elizabeth Thompson, Natasha Tomlin, Bart Upah, Erin Wadsworth and Courtney Hittepole, Claire Waggoner, Kathrin Wenke, Emilyn Whitesell, Cortnee Yarbrough, and Lindsey Zaragoza.

Index